K

DATE DUE

APR 2 8 1993	
OCT 1 8 1995	
OCT 3 1 1995	
FEB - 3 1996	
Feb 17	

BRODART, INC.   Cat. No. 23-221

SHARING THE DIFFERENCE

For ten years the influential women's studies journal *Tijdschrift voor Vrouwenstudies* has been the focus for the best Dutch feminist writing. This selection of articles from the journal, translated from the original Dutch, reflects the depth and wealth of Dutch feminist theories and the dynamism of the women's movement in the Netherlands. Focusing on four main themes: equality versus difference, theory and history, the body, and French thought and psychoanalysis, *Sharing the Difference* puts onto the international feminist agenda a new tradition of research and thinking in women's studies and feminist theory.

The editors: Joke J. Hermsen is Researcher in the Arts Faculty of the University of Utrecht. **Alkeline van Lenning** is Assistant Professor in the Social Science Faculty of the Katholieke Universiteit Brabant.

SHARING THE DIFFERENCE

Feminist debates in Holland

Edited by

Joke J. Hermsen and Alkeline van Lenning

Translated by Anne Lavelle

London and New York

First published 1991
by Routledge
11 New Fetter Lane, London EC4P 4EE

Simultaneously published in the USA and Canada
by Routledge
a division of Routledge, Chapman and Hall, Inc.
29 West 35th Street, New York, NY 10001

Typeset in 10/12pt Garamond by
Falcon Typographic Art Ltd, Edinburgh & London
Printed in Great Britain by
T. J. Press (Padstow) Ltd, Padstow, Cornwall

British Library Cataloguing in Publication Data
Sharing the difference: Feminist debates in Holland.
1. Netherlands–Feminism
I. Hermsen, Joke J. (Joke Johannetta)   II. Lenning,
Alkeline van
305.4209492

Library of Congress Cataloging in Publication Data
Sharing the difference: Feminist debates in Holland/
edited by Joke J. Hermsen, Alkeline van Lenning.
p. cm.
1. Feminism–Netherlands.   2. Feminist theory.
I. Hermsen, Joke J. (Joke Johannetta)   II. Lenning,
Alkeline van
HQ1658.S53   1991
305.42'09492–dc20   91–8989   CIP

ISBN 0 415 06138 5
ISBN 0 415 06139 3 pbk

CONTENTS

CONTENTS

ILLUSTRATIONS

NOTES ON CONTRIBUTORS

Rosi Braidotti is Professor and Chair of Women's Studies in the Women's Studies Department of the Arts Faculty in the University of Utrecht. She is the author of *Patterns of Dissonance – A Study of Women in Contemporary Philosophy* (1991), and of several articles on feminist theory, philosophy and psychoanalysis.

Sociologist Mieke Aerts has lectured at the University of Amsterdam's political and social sciences women's studies department since 1980. She is a co-founder of the *Tijdschrift voor Vrouwenstudies* and has edited a number of books on the history of women's organizations in the Netherlands. In addition to writing on feminist political theory, she is currently working on a book on Catholic women and politics.

Irene Costera Meijer is Assistant Professor in the Department of Women's Studies at the University of Amsterdam, teaching gay and lesbian studies.

Aafke Komter is Assistant Professor of Social Sciences at the University of Utrecht. Her Ph.D. thesis (1985) was on power in marital relationships. Her present research relates to power, gender and morality.

Marjan Schwegman teaches women's history and cultural history of modern Italy at the University of Amsterdam. She has published a biography of the Italian feminist Gualberta Alaide Beccari (1842–1906), a book on women in the Dutch Resistance (1940–1945), a book on the history of women's labour in the Netherlands 1870–1940 and several articles on theoretical aspects of women's history.

Hélène Vossen works in the Department of History at the University of Amsterdam. She is writing a dissertation on part-time education for working-class youth and the construction of sex and class differences.

Marianne Beelaerts read Dutch language and literature at the University of Utrecht, and is currently reading philosophy at Nijmegen University. For the past ten years she has organized programmes for academics designed to promote interrelations between the arts and sciences.

Saskia Grotenhuis is a Lecturer and co-ordinator of the women's studies programme of the Faculty of Pedagogy and Educational Sciences of the University of Amsterdam. She is working on a dissertation on girls' secondary schools, considering single-sex education and co-education in the Netherlands from 1920 till 1970 (the end of single-sex education).

Annemarie Mol came out of medical school as an anthropologist of medicine and studied philosophy in Utrecht and Paris. Her Ph.D. thesis looks at the conceptual changes in the recent history of Dutch general practice. She is currently studying 'Differences in Medicine' as a research fellow of the Netherlands Organization for Scientific Research.

Evelien Tonkens taught women's studies and philosophy for several years in the Department of Philosophy at the University of Groningen. She is currently engaged in research on rationality, professionality and the revolution of femininity in higher management.

Monique Volman has been working as a researcher at the Centre for Educational Research of the University of Amsterdam since 1986. From 1984–6 she worked as a research assistant in women's studies at the same university. She was awarded a degree in educational sciences in 1986 and has published several articles in the field of women's studies and education. She is currently working on a thesis about gender and computer education.

Joke Hermsen has worked as a researcher at the University of Utrecht since 1988. She is currently working on a dissertation on the philosophical conceptualization of sexual difference in the worlds of Mme de Charrière, Lou Andreas-Salomé and Ongeborg Bachmann.

Angela Grooten teaches philosophy and women's studies at the Universities of Amsterdam and Utrecht. In 1976 she published (with others) some of the first translations into Dutch of French texts on the psychoanalytical structure of the subject in Marxism, and of Althusser's *Freud and Lacan*. She has since pursued her interest in philosophy and psychoanalysis. Her current research focuses on the ontological structure of the subject in psychoanalysis.

Karen Vintges is a social philosopher. Throughout the 1980s she lectured at the University of Amsterdam, and is currently researching her Ph.D. thesis on the philosophy of Simone de Beauvoir.

ACKNOWLEDGEMENTS

This book celebrates the tenth anniversary of the Dutch Journal of Women's Studies (*Tijdschrift voor Vrouwenstudies*) and was made possible by the co-operation of the journal's editors: Janneke Plantenga, Evelien Tonkens, Odile Verhaar, Ingrid Visser, Monique Volman, and Hélène Vossen.

The editors would like to thank the Promotion Committee and Promotion Fund for Emancipation Research (Stimuleringsgroep Emancipatie Onderzoek) of the Ministry of Social Affairs and Employment for financing the translation of this book. In addition, some funding was provided by the Countess van Bylandt Foundation (Gravin van Bylandtstichting), the core Research Women's Studies Workgroup (Onderzoekszwaartepunt Vrouwenstudies) of the University of Amsterdam, and the Board of Emancipation (Emancipatieraad) of the University of Amsterdam.

With the exception of chapter 8, which is translated by the author Annemarie Mol, translations are by Anne Lavelle.

INTRODUCTION:
DUTCH TREATS
AND OTHER STRANGERS

Reading Dutch feminism

Rosi Braidotti

This is a collection of selected articles from the Dutch Journal of Women's Studies (*Tijdschrift voor Vrouwenstudies*), the most influential publication in this field in the Netherlands. The foreign reader may need a few guidelines in order fully to appreciate the importance of this collection. Over the last twenty years, much ink has been spilled over cultural phenomena such as 'French feminism', 'Anglo-American feminism' and other 'hyphenated' sorts of feminisms. Some have argued that these expressions are all misnomers that fail to account for the complexity of nation-specific women's movements and related cultural phenomena. Nevertheless, these intercultural cross-fertilizations have played a major role in the international debate and continue to contribute a great deal to setting the theoretical agenda.

French feminism in particular developed into quite a widespread international theoretical movement, with its own distinct features. It therefore is represented in this, as in other recent feminist collections, as a specific section of its own. Whereas 'French feminism' has become a shorthand term for 'theories of difference' and other deconstructive approaches, a new series of translations of texts from 'Italian feminism', which have just been published in English, seem to promise a more synthetic approach, where the issue of politics and of theoretical practice are articulated anew.[1]

I find it extremely significant that from the very start of its existence, the journal has been sensitive to and interested in many international forms of feminist thought: the article by Marjan Schwegman (Chapter 4 below), 'Gualberta Alaide Beccari and

1

the tempting perspective of the moral regeneration of humanity' testifies to this.

So far, however, 'Dutch feminism' has hardly hit the international headlines. Such neglect is unjustifiable, considering the depth and the wealth of Dutch feminist theories, and the dynamism of the women's movement in this country. This is consequently a very timely collection, that puts on the international feminist agenda a new tradition of research and thinking in women's studies and feminist theory. It also contributes to a better understanding of the complex phenomenon that is the women's movement in a small but highly complex country, such as the Netherlands. Last but not least, we hope it will also help the foreign reader to develop a heightened perception of the variety and diversity of cultural traditions within the monolith known on the other side of the Channel as 'the Continent', and on the other side of the Atlantic as 'Europe'.

However vague it may be, over-determined as it is by centuries of conflicting history, the notion of 'Europe' has at least one significant meaning: as a geo-political location. And by any standards or calculations, the Netherlands lie at the very heart of it. This geographical factor, far from being a mere contingency, turned into a historical and cultural vocation. The Netherlands, its culture and society, have always functioned as the gateway to the Continent, the bridge towards the heart of the Old World. Holland as a gateway, a point of transition.

It is hardly surprising, then, that Dutch feminism displays the same features: as the crossroads of Europe's multi-faceted women's movements, the point of intersection of many different feminist cultures and traditions. The Dutch in general are well and widely read: in the feminist readership it is not uncommon to find widespread knowledge of the French, American, German and English feminist sources. This awareness of international literature, coupled with the strong local tradition of feminist practice, makes the Dutch feminists a sort of melting-pot of feminist cultures. This collection is good evidence of this fact: you will find articles about Italian, French and English-language feminist theories, read from a local and highly specific perspective.

For instance – one of the most polemical and much talked-about controversies of the feminist 1980s: the so-called 'equality versus difference' debate, started off in the Netherlands as a purely local discussion, generated by the intellectual dynamics of the women's studies movement in the universities. In the course of time, this local discussion merged with the wider international developments in American theory and especially in French theories of deconstruction and the philosophies of sexual difference.

This attitude is clearly reflected in the articles selected for this collection, which range through a very wide spectrum of cultural and theoretical traditions. This is the case not only in fields such as history, where different cultures can be and even are expected to be turned into objects of study, but also in the actual methodological frameworks adopted in the different articles. The reader will find in this collection approaches drawn from post-structuralism, others from a more empirical standpoint, as well as a variety of combined approaches.

This distinguishing feature as a theoretical melting-pot, however, is the antithesis of American-inspired heterogeneity and pluralism. In the Dutch feminist traditions, you will find that qualities such as an openness towards foreign cultures and countries, a receptivity towards ideas from abroad and a willingness to understand the other's point of view, are praised *per se*, as a correct intellectual and moral position. They are an end in themselves, and consequently do not aim at producing one synthetical standpoint, however pluralistic.

The leading writer and literary theorist Maaike Meijer has however pointed out[2] that, as far as the Dutch women's movement is concerned, this attitude, far from being innate, is itself the result of a series of disagreements and conflicts between different groups and factions of the movement, which characterized the feminists through the 1970s. Heterogeneity was then the main feature of the Dutch, as of most women's movements the world over: the polite revisionism of the 'emancipation-minded' members of the MVM (man–woman-society) was opposed to the radicalism of the consciousness-raising groups; the different lesbian parties contended with their heterosexual sisters and among themselves; the old communists versus the new Marxists and both versus the Dutch liberals, and so on. Thus, the attitude of receptivity and willingness to contextualize the other's point of view was developed gradually through this rather familiar tale of frictions, factions and in-fightings.

To the foreign reader, this tolerant and almost self-effacing quality may appear at first puzzling: this Dutch feminism which is not one, this melting-pot of so many different traditions and political genealogies seems to escape rigid classifications. Its features, contents and intellectual focuses are so many, and often so contrasting, as to avoid strict definitions. To appreciate this fact, and not see it as a mark of elusiveness, one needs to take into account the paradox that is Dutch cultural identity as a whole: a cultural identity whose main strength consists in asserting or pretending that there is no such thing as a Dutch identity. I incurred the wrath of many dear colleagues by suggesting that this approach, obviously inherited from negative theology in that it defines by *not* defining, is nevertheless a characteristic cultural mark of 'Dutchness'. It was pointed out that only a non-Dutch person would see it that way. Thereby proving my point.

One factor, however, should be stressed as the distinctive feature of Dutch identity: it is the so-called 'pillarization' of society, that is to say the division of the national income among separate and often conflicting groups. The Dutch deal with their differences by sharing, that is distributing wisely the available capital – be it material or symbolic. The best example of this system is the attitude the Dutch adopt towards different brands of religion: for such a small country, the Netherlands can display a huge variety of denominational labels. The same applies to the structure of the media and communications systems: broadcasting and TV time-slots are allocated evenly to all the political parties in such a way as to avoid domination of one group. Special care is taken to prevent the power of money controlling the kind of media and information that is provided. Feminist historians have argued that the pillarized system actually favours the emergence of women's organizations and sees them as major vehicles of social change.[3]

Where the heterogeneity of the Dutch feminist approach differs from its American counterpart is that it is firmly located in a strong autochthonous tradition of struggles for the emancipation of women. This tradition is relatively recent, as it is for other European countries: it is in this century that organized women's movements claimed for basic rights. Women activists cover the whole political spectrum, from reformist Christian groups to left-wing organizations, all the way to autonomous 'radical feminist' groups. It also relies on a very lively tradition of women's writings and cultural traditions.

The development of the latter is quite significant: in her authoritative study of Dutch women poets, Maaike Meijer[4] stresses how quantitatively and qualitatively remarkable is the Dutch female poetic tradition; she also argues that both the output and its quality have picked up since the Second World War. Meijer also points out[5]

4

that in the wake of the feminist movement, from the end of the 1960s, a network of separatist 'women's houses' was established all over the country; right through the 1970s some twelve feminist bookshops and many cafés came into existence in all major and middle-sized cities; feminist/lesbian publishing houses also came into existence. All these functioned as cultural centres, real venues for literary, artistic and musical manifestations: in Holland as elsewhere, the 1970s saw major public festivals and concerts. Very significant as an indicator of the feminist cultural revolution is the large number of journals and magazines, to which I will return later.

An important component of the feminist cultural movement was and still is lesbian; the lesbian organizations, however, did not emerge until recently from the extensive gay organizations, which were massively male-dominated (their acronym was COC) and not at all inclined, till the late 1970s, to take the feminist standpoint seriously.

By the late 1980s, feminist theatre, film and music were making their way into the dominant cultural venues and television was sensitive to the feminist presence. Dutch women film-makers, some of whom, like Marleen Gorris (*The Silence around Christine G.* and *Broken Mirrors*), have acquired a considerable international reputation,[6] are close to the women's movement. Moreover, in a very Dutch spirit of entrepreneurial creativity, some feminist writers founded in the 1980s the Anna Bijns Prijs as a major literary prize awarded to the 'female voice in literature'; named after the leading Dutch medieval poet, it aims at matching the highest literary awards, which are still massively male-dominated.

The Dutch women's studies movement is therefore a very extensive network, which provides the groundwork for the Dutch women's movement; it is also an extremely organized culture that has emerged relatively unscathed from the political and economic backlash of the 1980s. It is this firm implantation in local realities of struggle and political activities that provides the impetus for the cosmopolitanism of the Dutch feminists. They are not only extremely localized but also highly international in their outlook.

SITUATED KNOWLEDGES[7]

One of the first things the foreign reader needs to understand about the Netherlands is that it possesses one of the most efficient and highly sophisticated systems of institutionalized feminism in Europe. The government supports directly the bulk of the intellectual, teaching and research organizations of the women's movement and has a long-standing tradition of financial support and political backing for women's issues.[8] At present, about 200 women's studies and feminist scholars are employed in various universities across the country, at every professional level, from full professors to graduate students. It must be added, however, that many of these only hold part-time jobs and that a great deal of the intellectual work of the movement rests on the willing shoulders of volunteers and of dedicated feminist activists. In this context, it is nevertheless hardly surprising that a great deal of documentation and scholarly information is available about the field.

It must be stressed, however, that the wealth of available data on feminist research in the Netherlands is not due only to state intervention, but also to the autonomous efforts of women's organizations outside institutional structures.[9] While discipline-based organizations continue to promote women's studies,[10] special mention should be made of the International Archives for the Women's movement, which have provided for years a point of reference for feminist activists and scholars.[11] When you consider that, to date, there are so few Europe-wide surveys available of women's studies research and teaching facilities in the community,[12] the Dutch surely appear to have the edge.

Let us go back to the institutionalized nature of Dutch feminism. The intensive state support accorded it can be best understood in terms of some features of the Dutch political system, which in turn must be referred back to Dutch history. As Simon Shama argues,[13] the joint influence on the one hand of religion, and especially in certain geographical areas, of Calvinism, and on the other of capital accumulation is absolutely crucial to an understanding of the Dutch political system. It has produced, among other things, a contradictory tradition of self-castigating inhibition, charity and denial of earthly pleasures, even in their desirable cultural forms, such as art and high culture. It has also resulted, however, in a very pleasure-prone, permissive and highly tolerant spirit of enjoyment of one's well-earned wealth. The paradoxical mixture of Calvinism, Puritanism and of the desire to escape therefrom constitutes one of the main features of Dutch society.[14]

Shama concludes that the openness and receptivity towards one's neighbours, local or foreign, is based on the shifting grounds of these equally powerful, though eminently contradictory, historical traditions. They coincide in the much-envied and highly admired Dutch 'welfare state' – the state as all-nurturing mother;[15] the very same state that, thanks to intense feminist action, has learnt to support women's emancipation and to see feminism as a governmental priority. Although Simon Shama's reading of Dutch culture has been the object of some criticism in the Netherlands, where it was met with mild scepticism, I think his insight is useful for any foreigner who wants to approach the enigma of Dutch cultural identity.

In order to assess the extensive institutionalization of Dutch feminism, one needs therefore to contextualize it a little. Thus, one needs to keep in mind one of the major paradoxes of Dutch society, as far as the condition of women is concerned. It is the paradox of a general condition of women that is, in economic and political terms, among the most backward in Europe. In terms of integration into the labour force, state support for child-care and the general professionalization of women, the Netherlands does not stand out as a path-setter.[16]

To this rather discouraging social reality of women, there corresponds a brilliantly integrated, politically active and intellectually alive feminist movement. That in such a context the state should support feminism as one of the sources of women's social emancipation and political integration comes as no surprise.

In her outstanding analysis of the relationship between the professionalization and modernization of women and traditional Dutch political structures, especially the model of 'pillarization', the historian Berteke Waaldijk stresses the important role played by traditional women's organizations within the 'pillarized' system. She argues that they provided a much-needed link between the top layer of the state apparatus and the base and, as such, contributed a great deal to the setting up of the Dutch welfare system.[17]

Certainly, that so much support should have been won is primarily the merit of the women's organizations that campaigned for women's rights and revendications.

Of course, such a high degree of institutionalization and state intervention does not escape difficulties and resistance: While the Dutch government, bent on an effort of modernization of its female population, is marketing the emancipation of women more and more in terms of participation in the labour force, feminist opposition to the process has also been rising. This takes many different forms: from the radical wing claiming post-1968 rejection of institutional practices,[18] to the more recent 'care-oriented' defence

of the traditional feminine sense of the private sphere and of nurturing values.

This revendication of areas of experience traditionally associated
with women, as opposed to massive state intervention through the
welfare system, does not aim to glorify an essentialized femininity.
It rather attempts to preserve both some margins of individual
autonomy, as opposed to the government's emphasis on integration
into the labour market, and also some form of resistance against the
power-system and the hierarchy that characterizes it.

A JOURNAL IS A JOURNAL IS A JOURNAL IS

The vitality of Dutch feminism can best be testified to by the
breadth and variety of its publications. Maaike Meijer noted that
the Dutch feminist/lesbian press has always shown an enormous
diversity: the most widely-read feminist journal of the moment,
Opzij, has a readership of about 50,000. Notable too is the presence
of several feminist literary journals such as *Chrysallis, Lover, Lust
en gratie* and *Surplus*. The more specialized press is also important:
for example *Ruimte*, the magazine for women in the visual arts,
and the gay/lesbian cultural magazine *Homologie*. Very encouraging
also is the presence of relatively new and young publications, such as
the undergraduate women's studies journals *Brjllantine, Dynamiek*
and *Pheme*, which affirm the vitality and the continuity of the
feminist tradition among the younger generation. In this rich and
varied context, the Dutch Journal of Women's Studies has played a
leading and path-setting role.

Interdisciplinary

The Dutch Journal of Women's Studies was started as an unasham-
edly intellectual academic journal in 1980. Its appearance, however,
was due entirely to the political sagacity and administrative flair
of a few women's studies researchers in the university system. I
happened to attend the fifth birthday celebration of the journal, in
Amsterdam: an event that was marked by an international congress
in which researchers and representatives of feminist journals from
most European countries participated. If vitality and enthusiasm were
already evident then, on the day of its tenth birthday the journal can

boast of having come of age. It has gained widespread recognition as a serious academic journal and is accepted as the main scientific publication for feminist researchers in the country.

The interdisciplinary nature of this medium leaves it open to contributions from different areas of enquiry, ranging from the social sciences to literary theory, but also to biology and economics. This cross-disciplinary approach makes it a very receptive and exhaustive tool of research and analysis. But there is more to the interdisciplinarity than just a variety of subject matters. The journal also offers new perspectives on the methodological foundations of interdisciplinary work, by casting a critical look at the boundaries and connections between the disciplinary fields themselves.

Thus, over and above the heterogeneity of the subject matter, the focus is on feminism as critical theory, that is to say as a discourse that throws open the very foundations of the disciplines as we have learnt to know them. Here the influence of Foucault is very striking. The Dutch Journal of Women's Studies can be compared favourably on this point to the British journal *m/f* in that it combines a flair for cross-disciplinary perspectives with a distinct intellectual style of its own. Both are strongly influenced by 'post-Marxist' theoretical frames, especially French philosophies of difference, deconstructive critiques and theories of subjectivity. In the complex landscape of European feminism, these two journals represent a unique attempt to move beyond the more constricting aspects of classical and especially of historical materialism, while remaining attached to such notions as praxis or theoretical practice, the importance of science and especially the idea of the social and political accountability of intellectuals.

Symptomatic of this approach is Annemarie Mol's contribution to this collection: 'Wombs, pigmentation and pyramids (Chapter 8). This text shows most convincingly and with highly characteristic wit that Dutch feminist theory is actively resistant to a global synthesis, in that it does not wish to develop 'one formal theory of scientific knowledge'. The aim is rather to expose the co-extensivity and therefore the compatibility of disciplines as divergent as biology and the social sciences.

On the cutting edge of contemporary feminist theory

The variety and depth of the texts published in the Dutch Journal of Women's Studies over the last ten years have contributed in a decisive manner to setting the agenda of feminist theory and women's studies research. One of the most significant examples of this leading role played by the journal is the so-called 'equality versus difference debate'. The crucial question here was less one of assessing the compatibility of the two respective lines of thinking, than to work towards a political resolution of the different forms of political action each line actually implied. The question then became: 'How can we analyse the tension between strategies that emerge from an equality-based approach and those that are elaborated within theories of difference?' Although the debate was very passionate in this country, it certainly took a more productive form in the Netherlands than it did, for instance, in France. There it acquired a particularly polemical and negative twist, the criticism of 'écriture féminine' and the philosophies of sexual difference merging with the attacks against the women's group 'Des femmes', also known as 'Psychanalyse et politique'. This group, foremost amongst whom were Cixous, Irigaray and A. Fouque, were largely responsible for popularizing these ideas. This situation led to a climate of hostility and conflict among women that did considerable damage to the feminist cause.[19]

The debate in the Netherlands also remained a more nation-wide discussion than it could ever be in the English-speaking world where the debate was not only fragmented because of geographical spread, but was also over-determined by problems of translation of the French texts. It is significant that the texts of Luce Irigaray, who is in my opinion the single most important theoretician of sexual difference, have been available in English only since 1987. It is also very important to remember that the 'difference' debate originated in the USA in literary theory circles and mostly in literature departments in the universities. This disciplinary specificity gives to the American form of the debate a very different configuration from most of the European ones, and also accounts for the *en bloc* rejection of difference by social and political scientists.[20] One would have to turn to Italy to find a mixture of theoretical sophistication and political awareness in approaching such a complex debate comparable to that in Dutch feminism.[21]

The articles presented in the first section of this collection spell out quite clearly the terms of the Dutch debate: for the authors it seems clear that the actual concepts of equality and difference should not be discussed apart from the historical and philosophical processes of conceptualization of sex-differences. As Mieke Aerts argues very forcefully in Chapter 1, 'Just the same or just different?', the respective concepts of equality and difference are committed to different feminist political traditions.

In a different vein, Irene Meijer, in the following chapter, points out that the debate about equality versus difference leads to the dilemma of 'biologism', in that it over-emphasizes the differences between men and women. In Meijer's opinion, it would be theoretically and politically more profitable to plead for a relationship other than the classical sexual division of labour between the sexes.

In Chapter 3, Aafke Komter points out that equality and difference, far from being necessarily opposites, presuppose each other in a subtle and problematic mutual dependence.

The emphasis thus placed on the historical, that is specific, nature of this theoretical debate has protected the Dutch from easy simplifications and one-way reductions of the problem. It has therefore bred an intellectual climate that is conducive less to oppositions than to new coalitions of theoretical interests.

Concerned with theory and/as practice

In spite, or rather, because of its intense theoretical agenda, the journal has always made a point of relating recent theoretical developments to concrete issues of social and political relevance. This is the approach defended, for instance, by Saskia Grotenhuis in her article, '"Let the body talk", or can children learn to protect themselves against incest?' (Chapter 7). The task of understanding not only how the sexes function and how their differences are constructed, but also what can be done to change the power system is a recurrent one in this collection. It is especially important to the section on 'the body'.

This section combines several approaches to 'the body' within feminist research, from a theoretical as well as an empirical point of view. The terms of the Dutch debate on this issue see a combination of influences, from psychoanalysis to more traditional forms of materialism. As in other cultures, many Dutch theoreticians regard with suspicion any reference to the 'body', fearing the trap of biological determinism. Under the influence of more recent post-structuralist developments, however, more Dutch feminists have come to view the bodily self as a valuable starting point in the struggle against power-structures. What provides the point of consensus here is the notion that the female bodily subject is the active agent of social transformation and change.

This renewed emphasis on the body as a positive concept has also led to reconsidering the parameters of materialism, in favour of a more situated, or specific kind of materiality: that one's body be one's location in reality turns, therefore into both an epistemological and a political starting point.

The article by Evelien Tonkens and Monique Volman, reprinted in Chapter 9, is representative of this approach: the authors discuss several approaches to both the criticism of sexual violence against women and the strategies of defending a female sexuality that is different from the male-dominated one. If we situate this approach in the international context, we can see that, once again, Dutch feminists avoided the pitfalls of both biological reductivism and prescriptive moralism, approaching the subject of pornography from a variety of mutually enriching angles. This attitude rests to a large degree on a carefully balanced mixture of theoretical and empirical elements.

Critical of power/knowledge

The journal always put a high priority on the critique of knowledge, of scientific concepts and methods. These theoretical frameworks are compared to empirical feminist research, as Hélène Vossen shows in Chapter 5, 'Productions of sexual differences in Catholic "Life Schools"'.

This kind of approach favours analysis of the multiplicity, ambivalences and paradoxes of the very historical sources which it employs. The emphasis on multiplicity has also been inspired by contemporary French philosophy and most of the feminist historical research in Holland can partly be seen as a combination of French theories and empirical results. Once again, the interdisciplinarity is strong, as evidenced by Marianne Beelaerts' contribution to this collection, 'The problems of the young, intelligent woman', a re-appraisal of a nineteenth-century novel in a way that successfully combines literary and historical sources.

We should look further at the discipline of history in the Dutch intellectual context. This country can boast of being the first in Europe to have 'women's history' adopted as a compulsory examination question for the final secondary school examination.[22] With an extensively organized network of feminist historians, Dutch feminist history is one of the most active and innovative areas of feminist research today. The many women scholars, feminist publications, international events and training sessions on feminist and women's history that originate in the Netherlands are evidence of this vitality. This disciplinary field is consequently one of the better known outside the country.

Close to, but not the same as, the French connection

The influence of French theoretical traditions and of French feminist theories is very strong in the *Tijdschrift*. The movement of ideas from France generally known as 'post-structuralism', 'postmodernism' and 'theories of sexual difference' has played a very important role in Dutch research in the field of womens' studies. Joke Hermsen's chapter on 'Baubo or Bacchante? Sarah Kofman and Nietzsche's "affirmative" woman' is a significant example of this. Very aware of the latest international developments, and very keen to assess them in their own terms, Dutch feminists have been among the first in Europe to recognize the importance of renewing the theoretical frameworks of feminist thought, adapting them to changing political and scientific conditions.

The Franco-Dutch connection, however passionate, is nevertheless a marriage of reason and is not without traces of ambivalence and conflict. One criticism often voiced is that the French theoretical standpoint is useful in that it delivers relevant and innovative tools for the analysis of social and cultural patterns, but it is also paradoxical in that it tends to reinforce the very phallocratic structures which it criticizes. As if the mimetic trap were somewhat inevitable, the French deconstruction of the primacy of phallocentrism ends up in the paradoxical reassertion of the very power it denounces. Angela Grooten, for instance, highlights in her contribution to this volume the paradox of the phallocratic ends of Lacanian psychoanalysis.

Despite these difficulties, it becomes increasingly clear that French theories can provide an inspiring answer to questions such as, 'How can we lay the foundations for feminist politics or feminist ethics?' Karen Vintges, in Chapter 12, 'The vanished woman and styles of feminine subjectivity', gives a clear example of this kind of approach. On the basis of Foucault's notion of the 'aesthetics of existence', she maintains that feminist cultural constructions should be represented as autonomous ethical discourses that no longer base themselves on general assumptions about womanhood.

ROSI BRAIDOTTI

CONCLUSION

This collection does not claim, nor does it even attempt to be exhaustive. If it be representative, it is of a movement of ideas and of academic feminism that is extremely contextualized and well-defined. Because of its highly focused structure, this volume constitutes an ideal introduction to the very complex, rich and varied world of Dutch feminism. In a country where the welfare, pillarized social system actually favours the emancipation of women, Dutch feminists have been able to strike a note of radicalism without losing touch with their specific historical and cultural tradition. In a culture that does not favour high-flown theorizations, they have found the right mixture of conceptual and empirical know-how. Last but not least, Dutch feminist scholars continue to keep open the road of genuine cross-disciplinarity and intercultural exchanges, thereby practising the art of consensus-making. I find their intellectual style extremely innovative and a source of inspiration for feminist theory today.

NOTES

I wish to thank the editors of this volume for their assistance. Special thanks are also due to Anneke Smelik, Maaike Meijer, Berteke Waaldijk and to J. G. Veldhuis, Chairman of the Utrecht University Board, for their inspiration.

1 P. Bono and S. Kemp (eds), *Italian Feminist Theory*, Oxford University Press, Oxford, 1991.
2 In an informal discussion held at the women's studies department in the Arts Faculty of the University of Utrecht in January 1991.
3 Dutch historian Berteke Waaldijk argues that the 'pillarization' system, which American political scientists usually describe as 'consociationalism', in fact favours the existence of women's organizations and allows them a major role within each 'pillar' of the social system. Thus, a tradition of women's political organizations existed in this country prior to the advent of the women's movement.
4 M. Meijer, *De lust tot lezen* (The desire for letters), van Gennep, Amsterdam, 1989; it also contains an English summary.
5 In an informal discussion, for which I thank her.
6 For an enlightening feminist appraisal of M. Gorris' work, see Anneke Smelik's article on *Broken Mirrors*, in 'Het Stille Geweld' *Tijdschrift voor Vrouwenstudies* (Journal of Women's Studies), no. 38, 1989, pp. 235–53.
7 The expression is Donna Haraway's, in her article: 'Situated knowledges', *Feminist Studies*, vol. 3, 1988, pp. 575–99.
8 As an example of the sort of advanced work achieved by Dutch academic feminists, one could name the main bodies that stimulated

research activities in this field. The first is STEO, the Promotion Committee for Emancipation Research, which was set up by the Dutch government to stimulate women's studies in the academy. Apart from setting priorities and subsidizing new research, STEO published a number of important studies on the structure and progress of women's studies. By far the most significant, translated into English, is Margo Brouns' *The Development of Women's Studies in the Netherlands*, Rion, Groningen, 1989. This remarkable document analyses fifteen years of thinking and planning for women's studies, setting out the trends and major lines of theoretical development. Another interesting document is the progress-report on women's studies which spells out new directions in research: C.G.M. Gremmen and J.A. Westerbeek van Eerten, *De kracht van Macht* (The force of power), Steo, The Hague, 1988. See also M. Brouns and A. Schokker, *Arbeidsvraagstukken en Sekse* (Questions on labour and sexuality), Steo, The Hague, 1990.

9 Another interesting organization is the Dutch women's studies organization (Nederlands Genootschap Vrouwenstudies), which has promoted research and teaching at grass-roots level, also setting priorities and publishing in-progress reports. On the international front, the association is one of the organizers of the Europe-wide network WISE. In addition it has published several useful brochures, among them a guide to funds and financing in the field of women's studies. This is actually a significant document in itself, in that it maps the 'pillarized', that is to say the widespread, distribution of feminist funds in this country: T. van den Heuvel, C. Verheyen, J. Oldersma, E. Kas (eds), *Nieuwe Geldpotten* (New funds), Slov/Steo, The Hague, 1987. The women's studies organization also publishes specialized disciplinary guides to feminist research: M. van den Burg, *Thema en disciplinennetwerk vrouwenstudies* (Thematic and disciplinary networks), Nederlands Genootschap Vrouwenstudies, Utrecht, 1989. Also available are documents about future trends in the field: *De toekomst van ons vak*, ed J. Oldersma and Micke Verloo, 1990; and a study on the employment opportunities available to women's studies graduates, L.C. Nicolai: *Werken met vrouwenstudies*, 1989.

10 For instance, the association that aims at developing research in the social sciences – SISWO – has contributed greatly to the growth of feminist research through various publications. The study on academic women and their professional opportunities is of special interest: E.K. Hicks and G. Noordenbos, *Is Alma Mater vrouw-vriendelijk?* van Gorcum, Assen/Maastricht, 1990.

11 The International Archives for the Women's Movement is an extremely important organization: it was started in the 1920s and provides both documentation and research advice. It publishes a quarterly inventory of women's studies, *All'Erta*, and has produced several interesting studies, for example, I. Jungschleren, *Bluestockings in Mothballs*, 1982; C.A.M. Vansuyt, *Een koekoeksjong in het wetenschapsnest*, 1986.

12 See the report drafted by the Franco-Belgian journal *Les Cahiers du Grif*, for the EEC, in 1988. Also the special report of the EC Commission on Women's Studies: Supplement no. 18 to *Women of Europe*, 1984.

13 In *The Embarrassment of Riches*, Collins, London, 1987.

14 For a discussion of Schama's work, see *Bijdragen en mededelingen betreffende geschiedenis der Nederlandern*, 1989, pp. 39–55.

15 The expression is Annemarie Mol's.

16 According to a recent EEC survey, about 27 per cent of Dutch women are in the workforce, though only about 15 per cent of married women actually work. About 32 per cent of women with a child under 10 were employed in 1988, as opposed to 91 per cent of men in the same category. Single mothers are less likely to be employed than any other social category: the percentage is about 18 per cent. These figures make much more sense when one considers that publicly funded childcare services are few and far between; the best estimate is that there is provision for 1.5 per cent of children under 3, and a further 10 per cent attend playgoups for a few hours a day. With maternity leave extended to 16 weeks, during which period women receive 100 per cent of their salary, and no parental leave officially approved for the father, it is clear that the incentive for women's integration into the labour force is extremely low. These figures are taken from the report of the EC Commission, 'Childcare in the European Community, 1985–1990', published as a supplement to *Women of Europe*, no. 30, August 1990.

17 See B. Waaldijk and G. Dimmendaal (eds), *Groniek: Groninger Historische Tijdschrift* no. 97, 1987, special issue on women and the welfare state; in particular, see B. Waaldijk's contribution: 'De verzorgstaat een vrouwen geschiedenis', pp. 123–35.

18 This took the same form in the Netherlands as in most western countries: the rejection of institutionalization, and emphasis placed on consciousness-raising and direct challenge to patriarchal codes. One distinguishing feature of the radical wing, however, is that the lesbian presence was probably more visible and vocal than elsewhere: for instance, radical critiques of enforced heterosexuality were articulated well before A. Rich's famous formulation of 'compulsory heterosexuality'.

19 For a detailed account, see C. Duchen, *Feminism in France*, Routledge, London, 1986.

20 The actual analysis of the American debate on equality versus difference is only beginning to be written. For an enlightening approach, see the recent special issue of *Feminist Studies* on deconstruction, 14 January 1988.

21 The main spokeswomen of the Italian debate are the philosopher Adriana Caverero, the theoretician Luisa Muraro and the politician Livia Turco, of the women's commission of the Italian Communist Party. Their common point of reference is the work of Luce Irigaray and their impact on English-language feminist theory has been assessed by T. de Lauretis in her introduction to the English translation of the group's political manifesto, *Sexual Difference – A Social-Symbolic Theory*, Indiana University Press, Bloomington, 1990.

22 On this point, see the extremely important article by M. Geever, 'Pivoting the centre. Women's history: a compulsory subject for the final written examination in history in all Dutch secondary schools in 1990 and 1991', forthcoming in *Gender & History*, vol. 3, no. 1, Spring 1991, pp. 85–105.

Part I

THE EQUALITY–DIFFERENCE DEBATE IN THE NETHERLANDS

INTRODUCTION

The discussion which will go down in Dutch feminist history as the 'equality versus difference' debate was chosen by the editors of the *Tijdschrift voor Vrouwenstudies* (Journal of Women's Studies) as the theme for the congress to mark its first lustrum in April 1985. Thus, this debate had been ongoing in Dutch women's studies circles for three years when American historian Joan W. Scott's innovative 'Deconstructing the equality-versus-difference debate: or, the use of post-structural theory for feminism' appeared.[1]

The international congress heard guest speakers Michèle Barrett, Rosi Braidotti, Elisabeth Cowie, Mary McIntosh, Ryana Rapp and Judith Walkowitz on the question: 'Do the concepts "equality" and "difference" form a dilemma?' This debate had been anticipated twelve months earlier by Mieke Aerts, a sociologist and one of the co-founders of the *Tijdschrift voor Vrouwenstudies*. Her article 'Just the same or just different?' gave the impetus for this debate. Aerts argued that even if a dilemma existed, that did not necessarily mean the two concepts were in opposition to each other, and that one had to choose one or other position, as was often suggested. In her view, although the concepts of 'equality' and 'difference' are usually presented as theoretically and politically distinct, they are committed respectively to two different Dutch feminist traditions – '*equal rights feminism*' and '*ethical feminism*' – which are closely interwoven and even presuppose each other historically as well.[2] If there is a dilemma, then it should not be resolved by opting for one or other position.

The Dutch feminist scholars who organized the congress argued in the same vein. They also suggested both concepts presuppose each other in the sense that they have no meaning without each other. Considering both equality and inequality is, of necessity, based on

19

thinking about differences. Questions were raised such as, 'On what concept of difference is that in/equality based?' 'Difference' should not be opposed to 'equality'; having a critical function, 'difference' was also needed to attain a certain type of equality in order to prevent an equality based exclusively on men's terms (the 'feminization' of equality). The conclusion was that 'difference' is integrated into the concept of 'equality', and vice versa.

The subsequent discussion examined questions such as whether feminists should be concentrating on sexual difference, or whether they should focus on the relationship with other structuring differences such as 'ethnicity', 'class' and differences in sexuality? Does opting for equality preclude respect for difference, and for different kinds of differences in all their diversity and variety? And is the recognition of sexual difference not *the* precondition for non-hierarchical differences, or is difference just another term for fragmentation?

On a more political and strategic level, the dilemma showed (and shows) up everywhere. Take for example the question on the (recently repealed) law prohibiting nightwork for women. In their striving for equality, should women attack a law which implies equality in the sense of equally bad treatment? Or should they defend special treatment for women and, in so doing, implicitly agree with the concept of sexual difference upon which that law is based? And what position should be taken in the discussion on the government's campaign to encourage girls to choose less traditional 'feminine' subjects at school, or to opt for a less 'typically feminine' education? Should girls follow that advice and choose 'typically masculine' subjects, acquire 'masculine' qualifications in order to have equal chances on the labour market? Or should the assumed hierarchical distinction between 'feminine' and 'masculine' jobs and qualifications be thrown open to discussion? (And a related question: would it be more advantageous for girls to learn these 'masculine' subjects through general, 'gender-neutral' courses, or through special courses designed for girls and adapted to what is supposed to be of interest to girls, that is, based on very stereotyped meanings of femininity?)

From the second half of the 1980s, the debate on how to relate 'equality' to 'difference' and vice versa, which had been fairly abstract and theoretical, turned out to be fruitful for concrete studies in the field of women's studies. In addition, the explicit influence of French deconstructivist philosophers such as Derrida, Foucault and others led to the debate developing a heuristic function. The ways in which sexual difference (that is, in fact, women's identity as different from men's) is historically and socially constructed in various specific situations (also defined as inequality), became the subject of studies by a large number of feminist scholars. The consensus underlying this type of research – the two concepts cannot do without each other – did not imply there was no dilemma. Some feminist scholars saw the dilemma as an inspiration rather than an obstacle.

In the context of women's studies research, the questions raised on the problematic nature of the 'equality–difference' relationship also have a political impact. Does analysing the construction of sexual difference in the way a large number of women's studies researchers did (and still do) mean the social (in)equality aspect is neglected? Does it make sense to say that as a result this type of research is less 'political' than so-called 'emancipation studies'? Is the related distinction between 'feminist' and 'emancipation' studies structured along these lines a valid distinction?

Whether the problematic nature of the equality–difference question at the heuristic level should be seen as an obstacle or not resulted in the following debate. In 1987, women's studies scholar Irene Costera Meijer wrote the article published here which gave a further impulse to the debate. In 'Which difference makes the difference?' Meijer argues that thinking in the terms in which the dilemma is posed, that is, with its emphasis on the difference between men and women, prevents consideration of the way this difference is also constructed through other differences, such as the division of women into 'genuine' and 'other' women. She stresses the importance of analysing *how* and *which* differences among women (and among men) are made relevant and useful for the construction of 'the' difference as a relationship of inequality. She proposes shifting the central theme of women's studies to the 'sexual division' among one sex, and away from 'the' difference between the sexes.

The third chapter in this section was written by social psychologist Aafke Komter. The point of her contribution is clear from the title – 'The construction of dilemmas in feminism'. According to Komter, the so-called dilemma does not exist. Like Meijer, she criticizes the problematic nature of the 'equality versus difference dilemma debate', but she comes to a different conclusion. She argues that the hypothesis that equality and difference presuppose each other does not clarify matters but creates even more confusion (because of the very ambiguous nature of the concepts used). Concluding that the dilemma is a false one, she argues that it makes no productive contribution and even has a counter-productive effect on research. The dilemma does not originate from the nature of things, but should be seen as the invention of some ('constructivist') feminist scholars. Her solution to the 'dilemma problem' is pragmatic: one should choose either the 'equality' or the 'difference' approach depending on the situation.

Today, the debate on difference–equality no longer concerns the question of whether or not there is a real 'dilemma', and if this should be seen as an obstacle. According to feminist scholars who now use the concepts of difference–equality as an analytical tool, the way both concepts are interwoven in a tense but ever-changing relationship generates new, interesting questions. This is borne out by a great many research projects, and even a complete research programme carried out by one women's studies department.[3]

So although there is an ongoing tendency in women's studies to analyse the genderedness of cultural practices in terms other than explicitly sexual difference (or 'equality'), the ever-changing relationship between equality and difference can still be said to function as a fruitful feminist heuristic method, structuring entire research programmes.

NOTES

1 Joan W. Scott, 'Deconstructing the equality-versus-difference debate: or, the use of post-structural theory for feminism', in *Feminist Studies*, vol. 14, no. 1, 1988.
2 'Equal-rights feminism' tends to deny and minimalize sexual differences because it considers differences between the sexes as an obstacle to social and economic equality. 'Ethical feminism' stresses sexual differences based on the argument that they cannot and should not be denied in the battle for equality.
3 The two professors of women's studies at Utrecht University described their department as 'sexual difference' studies.

1

JUST THE SAME OR JUST DIFFERENT?

A feminist dilemma

Mieke Aerts

In the following article I will attempt to demonstrate that a historicizing approach to what we now call 'sexual difference' can make an important contribution to the breakdown of differences which have carved out a niche within and outside the women's movement. In view of the current condition of (feminist) historiography, I am concerned here with formulating tentative assumptions based on heterogeneous research material from the United States and Germany.

There are strong indications that since its very beginnings in the early nineteenth century, the western feminist movement has been plagued by a dilemma around the concept of sex. On the one hand, feminists strove after verbalization of the specific position of the female sex, and on the other, they emphasized that this specific position was not self-evident. In itself, the conclusion that sexual difference exists but does not suddenly emerge out of thin air is not a dilemma; at most it is a rather meaningless pronouncement. However, as soon as that pronouncement is elaborated into an argument, the underlying contradictions of its composition become clear, and people are apparently forced to emphasize one or other element for the sake of consistency. Viewed in this light, and with some reservations, one could talk about two traditions in the feminist movements of western Europe and the United States.

In one tradition the emphasis is placed on the social injustice done to women. Women are subordinated, discriminated against, oppressed; in comparison with men, women receive second-class treatment; they are continually told they are different from men, so that they will resign themselves to the fact that they do not have the equal rights to which they are entitled. In this tradition, sex is a product of male power. It is not that people do not recognize a difference between men and women, but people dispute in all kinds of ways that this difference should lead to social inequality. For example, by stating that differences between women and differences between men are at least as great as those between women and men; that there may be biological differences between the sexes but they only acquire meaning in a social context; and furthermore that differences identified through biology and psychology are exclusively a result of centuries of unequal treatment and sex-specific socialization. As soon as women have the same rights, opportunities and options as men, the concept of sex will die out as a social structuring principle and make way for an enormous variety of human individuals.

In contrast, the parallel tradition argues that the female sex cannot in any way be reduced to an invention of men – that men should be so lucky! Women definitely share something that men have no part in: a specific connection to the reproduction of humankind (motherhood, children) and a certain sensitivity and emotionality. What women have in common is a difference with regard to the other sex. Some believe this difference developed biologically and others historically. Furthermore, it acquires shape in the feminine experience. This is oppressed in male societies, and can only be made socially effective through the efforts of feminists, which in fact implies a transformation of the whole social order. The intended aim is not so much the abolition of the category of sex, but the ultimate equality of both sexes.

As already noted, some reservations are needed in differentiating these two traditions, if only because the poor state of affairs in feminist historiography necessitates these. Research appears to indicate that during the first feminist wave (c. 1850–1920) the equal-rights perspective dominated in the US and the UK, while the women's culture perspective was most prominent in continental Europe. It would appear that, with the exception of the UK, this state of affairs has been completely reversed during the second feminist wave. But how far are appearances deceptive and, particularly important, why does one and then the other perspective gain the upper hand? These questions need further research. Moreover, an important argument for maintaining reservations is the possible polemic tenor of this differentiation. This is a point to consider carefully.

In the history of the feminist movement other divisions in

perspectives, traditions or argument structures can be discerned. One division that is well known is that between bourgeois and socialist feminists, or between collectivists and individualists. This kind of division continually links up with differences which were and are identified and applied in the political struggle by feminists among themselves and often outside the women's movement. A notorious example is the fierceness with which the socialist Clara Zetkin labelled a section of the women's movement of her time as bourgeois, and thus as bigoted and focused narrowly on the interests of their class.

In the same way, the differentiation applied here between a tradition in which the female sex is perceived as the product of social oppression, and a tradition which emphasizes the inherent characteristics of the female sex, goes back to a political point of contention, which is recognized as such, both within and outside the feminist movement. And it involves all the manoeuvring and taking up of positions that goes with it. The most neutral catch-words for the two positions are 'equal-rights feminists' versus 'feminine-value feminists', or in the Netherlands at the turn of the century, 'rationalists' versus 'ethicists'. Obviously, there's a lot of less elevated language flying back and forth, such as 'insensitives' versus 'romantic fanatics', and 'radicals' versus 'conservatives' (or even 'fascists'). The Dutch Marxist historian Jan Romein's evaluation is typical of this counter-positioning: 'Emancipatory movements usually recognize two tendencies: one which advocates equality with others, and one which wants consideration and recognition of their inherent characteristics. The latter always runs the risk of moving in a conservative direction.'[1] Only the tradition which emphasizes the difference between men and women is seen as potentially conservative. It would seem that by definition the equal-rights struggle is in no danger of that fate.

If in this article I want to focus on the distinction between these two traditions, my objective is not an evaluation in Romein's sense. I am not concerned here with such a negative assessment or with the notion that both traditions assume a different stance, but with the fact that both points of view are concerned with the same question. In other words: before making any kind of pronouncement on the comparative merits of one or both answers to the question about the meaning of 'sexual difference', it could be useful to look at the question itself historically.

At first sight, anthropological and historical studies appear to simply confirm the existence of sexual differences in all social formations. They indicate that women take up different positions from those taken up by men, and that in most cases these positions are subordinate. However, when the results of these studies are scrutinized more closely, it turns out to be impossible to reduce them to one or more constants (which could then form the nucleus of sexual difference). Without bending the data, one cannot get any further than establishing that it is the women who bear the children. It is nowhere near the case that in all societies women have exclusive care of the children or that men have most power in public life, aside from the complications which arise because child care and public life have different meanings in different societies. Even points which are self-evident to western eyes, such as the idea that women are not as strong as men, are sometimes seen differently in other societies.

Feminist researchers such as Michelle Rosaldo have recently pointed out that the contradiction between an apparent universality of sexual difference on the one hand, and an irreducible assortment of empiric data on the other, also stems from the way in which sex and sexual difference is studied. It would appear as though sex is perceived as a product of social relations between people, but in fact the opposite is the case. Because anthropologists and historians apply themselves to answering the question 'What do men do and what do women do?', the question on the development of sex remains implicit. No one questions what 'men' and 'women' are, for this is assumed to be known, and is thus shoved aside to a pre-social level which is then often equated with the biological and/or psychological. No other apparently universal asymmetry (e.g. that between the rich and the poor) is studied in this way. No one applies the pattern of 'What does the one group (the rich) do, and what does the other (the poor) do?' to reach a conclusion on differences between people. By the same token, we should not be applying this kind of approach to the asymmetry between the sexes. That this still happens merely indicates that western historians and anthropologists are preoccupied with a dichotomy which is self-evident to them. Where does this preoccupation come from?

Various studies around this theme produce a summary picture of a history which is less than than 200 years old. It looks something like this: there have, of course, been contrasting sex stereotypes doing the rounds in western Europe for a lot longer, but in the last three decades of the eighteenth century a qualitative change took place. A growing stream of publications, from behavioural manuals to philosophical meditations, arose in which the contrast between the sexes was advanced with ever-increasing systemization as a central principle of social organization. Coupled to this was a tendential breaking down of class-linked attitudes to the correct relationship between the sexes in favour of one dominant ideal which primarily linked up with older ideas on the correct relationship between man as head of the household (patriarch) and the woman as his subordinate and obedient housewife. This ideal begins to look rather different because the sexes are perceived more consistently as each other's opposites which together form a human whole. In contrast to the past, only the woman is still defined by housekeeping and the family, while in addition the scope of sex as a social category has been expanded extensively. It is now made up of a combination of nature, social destiny and inner being, whether God-given or not. According to historian Karin Hausen, the whole looks like this:

Man		**Woman**	
destiny		*destiny*	
	outside		inside
	distance		proximity
	public life		home life
activity		*passivity*	
	energy, (will)power		weakness, surrender
	determination		instability
	bravery		modesty
doing		*being*	
	independent		dependent
	purposeful		industrious
	acquisitive		preserving
	giving		receiving
	persevering		accommodating, self-denying
	violent		loving, good
	antagonistic		sympathetic

rationalism	*emotionalism*
mind	feelings
sense	experience
thinking	receptiveness
knowledge	religiosity
abstraction	understanding

virtue	*virtues*
dignity	chastity
	decency
	charm
	tact
	ability to enhance
	beauty

The polarization of the characteristics represented in this diagram is not based on a simple accumulation of disparate beliefs. It was typical of the reversal which occurred at the end of the eighteenth century that those differences in position and behaviour between men and women which had formerly emerged here and there, were now systematically dealt with, and along a number of channels simultaneously. Not only 'old' established institutions such as the churches and the law, but also the sciences (anthropology, biology and medicine) and literature (novels), played an important role. In recent years, the interconnected 'programme' which thus emerges has been called 'the cult of domesticity' and sometimes 'the cult of true femininity'. These terms indicate that this programme developed sexual difference primarily through the regulation of the 'feminine'. That this programme was highly successful needs no further explanation here. In the second half of the nineteenth century it was extended to more areas of social life and in increasingly large groups of populations in western Europe and the United States, and was able to maintain itself right up to the present day, although more and more cracks are appearing in the façade. Only two questions remain: What are the social backgrounds to the emergence and establishment of this 'invention of the modern sex'? And in view of this, what can be said about the division in feminist traditions sketched above?

Where the description of the 'cult of true femininity' is still fairly fragmentary (primarily as regards relations in western Europe), it necessarily follows that indicating social backgrounds will be the same. Nevertheless, most researchers have come up with the same explanations. These come down to the polarization of the sexes as a junction in the (re)structuring of social relations in western society after the overthrow of the feudal estates – in short, a junction in the establishment of the bourgeoisie's socio-cultural and political hegemony, with retention of male dominance. This involves a number of contradictions which all have somehow to be reconciled. In the first place, there is of course the much-discussed division between men's work and the family, which is not only evident among merchants, manufacturers and industrialists as is sometimes thought, but also exists among civil servants and professionals. In the second place, there is the problem of finding a validation for social hierarchy in a society which, according to the law, consists of equals. And, finally, there is the necessity of neutralizing criticism of the culture of money and profit, rationalization and fragmentation. In the development of 'true femininity', the division between men's work and family life could be seen as both necessary and complementary. The validation of social asymmetries based on 'natural' differences offered a way out of the equality ideology, which had something to offer to the poorest: 'not less, but different'. And something similar applied for the thinking which allocated women the task of devotedly cushioning the failings of commercialization and disenchantment. But the strategic application of sexual difference doesn't end here. It has more uses. In the course of the nineteenth century, a host of other uses were added (nationalism, population politics, imperialism, sexuality). Sex proved to be the link *par excellence* between what is designated as the level of the micropolitical ('the personal') and that of the macropolitical (the state).

Obviously, a little reservation wouldn't be out of place here. Most of the social backgrounds to the femininity cult summarized here have a rather flat recognizability value which leaves much to conjecture about the exact source of this and that. One of the main questions that comes to mind is the extent to which and the way in which these relations were able to penetrate classes other than the bourgeoisie, from which they initially borrowed their content in reality.

In view of the research on the history of western European sex constructions sketched here, the dilemma round sex in the feminist movement can to some extent be clarified. Against a backdrop of the ideal of civil equality and the undermining of the patriarchal authority of men, subordination of the (house)wife became visible as inequality. Here, of course, lie the roots of the 'equal rights' tradition. The invention of the modern female sex at the end of the eighteenth century was initially a competitive social action programme, aimed against struggles for equal rights. But only the generalization of femininity into a social category created a climate in which a general (mass) movement of women became possible, through which a striving after equal rights could also find a new breeding ground. Important feminist concepts such as sisterhood are clearly related to the culture of feminine values which was coupled to the invention of the female sex. And a notion like 'autonomy' performs a kind of bridging function.

Instead of placing the two traditions diametrically opposite each other, it would be more correct historically to see each as the other's prerequisite. It would also be misleading to connect one tradition more with conservatism than the other, as Jan Romein does and many liberals and left-wingers with him. After all, both traditions are product and producer of a modern bourgeois (self-) concept of femininity. Moreover the idea that women 'are just different' and the idea that women 'are just the same' can both be applied to deny the necessity of a feminist movement. As in so many dilemmas, the solution probably does not lie in choosing one side or the other. Just as Minoan acrobats are supposed to have done, feminists will have to take the bull by both horns in order to swing themselves in a graceful gesture over the animal's head. And like everything that looks effortlessly beautiful, that will take a lot of hard work.

NOTES

This chapter was originally published as an article 'Gewoon hetzelfde of nu eenmaal anders? Een feministisch dilemma', in *Dilemmas van het feminisme, Te Elfder Ure 39*, November 1986, vol. 29, no. 1, pp. 4–14, and before that in *Wending*, February 1984.

1 *Op de breukvlak vantwee eeuwen* (On the breakpoint of two centuries), Part II, Brill/Querido, Leiden/Amsterdam, 1967, p. 362. Romein comes to a fairly positive judgement on conservatism in the ling run in 'Het conservatisme als historische categorie' ('Conservatism as historic category') in *Historische lijnen en patronen* (Historic lines and patterns, a selection of his essays), Querido, Amsterdam, 1971, pp. 511–35.

REFERENCES

Please note that this literature list was topical in 1984 when this article first appeared. A whole body of research has, of course, appeared since that date.

Works that are representative of modern historical research into the origins of the position of women in relation to the problems outlined above:

Karin Hausen, 'Die Polarisierung der Geschlechtscharaktere - Eine Spiegelung der Dissoziation von Erwerbs- und Familienleben', in *Sozialgeschichte der Familie in der Neuzeit Europas. Neue Forschungen* herausgeg. von Werner Conze, Ernst Klett, Stuttgart, 1976, pp. 363–93.

Nancy Cott, *The Bonds of Womanhood. 'Woman's Sphere' in New England, 1780–1835*, Yale University Press, New Haven and London, 1977.

Anneke Coutinho-Wiggelendam, 'Vrouwenemancipatie rond de eeuwwisseling en het verzet daartegen. Een vergelijkend onderzoek naar feminisme en anti-feminisme in Nederland in de periode 1870–1914' ('Women's emancipation at the turn of the century and resistance to it. A comparative study of feminism and anti-feminism in the Netherlands, 1870–1914'), in *Tijdschrift voor Vrouwenstudies*, 6, 1981, no. 2, pp. 214–41.

Michelle Z. Rosaldo, 'The use and abuse of anthropology: reflections on feminism and cross-cultural understanding', in *Signs*, vol. 5, no. 3 (Spring), 1980, pp. 385–417.

Siep Stuurman, *Verzuiling, kapitalism en partriarchaat* (Sectarianism, capitalism and patriarchy), SUN, Nijmegen, 1983.

A work that focuses on the historic meaning of anthropology:

Rosalind Coward, *Patriarchal Precedents. Sexuality and Social Relations*, Routledge & Kegan Paul, London, 1983.

2

WHICH DIFFERENCE MAKES THE DIFFERENCE?

On the conceptualization of sexual difference

Irene Costera Meijer[1]

'Difference' and 'equality' of the sexes is a popular topic among feminists. Points of discussion range from the possible existence of a specific women's writing tradition (as a result of the Anna Bijns book award for feminist writing) to a specific women's sexuality (discussions on the compatibility of sado-masochism, prostitution and feminism), girl-oriented mathematics courses, or a separate interest in bio-technology. However, one question arises continually – are women different from or the same as men?

It is to Mieke Aerts' credit that she pointed out the relative distinction between the 'equal-rights tradition' (equality) and the tradition which generates a more critical approach to social and cultural values (difference).[2] Socio-political and legislative approaches may strive after equality, but at present they cannot get round difference. As a result, equality often has to be effected through measures whose point of departure is difference. Examples of this are affirmative action on the labour market, or more encouragement for girls in technical and science subjects. Moreover, in the reasoning behind equality, difference is frequently brought into play. In order to make certain kinds of work more accessible to women, it is said on the one hand that women will do them otherwise, but better (difference). Women are more democratic and would therefore be more effective managers than men. On the other hand, women could keep a battleship in service just as easily as men (equality), while more women on board would mean a considerable improvement in the work climate (difference).

In contrast, the critical tradition within feminism places primary emphasis on the difference between the sexes, but this is done in order to exact in the end an equal evaluation of femininity. For example, 'Women for Peace' stresses the special relationship women have with peace and war issues, but they want to have as much say as men in the acquisition and placing of weaponry, let alone an equal evaluation of the 'female' point of view.

The equality sought by the 'equal-rights tradition' can only be achieved if the feminine (difference) is valued more highly. The 'difference tradition' considers otherness a desirable position because it is critical of cultural structures. Yet this other human being will only be able to use her influence to its fullest capacity when she is taken equally seriously. Difference and equality appear to presuppose each other. This makes it impossible to link both notions separately to socio-political and legislative equal-rights feminism, or its critical sister. Hence difference *and* equality.

The fact that many a politician or scientist becomes involved in the difference-and-equality debate is not so much because it is irrevocably linked to every feminist policy or science. Their engagement stems more from the discovery that the question 'Are women the same or different?' is not a question but a serious dilemma for which no adequate solution has yet been found. Choosing the side of equality means denying the unequal position of women. Choosing difference implies the continuation of sexual inequality.

The romantics among feminists will sometimes force a solution by simply ignoring the masculine, or by choosing a perspective such as 'androgyny'. Unfortunately, this doesn't really solve much of anything. The former option's point of departure is that women are collectively distinct from men. This is probably an erroneous but in any case a premature conclusion. The latter option is a non-starter as no one could manage to analyse androgyny in terms other than masculine and feminine, and so the dilemma looms once again.

The presupposition in the dilemma is that a person's 'sex' is always expressed in terms of difference and equality between women and men, femininity and masculinity. Up until now, men have always formed self-evident comparative material for women. My aim in this article is to undermine this presupposition. In my view, there is much to be said against the self-evidence of the starting point that women and femininity – if they are not already seen as extensions of each other – are in any case set against men and masculinity. I will not explore this hypothesis using the ambivalent character of difference and equality.[3] Many feminists have already come to recognize the importance of this dilemma in feminist activities and analyses. Strangely enough, there appears to be a lot less interest within women's studies itself in the academic counterpart of difference versus equality – the biologism/reproduction of femininity dilemma. If research conceives women as 'different from men', if 'men' or 'masculinity' disappear from view, femininity will invariably degenerate into an exclusive characteristic of women. In their turn, these 'women' are recognized by their biological appearance (biologism). If 'equality' is the starting point of feminist research/women's studies, femininity will function as a separate category which does not necessarily coincide with 'women', but can also characterize 'men'. The meaning of the feminine (emotional, peace-loving, passive, non-violent, intuitive, etc.), however, changes little or not at all.

As I see it, in view of the terms used to express the dilemmas – women and femininity alongside or opposite men and masculinity – the biologism/reproduction of femininity dilemma can be seen as the academic counterpart of the 'different from or equal to men' feminist dilemma. There is a question of *reproduction of femininity* when the feminine within the research does not appear as a contextual variable, but is endlessly reproduced, in other words continues to retain the same meaning. In this case, femininity is not necessarily tied to one sex as it is in *biologism*. There is a question of biologism when femininity can be traced back to the (biological) category women; when what women say, do, think, or how they are characterized, appears in the research as feminine. However, femininity in this case has no fixed form or content.[4]

Marijke Mossink provided an example of reproduction of femininity in an article on her research.[5] Mossink was studying two important Dutch women's peace organizations during the inter-war years – the General Dutchwomen's Peace Union (ANVV) and the Dutch section of the Women's International League for Peace and Freedom (WILPF). She describes her initial aim as examining how 'definitions of femininity' were established in both unions. To that end, she listed all the pronouncements on 'women and peace'.

But there was a problem. They were all so uniform: there was hardly an observable change over the years, and it made no difference whether the pronouncements came from WILPF or the ANVV. That woman=mother=peace seemed an uncompromising given. I think I realized at this point that it wouldn't be enough to limit myself to a reflection of the 'definitions of femininity' in both unions. It seemed so unlikely that there was no difference between feminist pronouncements made in 1915 and the ritual appeal to women as mothers in the Women's Peace March of 1936.[6]

To escape reproduction of femininity, Mossink formulated her research aim as follows: 'My actual goal is to show that there was nothing in either union which was not "feminine": every point of view, every activity, every meeting can be seen as a "construction of the feminine".'[7] However, whether she can also get round the second pitfall, biologism, is open to question. Because the unions are *women's* organizations, everything in both unions is conceived as feminine.

When Mossink considered women as the same as men in principle, when she studied 'definitions of femininity' (independent of the sex of those who expressed them), it appeared that the feminine was an unchanging and unchangeable category. Conversely, now the point of departure of her research is that women form a separate category (other than men), femininity may indeed change, but biologism appears almost inevitable.

Is a reading of sexual difference possible in which researchers do not lapse into biologism or reproduction of femininity? Are the dilemmas inevitable, or can difference, or equality, be conceived in terms other than man/masculinity and woman/femininity? Can the feminine only take shape and acquire content in a relationship with the masculine (and vice versa), or is there something outside the relationship with the masculine? If women's studies wants to substantiate its political aim, if women's studies wants to demonstrate how women and femininity are contextual variables, then it will have to face up to these dilemmas in one way or another.

Perhaps it is possible to get round these dilemmas by taking as focal point a relationship other than the masculine/feminine. It seems to me high time to look sideways, at what has been going on among women and among men. First, I'll give an example of research into the changing meaning of masculinity. Then I'd like to cite two studies which demonstrate the changing meaning of women and femininity. Finally, using a recent feminist debate I will examine how far feminism itself offers an indication of the direction in which we should be seeking a solution to the dilemmas.

Little research has appeared on shifting sex-specific dividing lines within a sex. Quite by accident, I stumbled across a study which provides an illustration of both the problem and the solution. A Dutch cultural anthropologist, Anton Blok, studied the meaning of 'honour', 'sense of honour' and 'codes of honour' in a Mediterranean shepherd community.[8] According to Blok, the concept of honour functions as the most important term in giving meaning to masculinity in Sicily (but also in remote mountain villages in Greece and Spain). He developed this proposition by studying the distinction between real, honourable men and unmanly, dishonourable cuckolds. His study can be seen as research on the shifting dividing lines between real and unmanly men, or, to use his terminology, between virile men and cuckolds. He compares the concept of honour in Mediterranean shepherd communities with modern western European concepts of honour and concludes that masculinity today does not have such strong links to clearly defined codes of honour. 'A person's appearance and especially their physical strength, increasingly less often determine their social position, their sense of worth, their personal identity, their honour.'[9] 'Honour' is no longer an important, and certainly not *the* most important, criterion which distinguishes real men from their more unmanly brothers.

We could have expected Blok to provide us with two lists of typologies which are applicable to virile men and cuckolds respectively, because in his research honour functions as a divisive mechanism between men. Women in Mediterranean agricultural communities have no honour. 'Women are seen as possessions – as part of a patrimony – and at most can claim virtue.'[10] Although honour does not play a role among women, Blok still presents differences between *men* as a *masculine/feminine* diagram. His point of departure is that the logical relationship between honour and shame – presented by him as a complementary opposition – is a transformation of the logical relationship between masculinity and femininity.[11] His lists are, therefore, as follows:

1.	honour	shame
2.	manly (masculine)	womanly (feminine)
3.	men	women
4.	testicles	virginity, chastity
5.	ram	(billy) goat
6.	sheep	goats
7.	virile man	cuckold (billy) goat
8.	strong	weak
9.	brave	cowardly
10.	right	left
11.	pure	impure
12.	silence	noise
13.	ram's horns	goat's horns
14.	god	devil
15.	good	evil
16.	wild	tamed (castrated)
17.	meadows	home
18.	outdoors	indoors
19.	public	closed
20.	men's domain	women's domain
21.	dominance	subjection
22.	healthy	sick
23.	cheese	milk[12]

But if honour and shame are not applicable to women, how logical is this transformation? Blok fails to present a convincing argument that the (sexual) difference between men (in terms of honour) can be generalized to the difference between women and men.

Just take the fourth opposition. In shepherd vernacular, a man with testicles means a man with guts, a brave man. What virginity and chastity are doing there does not become clear from his argument. Conversely, Blok himself supplies the following story:

In the village where I carried out my research, there was a woman who through circumstances had to take care of a lot of matters normally handled by men. She did this in a vigorous way, which commanded respect. One of my informants described her as 'una donna a chi mancano i conglioni' ('the only thing she lacks is testicles'). The man emphasized this standard expression with a characteristic gesture: using a spiral movement, he moved both fists downward and held them in a demonstrative manner in front of his underbelly.[13]

Thus, something that was typical of men – having testicles – did not appear to be unfeminine. This woman's womanhood was not questioned. In this shepherd community, having testicles, having courage and daring, functioned as a general description and a specific characteristic of real men. If they were cowardly, did not have testicles, then they weren't real men. So, in this list of oppositions, testicles should be paired with cowardliness, a category of unmanliness, and not the typically feminine quality introduced here.

There is a further example in the 23rd opposition, cheese–milk: it was unthinkable, because it was unmanly, for men to drink milk. Milk was good for women, the elderly and children. Conversely, eating cheese does not tarnish the womanhood of women.[14] So the criterion for manliness is not cheese, but the refusal to drink milk. The opposition should read drinks versus does not drink milk.

In his research, Blok introduced a lot of empirical material which illustrates how 'unmanly'/'feminine' and 'unfeminine'/'manly' are not interchangeable notions. But because Blok apparently did not fully realize that not all sexual differences between men have to do with womanhood/femininity, femininity becomes a caricature. By applying this kind of masculine/feminine classification, he furthermore attributes characteristics to women which are abso- lutely at odds with his sources. Conversely, if he had presented his research material not as a masculine/feminine list, but as a masculine/non-masculine list analogous to his research question – the shifting criterion for masculinity – he would have been more convincing in his attempt to demonstrate that the concepts men and masculinity are changeable and changing categories. Had he done so, then there would have been no question of a reproduction of masculinity in Blok's research (honour here and now means something quite different from then and there). And he would also have obviated the biologistic side of the dilemma. Whether someone is considered a man in the shepherd community is dependent on (a specific meaning of) honour and is not determined by his biological appearance. In modern western European communities, honour is not a precondition for manhood. The concept has lost importance as a criterion that distinguishes between real men and 'other' men.

The research material shows (in spite of Blok's interpretation of it) that the notion of the unmasculine is entitled to its own inde- pendent status. Men are not 'non-women', and unmanliness is not equal to femininity. The sexual difference Blok analysed exists and changes by the grace of masculine/unmasculine. Using this example, I would like to emphasize how important it is for researchers to ask themselves to what extent, and under which conditions, differences between men and between women are connected to each sex. Sex does not automatically fall neatly into two oppositions – man(ly) and woman(ly). Other women and other men can function just as easily as the opposite sex.

After the other men (cuckolds), I would like to cite two studies concerning a group of other women, that is, 'other than genuine or real' women – homosexual or lesbian women. In the Netherlands, lesbianism, homosexuality among women, functions as an important category of unwomanliness. As a result, for a long time lesbians or homosexual women were not considered genuine women. The studies on divisive mechanisms between women examined here suggest that it is easier to avoid the pitfalls of biologism and the reproduction of femininity if the sexual difference within a sex is the aim of the analysis.

A sound example of changes in unwomanliness over *time* is provided by Annemiek Onstenk in her book *Van brede schouders tot hoge hakken* (From broad shoulders to high heels), which examines the changing image of lesbian women within the COC (the Dutch organization of and for lesbians and homosexuals).[15] In her book, she describes how, in the years after the Second World War, the difference between genuine women and homosexual women became increasingly smaller. She quotes a comment made by a woman in 1964 (in *Vriendschap* (Friendship), no. 102, 1964): 'A lot of things that used to be considered too tough for women are now normal: smoking, drinking, wearing shirts, driving cars . . . the lesbian woman who enjoys all these things to her heart's content no longer differentiates herself in this way from the normal woman.'

An example in which it is not time, but *place* which is the distinguishing factor, is provided by Myriam Everard in an article on lesbian historiography in the Netherlands.[16] She discovered that at the beginning of this century Sapphism among working-class women was considered extremely unwomanly, and sometimes even as manly. On the other side of the coin, the passionate bosom friendships which blossomed between bourgeois women gave almost no cause for consternation.

Both studies show just how mobile womanliness is. Under certain conditions (upper-middle class), passion among ladies had no sexual meaning, but woe betide the working-class woman who 'kept company with' a likeminded friend. Under other conditions, it appeared that the unwomanliness of activities such as smoking, drinking and driving was transitory.

If the minimal aim of women's studies is to point out the changeability and changeableness of women and femininity, it would seem more sensible and useful to concentrate on a relationship other than sexual difference (masculine/feminine). Making visible the shifting meaning of the feminine could prove impossible if the masculine is retained as sole opposition (and vice versa, of course). I would like to suggest turning attention within women's studies away from sexual difference and focusing it on sexual difference between women. To my mind, research on the changeableness and changeability of *unfemininity*, analyses of the changing relationship between femininity and unfemininity, genuine women and other women, the difference in equality/sameness, could make possible the avoidance of biologism and the reproduction of femininity.

An example taken from feminism's most recent history best illustrates this point. In the early 1970s, feminists came across the problem of how and under what conditions sex could appear as an unequivocal category. Their attention was also focused on the changing demarcations between 'genuine' and 'other' within a sex postulated as a unit. I analysed the criteria which were applied by contemporary feminist magazines to distinguish 'genuine' women from their 'unfeminine' counterparts.[17] The formulation of these dividing lines was accompanied by fierce discussions. Paarse September (Purple September) – the Netherlands' first radical-feminist action group – initiated this debate in 1972.

The immediate cause was the question of whether homosexual women could be feminists, or whether their other 'nature' would discredit feminism. Being a genuine woman was seen as a precondition for making valid feminist statements. 'If you're seen as a "homo-woman" [gay woman], then you're suddenly somebody else, and what you say about women's rights is no longer valid.'[18] Your feminism was said to have developed from rancour and penis envy. Only genuine women's feminist views appeared to be taken seriously. The question of whether homosexual women were (genuine) women and could also participate as lesbians in feminist activities was the starting point of a debate on feminism and lesbianism which would go on for more than a decade.

The central point in this debate was whether lesbians – and later also feminists – were women. This was a totally different matter from the question of whether all women were the same. The point of these discussions was not the recognition of the existence of various femininities or differences between women, but whether all women were women. It concerned the difference, not between the sexes, but between women.

Under the slogan 'compulsory heterosexuality and lesbianism as a political choice', feminists discussed their own conditions of existence for more than ten years. They differentiated between the identity issue (how to give yourself form and content) and the sexuality issue (how to handle your relationships). The first four years of this debate (1971–1975) were interesting because a great reversal took place in the evaluation of 'women' and 'femininity'. If in 1972 there was still an all-pervasive sense of a feminist difference in terms of 'we women' versus 'them, "homo-women"',[19] by 1975 the difference had become less simple. In the intervening period, a number of new women had emerged who defied classification in these simple categories: the 'married homophile woman', feminists who considered 'their lesbianism as a political choice against the heterosexual norm'; the 'woman-identified women'; (heterosexual) feminists who discovered lesbianism as an 'extra dimension'; and the feminists who 'just happened' to be lesbians – the 'lesbian feminists'.[20]

In the space of four years, the phrase 'we women' made way for 'we feminists'. The criterion for participation in the women's movement shifted from 'feminine' to 'unmasculine'.[21] In 1975, it was the turn of women who identified with men and preferred a 'masculine' sexuality – i.e. an unequal, dominant sexuality in which women functioned as (sex) objects, and which was oriented towards achievement and technique – to be excluded from the title of feminists. *Les extrèmes se touchent.* There was no place any more within feminism for the 'genuine', 'heterosexual-woman'[22] and the 'male-identified lesbian'.[23]

In the area of sexuality, feminist meant 'unmasculine', in other words, not enjoying 'male' sexuality. At the identity level, on the other hand, feminist meant 'unfeminine'. Feminists were not supposed to fulfil typical female role patterns. The lesbian evolved within feminism from an excluded to a privileged category. In 1973,

41

a leading and well-known Dutch feminist put it like this:

> Lesbian feminists could be an example for other women in the way they deal with their relationships and search for their own identity. In relationships without men, all the warmth doesn't have to come from one partner, and eroticism can finally be stripped of dominance. Furthermore, lesbian women are confronted more irrevocably and sooner than others with the question: who am I, myself, apart from a (potential) wife? What do I want to do with my life? If lesbian feminists could describe how they have given form to themselves and their erotic relationships with women, that could mean a great stimulus for feminism.[24]

If women's identity was at issue, a division was made between femininity and non-femininity. Which women were feminine, and which were not? In the identity issue, the lesbian functioned as a *'non-feminine'* category. 'Socially speaking, they fall outside the pattern of the bread-winning man and the wife who takes care of the family. . . . They demand the right not to behave as women are supposed to, and they do not conform to the female sex role of the soft woman.'[25] Feminists distinguished 'genuine' from 'other' women. And a whole new range of identities for women was the result of that distinction.

It is true that a division also occurred in the domain of sexuality, but this was couched in terms of 'masculine' and 'non-masculine'. The lesbian functioned here as a unifying factor for these new women. It served as a model for *'non-masculine'*, which was not oriented towards achievement or technique and not interwoven with power and violence. A lesbian sexuality was different from that of men. Although there is no question of diverse new sexualities for women – there was a striving after a recognition of a common sexual feeling – women did emerge (and this was new) as the *subject* of sexual pleasure.

The ambivalent, almost ambiguous, use of 'lesbian' (it could mean both non-feminine and non-masculine) made the debate around homosexuality and feminism – 'compulsory heterosexuality and lesbianism as a political choice' – a unique occurrence. The lesbian undermined the dilemma of 'difference and equality' where it stressed its distinction as a 'non-feminine' category. Therefore, in this sense, we can no longer speak in terms of 'reproduction of femininity', for it was the rift between lesbianism and femininity which generated a new sexual position and new identities for women.

Not everything women thought, wanted or did was labelled feminine in this feminist debate. Unfemininity and unmasculinity were, after all, important attributes of women. In the discussions on homosexuality and feminism, the dividing lines between genuine and other women, genuine and other feminists were extended time and again. By examining these changing borders, the changing meanings of 'unfeminine' and 'feminine' become visible, revealing the changing conditions under which women appear as a unit. In this sense, research on other differences between other sexes can avoid not only reproduction of femininity, but also biologism.

Lesbians are not, of course, the only category of 'other' women. The womanhood of whores, black women, or female factory workers – let alone combinations of these – was a point of discussion not too long ago.[26] Could it be that the central focus of women's studies should not be the notion 'femininity', but 'unfemininity'? I propose women's studies should give much more of its attention to groups of 'other women'. Research into the 'border differences' between genuine and other women, femininity and unfemininity, would not deliver us from the difference versus equality dilemma in itself, but phrases it in much more productive terms. It could make us more alert to new constructions of (un)femininity. A focus on shifts in borders could bring to light how we can expand our room to move, our behavioural and identity options.

NOTES

This chapter originally appeared as an article, 'Welk verschil maakt het verschil?' in *Tijdschrift voor Vrouwenstudies*, 4, 1987.

1 I would like to thank Tjitske Akkerman, Liesbeth Bervoets, Ines Orobio de Castro, Nelleke Vercouteren and Mieke Aerts for their comments on earlier versions of this chapter.
2 See note 3.
3 For an extensive exposition on the feminist difference versus equality dilemma, see M. Aerts' contribution to this book, pp. 23–31; N.F. Cott, 'Feminist theory and feminist movements: the past before us', in J. Mitchell, A. Oakley (eds), *What is Feminism? A Re-examination*, Pantheon Books, New York, 1986, pp. 49–63; A. Sommer, 'Het verschil en de gelijkheid. Inleiding bij de lezingen' ('Difference and Equality. An introduction to the lectures'), in *Tijdschrift voor Vrouwenstudies*, vol. 6,

no. 4, 1985, pp. 382–95; R. Milkman, 'Women's history and the Sears Case', in *Feminist Studies*, vol. 12, no. 2 (Summer 1986), pp. 375–400.

4 I have purposely chosen a definition which is as broad as possible. By allowing biologism to refer not only to the biological functions of women, but also to the biological category 'women' itself, I hope to avoid the, to my mind, dubious distinction which is often made between the so-called socially determined characteristics of women (gender) and her biologically-based qualities (sex). For this reason I prefer the term sex to gender. Sex is as much culturally, socially and historically constructed as gender. Using 'gender' as the central term potentially stresses an essential difference between sex and gender.

5 Mossink, 'Uit de duisternis het diepe in' ('Out of the darkness into the deep'), in *Heden, Verleden Vrouwen 1. Het Vrouwelijke Georganiseerd* (Present, Past Women 1. The Female Organized), compiled by M. Aerts, U. Jansz, M. Mossink, J. Withuis and published by the Women's Studies Department, Social Sciences Faculty, University of Amsterdam, 1986, pp. 175–92.

6 Ibid., p. 189.

7 Ibid., p. 178.

8 A. Blok, 'Eer en de fysieke persoon' ('Honour and the physical person'), in *Tijdschrift voor Sociale Geschiedenis* (Journal of Social History), vol. 6, no. 18, 1980, pp. 211–30.

9 Ibid., p. 226.

10 Ibid., p. 219.

11 Ibid., p. 219.

12 Ibid., pp. 222–3.

13 Ibid., p. 221.

14 Ibid., p. 223.

15 A. Onstenk, *Van brede schouders tot hoge hakken. Veranderende beeldvorming over lesbische vrouwen in de periode 1939–1965* (Changing representations of lesbian women in the period 1939–1965), SUA, Amsterdam, 1983.

16 M. Everard, 'Verandering en verschil. Lesbische geschiedenis in Nederland' ('Change and difference. Lesbian history in the Netherlands'), in *Lover*, vol. 10, no. 4, December 1983, pp. 198–201 and 253–4.

17 From 1985, I have been doing research on this debate under the title 'Echte vrouwen en andere vrouwen. Feminisme – homoseksualiteit, 1972–1982' ('Real women and other women. Feminism and lesbianism, 1972–1982'). The research examines the way the difference between 'Genuine' and 'Other' women acquires shape within the debate as a possible expression of a shifting area of tension between 'femininity' and 'sexuality'. The research will conclude with the systematic examination of the changing – historical – role of the lesbian in this process.

18 A. Meulenbelt in *Sekstant*, January, 1973.

19 At a lecture given in 1972 to the first forum on women's homosexuality in western Europe, Marijke Oort, a committee member of the then largest feminist organization in the Netherlands, Man–Vrouw–Maatschappij (Man–Woman–Society), said: 'Our [women's] view of homosexuality is linked to our view of ourselves. As long as we

continue to believe a woman is not a real woman unless she has a man, then we apparently also believe a woman can only derive her self-worth and identity from a man. . . . Until we begin to take sexuality among women seriously, we cannot take our own sexuality seriously, or we will continue to think sexuality cannot exist without specific, indispensable genitalia.' In *MVM-Nieuws* (MVM News), May, 1972, p. 11.

20 I will not go into the emergence of these identities, nor the context, intensity, place, principal figures or the debate's course. For more on these subjects, please see my article 'Echte vrouwen en supervrouwen. Feminisme en homoseksualiteit, 1972–1975' ('Genuine women or superwomen. Feminism and Homosexuality'), in *Te Elfder Ure 39 Dilemma's van het Feminisme* (Dilemmas of feminism), vol. 29, no. 1, November 1986, pp. 59–78.

21 An example as illustration: 'I did all those things that men normally do, the things we hate so much. . . . Then I came across a consciousness raising discussion group. And I acted like a real man there. . . . After a while, I withdrew because I'd become so confused about myself. My "role" had really started bothering me, but I didn't know what to do about it. It took me about a year to get out of the confusion. By that time, I knew I didn't have to behave like a man at all. . . . In the meantime, the women's centre had been set up and I met a lot of people there I used to know. . . . Almost no one saw how I had changed. I was judged and condemned for behaviour feminists especially should have understood. . . . That was six months ago, and I think I've managed to get rid of most of my old image.' Anonymous, 'Ik ben een homo' ('I am a homosexual'), in *Vrouwenkrant* no. 12, November/December, 1974.

22 On Femø, a feminist holiday island, Anja Meulenbelt was asked point-edly why she had an IUD. 'Because I still see myself as an appliance, I'm all prepared for the eventuality of wanting a man again, not that I think that's likely. . . . and then I got rid of the IUD, everyone applauds, an historic deed, after seven years of availability I have given back my body to myself.' Anja Meulenbelt, in *Sekstant*, November, 1974.

23 Meulenbelt in *Opzij* (a Dutch feminist magazine), March, 1974: 'The woman who comes up to me in the COC, chucks me under the chin and says: "isn't she a little darling", is, in my opinion, just as sexist as her paternalistic brothers and is absolutely not feminist.'

24 Joke Kool-Smit, 'De seringen bloeien, ('The lilac is blooming'), in *Opzij*, November, 1973.

25 Ibid.

26 In addition to the studies by Onstenk and Everard already mentioned above, see also: J. Walkowitz, 'Male vice and feminist virtue: feminism and the politics of prostitution in 19th-century Britain', in: *History Workshop Journal*, Issue 13, Spring 1982, pp. 79–93; N.F. Cott, *The Bonds of Womanhood. 'Woman's Sphere' in New England, 1780–1835*, Yale University Press, New Haven and London, 1977; J. Dowd Hall, 'The Mind that burns in each body: women, rape and racial violence', and K. Peiss, 'Historical notes on working-class sexuality, 1880–1920', in A. Snitow, C. Stansell and S. Thompson (eds), *Powers of Desire. The Politics of Sexuality*, Monthly Review Press, New York, 1983.

3

THE CONSTRUCTION OF DILEMMAS IN FEMINISM

Aafke Komter

INTRODUCTION

There has never been a lack of rapid classifications in 'theoretic positions' in women's studies. In current feminist circles you'll often hear that someone is 'pro difference', or conversely 'pro equality'. This kind of classification usually goes hand in hand with a condemnation of those who have opted for a position different from the speaker's own. One attendant advantage is that the sheep can be separated from the goats, and that the goats can distinguish themselves from the sheep.

The basis of the classification sketched above lies in the 'difference versus equality' dilemma that has been in vogue for some time now.[1] A further dilemma which is often mentioned in the same breath concerns the choice of sexual difference as a point of departure for women's studies, or the study of 'many differences in femininity'.[2]

In this article I would like to examine how far both these dilemmas are truly dilemmas, in other words situations 'necessitating a choice between equally unfavourable or disagreeable alternatives' (*Webster's New World Dictionary*). I will attempt this using as backdrop a somewhat older feminist debate: the debate on the possibility of a general theory of femininity. Feminist theory over the past two decades exhibits a strong tendency towards searching for general explanations for broad problem areas: 'gender relationships' or, more recently, 'femininity'.[3] As became apparent from a number of articles in the *Tijdschrift voor Vrouwenstudies*, feminists in the early 1980s began to doubt the possibility of a general feminist theory. In my view, these hesitations opened the way for the formulation of the dilemmas described above.

First of all, I would like to touch on the recent history of feminist theory. My intention is not to give an exhaustive overview, but to sketch the theoretic background from which the contemporary dilemmas emerged, and to evaluate these. Then I will attempt to describe the transition from questions concerning the possibility of a general theory to questions concerning difference and equality. Subsequently I will go into a number of problems which, in my view, are linked to the debate on difference and equality. In the conclusion I will come back to the question of the 'dilemma nature' of the dilemmas under discussion.

RECENT HISTORY OF FEMINIST THEORY: IN SEARCH OF A GENERAL THEORY

The Marxist perspective

The first call for a general theory on women's oppression dates from the beginning of the 1970s. At that time, various movements in feminism had evolved which differed greatly in their political and strategic aims. However, in a theoretical sense, these were frequently based on the same source – Marxism. Radical-feminist analyses in terms of the 'sex-class-system'[4] together with the socialist-feminist theory on (re)production relations in terms of 'patriarchy'[5] shared a common ancestry in Marxist theory.

The marriage between Marxism and feminism already contained the seeds of the process of theoretic feminism's division into different, often rival theoretic movements. This became clearly visible in the so-called 'domestic labour debate' in which diverse interpretations of the correct Marxist analysis of domestic labour vied for precedence.

Over the years, the marriage between feminism and Marxism was increasingly seen as an unhappy one[6] and a more or less strict divorce was advocated.[7] The women's movement in particular was demanding more attention for the differences between women themselves. Within women's studies there was a growing conviction that the earlier analyses in terms of the sex-class-system or patriarchy were too monolithic and failed to explain the way in which women differed from each other in their political, cultural and sexual loyalties, and through their identities as members of a specific class or ethnic group. Moreover, the economic focus of Marxist analysis proved inadequate where matters such as sexuality and motherhood were concerned.

The psychoanalytical perspective

A new, potentially attractive – and authoritative – marriage partner presented itself in the form of psychoanalysis. Authors such as Juliet Mitchell, Gayle Rubin and Nancy Chodorow provided new and important insights – from differing points of departure – into the psychological and ideological complexities of femininity, masculinity and sexual relations. They sparked off attention on the way in which 'sexual identity' or 'femininity' is constituted in the context of 'kinship systems', such as primary family relationships.

But the union between psychoanalysis and feminism was soon in trouble too. Was the Lacanian variant the most promising,[8] or could more be expected from the psychoanalytical tradition of object relationships articulated by Nancy Chodorow?[9] Both approaches shared a tendency towards certain universal concepts such as castration and the Oedipus complex, but the results of their analyses pointed in very different directions. In the former approach, the phallus was emphasized as *the* sex-linked symbol of meaning in our culture, and was seen as responsible for the fundamentally different ways in which women and men are inserted symbolically into our culture. The latter approach stressed mothering as *the* structuring principle of gender identity and sexual relations. But the almighty effect of the symbol of the phallus turned out to be difficult to explain from Lacanian thinking itself, and Chodorow's emphasis on the universality of the sex-linked psychological consequences of women's mothering were also criticized with increasing frequency. Her theory was said to neglect the essence of psychoanalysis – the unconscious – thus transforming psychoanalysis into a 'socialization theory'. The marriages between feminism and Marxism on the one hand, and between feminism and psychoanalysis on the other, had brought to light two serious problems. One was the discovery of the illusion of a 'given' feminine subject. The other, interconnected problem was that the stability of the object of feminism – once simply defined as 'women's oppression' - began to crumble. Not only was there a growing doubt about the analytical or theoretical usefulness of the concept 'women's oppression', but people also began to ask themselves what 'feminism' actually was.[10] In part, these developments appear to be the result of the increasing fragmentation of the women's movement as a political movement.

But the fragmentation within theoretic feminism itself also seems to have contributed to the increasing doubt about 'women' and 'feminism'.

In any case, the time appeared ripe for a new theoretic approach which was both in line with the decreasing certainty around the female subject as a given entity, and with the increasing hesitation on what the object of feminism actually was. This approach was found in the discourse analysis inspired by Foucault in which the primary focus is the constructed character of 'femininity'. A different train of thought concentrated more on gender as a relationship which is fundamentally structured by power. A short discussion of both approaches follows here.

The discourse analytic perspective

This approach considers femininity as constructed through a discursive plurality of positions. Categories such as sexuality, sex, gender, femininity, etc., have no fixed meanings. Research should be directed at the myriad ways in which the production of meaning concerning these categories comes about, and at the power mechanisms which play a role in this process.

Whereas in the past feminism had been concerned with the study of *results and consequences* of sexual relations, discourse analysis shifted attention to the *premisses* of these: what *is* gender? If there is such a thing as gender, how is it constructed? How can we talk of inequality when the category 'women' has no fixed meaning?

Although in this approach universalism – in the sense of general explanatory principles – appears to be absent (after all, 'femininity' is associated with continually shifting meanings and a plurality of differences), it is another species of a 'general theory', which in this sense is comparable with the Marxist and psychoanalytic perspective. After all, the power of the discourse is considered to be omnipresent and thus almighty: each social phenomenon or each social category is seen exclusively from the point of view of its discursive construction.

As with the Marxist and psychoanalytic perspectives, some problems adhere to the discourse approach also. First of all, through the emphasis on fundamental diversity and ambiguity, the concepts 'gender' and 'femininity' are in danger of losing their meaning as 'concepts', that is as conceptual labels which refer to specific, definable realities, altogether. The idea of 'women' as an underprivileged social category is in danger of being sucked into the bottomless swamp of continually shifting meanings. Is there any point in talking about 'women' when nothing enduring can be said? A rigorous anti-essentialism can literally lead to speechlessness, as is demonstrated by the untimely demise of the English journal *m/f*.

A second problematic aspect of discourse analysis is the underlying image of mankind. Although it is certainly true that on a general level people are continually occupied with the production and reproduction of meaning, too strong a fixation on the 'constructed' character of social reality can lead to a neglect of other relevant characteristics of people, such as their 'agency' – the fact that they are creatures who act – and their ability to change social reality through intervening in certain practices, or by inventing *new* meanings.

A third problem is that as a result of the preoccupation with the precarious status of the concepts 'femininity' and 'woman', the relevance of the concepts 'masculinity' and 'man' is in danger of being lost.

In contrast to common discourse analytical practice, in power approaches gender is considered emphatically as a relationship in which both 'femininity'/'women' and 'masculinity'/'men' play a role.

The power perspective

The most elaborated example of a power approach to explain gender relations is provided by Nancy Hartsock.[11] She has tried to design a general theory on gender, power and class. Based on a (somewhat adjusted) Marxist analysis, she arrives at a theory which attempts to explain both the sexual and class dimensions of dominance. She refers to the various ways in which Eros and power have become linked to each other in our western world and have structured sexual relations. The erotic dimension of power has assumed the form of opposition and dominance, Hartsock argues. Power and dominance have become associated with masculinity, and through this link a symbolic blend of sexuality, violence and death has come into being. A further facet of her theory is the conception that women's material world is structured in a fundamentally different way from that of men, which is said to be apparent from the division of labour between the sexes. In her analysis, Hartsock suggests '[laying] aside the important differences among women and instead [to search] for central commonalities across race and class boundaries'.[12] In her view of power, the exercise of power by one party is always at the expense of the other. Men and women 'share no common interest, and experience each other as threats to continued existence'.[13]

From Hartsock's power approach it is impossible to see women simultaneously as (socially constructed) gender *and* as having different sexual, political and cultural loyalties. Moreover, a questionable power concept emerges from her assumptions on fundamentally opposed interests of women and men, and from her view of power as a one-sided phenomenon: in her eyes power is exclusively oppressive and by definition based on conflict. Finally, her representation of the way in which women and men experience and give form to Eros is thickly larded with classic gender stereotypes.

However different in other respects, all the theoretic perspectives sketched above have a common point of departure in that they all have a certain pretension to generality. By this I mean that insight is sought into global matters such as 'femininity' or 'sexual relations' from the point of departure of a global analytical framework. The results of the various theoretic approaches are very diverse: in the case of Marxism, psychoanalysis and power, differences within the category women are neglected, whereas the discourse approach over-accentuates them. Both types of results, however, can in my view be traced back to theoretical pretensions of generality.

Explanations in terms of 'patriarchal (re)production relations', 'the female position with regard to the phallus', a 'one-sided power relationship' or 'constructions of femininity', can only offer interpretations of social reality on a very global level. Adherents of the psychoanalytical perspective, for example, repeatedly stated that the description of the various ways in which women and men are inserted into the symbolic order would produce a theory on the origins of femininity in our culture. And women who work with discourse analysis emphasize time and again that femininity is a discursive construction, that women, sexuality and sex are not 'given' but are socially constructed. Although broadly speaking these claims are not incorrect, they are not particularly informative when explanations of real aspects of the lives of real women are concerned, or when we want to know precisely how these aspects are linked to social constructions and how these in their turn are related to social, cultural, political or economic givens.

The most important difficulty with the theoretic approaches discussed here seems to be that both what has to be explained – gender,

femininity – and the explanatory principles – e.g. social constructions – are formulated in terms which lack theoretic differentiation
and empirical specificity.

In recent years, there has been a growing awareness within wom-
en's studies of the limitations of general theories. In the next section
I would like to examine more closely the theoretical developments
within women's studies which demonstrate this.

HESITATIONS ABOUT THE POSSIBILITY OF
GENERAL THEORIES

In 1983, the question was raised in the *Tijdschrift voor Vrouwenstudies* of the possibility of a general theory of femininity.[14] In the
ensuing discussion, Rosalind Coward gave an affirmative answer to
this question: according to her, psychoanalysis can offer a general
theory on the origins of femininity in our culture because the
dominant forms of gender constructions are described by it.[15]

Although they themselves make no clear pronouncements about
the question, Sommer and Dornekater perceive a fundamental
contradiction in Coward's view: 'Coward holds on to the contradiction of seeing women as a sex while still conceiving sexual categories
as discursive constructions.'[16] Here we see the first contours of
an emerging dilemma: recognition of sexual difference cannot go
together with recognition of various constructions of femininity.

This line of thought appears to have smoothed the way for a
new debate that became the theme of a conference held in 1985:
'Difference and Equality'. The central question on the 'strategies of
women's studies' was formulated as follows: 'Do women's studies
coincide with a theory on sexual difference and femininity, or
should the breakdown into many differences and femininities be
the central focus?'[17]

The dilemma between equality and difference was further elaborated in other publications.[18] Two traditions are discerned in
the history of feminism. One is based on 'equality' (women are
essentially equal to men and sexual difference is created solely by
social conditions), whereas the point of departure of the other is 'difference' (women are essentially different from men and femininity
should be accentuated and valued in a context of social equality).

Although equality and difference are considered as a dilemma,
at the same time the two concepts are seen as presupposing each
other. The solution to the dilemma is not to choose one or the other

position; the dilemma should be transcended in one way or another, but this is considered an almost impossible task.[19]

In Chapter 2 Irene Costera Meijer has sketched the dilemma between difference and equality as one of the most important pre-occupations of contemporary feminism. In her view it is 'a serious dilemma for which no adequate solution has yet been found'.[20]

Costera Meijer describes the dilemma as follows:

> Socio-political and legislative approaches may strive after equality, but at present they cannot get round difference. As a result, equality often has to be effected through measures whose point of departure is difference. . . . Moreover, in the reasoning behind equality, difference is frequently brought into play. . . . In contrast, the critical tradition within feminism places primary emphasis on the difference between the sexes, but this is done in order to exact in the end an equal evaluation of femininity. . . . The equality sought by the 'equal-rights tradition' can only be achieved if the feminine (difference) is valued more highly. The 'difference tradition' considers otherness a desirable position because it is critical of cultural structures.[21]

This dilemma, according to Costera Meijer, goes hand in hand with another – 'the biologism/reproduction of femininity dilemma'. Assuming that women are different from men can ultimately be traced back to biologism, whereas the point of departure of 'equality' carries the implication that the feminine or femininity is reproduced.

Costera Meijer sees a fundamental incompatibility between attention to sexual difference and the analysis of shifts in meaning of 'femininity': 'Making visible the shifting meaning of the feminine could prove impossible if the masculine is retained as sole opposition (and vice versa, of course).'[22] Here again we see the formulation of the dilemma whose first contours became visible in Sommer and Dornekater (see note 16). A way out of the dilemma, according to Costera Meijer, is to make different kinds of femininity, rather than 'sexual difference', the central theme of women's studies. Instead of using men and masculinity as an automatic comparison for women, she suggests focusing research on the analysis of 'the changing relationship between femininity and unfemininity, genuine women and other women, the difference in equality/sameness'.[23]

A number of problems are contained in the above view which

I believe are not limited to this specific view, but which also characterize other contributions to the debate on difference and equality discussed here. In the following section I will examine these problems more closely.

PROBLEMS IN THE DEBATE ON DIFFERENCE AND EQUALITY

In my view, the debate on difference and equality is clouded by four conceptual obscurities which I will expand on below:

1. In the debate on 'difference' and 'equality' we frequently hear 'Difference and Equality' or 'The Difference' and 'The Equality'. The capitals and the articles appear to suggest an unequivocalness of meaning which on subsequent examination does not exist. More-over, 'difference' is frequently set against 'equality' as if there was an opposition between the two concepts.

If we examine 'difference' and 'equality' more closely, we find that all kinds of semantic distinctions can be made within each of these terms. The list below is certainly not exhaustive, but I have placed alongside each other terms which can be considered as each other's 'correlates' or opposites:

'difference'	*'equality'*
– inequality	– equality
– non-resemblance	– resemblance
– diversity	– identity
– non-equivalence	– equivalence
– pluriformity	– uniformity
– asymmetry	– symmetry
– difference	– similarity
– distinction, e.g. opposition, polariz-ation, dichotomization, discrimination	– non-distinction

First of all, we observe that 'difference' and 'equality' are in no way necessarily each other's opposites. Logically, a more appropriate partner for 'difference' would be 'similarity' rather than 'equality'.

Also relevant to discussions on 'difference' and 'equality' is the distinction between 'difference' and 'distinction'. According to Anthony Wilden – from whom this distinction is borrowed – 'difference' indicates variations in size, frequency, division or organization of certain (social or physical) givens; he believes 'distinction' comes into being through a *decision* (conscious or unconscious) to establish a specific demarcation (between groups, between parts of a system, between fore and background, etc.).[24] For 'decision' we can also read here: agreement, rule, norm, treatment, attribution (of characteristics, for example).

By applying this distinction we can, for example, conceptually demarcate the socially generated gender differences in the disposal of diverse kinds (e.g. psychological and material) of 'resources' - 'difference' - from juridical and social rules and norms which imply a 'distinction' between women and men. Other examples of 'distinction' are the conscious or unconscious tendency to attribute various characteristics and qualities to either gender, and the broader cultural tendency to think about the sexes in terms of oppositions, dichotomies or polarities while there are at most only certain types of differences.[25]

If one overlooks the diverse semantic distinctions, and if one speaks about 'difference' and 'equality' before it has become clear what is meant exactly, one risks reifying these concepts, which will certainly not advance the debate.

2. It appears that the concepts of difference and equality have different functions and often no distinction is made between them in the debate. Difference and equality appear to act as:

- philosophical suppositions about what is feminine and what is masculine (e.g. social skills as feminine and cognitive capacities as masculine)
- description of aspects of social reality (e.g. women and men are 'the same' in so far as they are human beings, have certain cognitive and emotional options, whereas they are 'different' as regards their social positions)

- political arguments for an equal or different treatment of women and men (e.g. 'women are just as good as men in science', or 'women are better leaders than men', and therefore they should be treated equally/differently)

- political aims which people want to realize (e.g. social equality for women and men, or social differentiation in the positions of the sexes).[26]

In a recent article, Nancy Cott describes how the American suffragettes used both 'equality' and 'difference' arguments in their political struggle without having any trouble with a dilemma.[27]

Cott talks here about a 'salutary ambiguity'. This example shows how the meaning of the concepts difference and equality can vary depending on their function and context. 'Equality' and 'difference' as political *arguments* do not have to correspond with philosophical *assumptions* on the essence of woman which are the implicit or explicit point of departure. The American suffragettes clearly used both arguments because they saw them as politically opportune, regardless of their own views on the essence of woman. And to make it all just that bit more complicated: equality and difference as political *arguments* can, but do not have to, run parallel to equality and difference as political *aims*. For example, a political argument can be that women are equal to men and should therefore be treated equally. However, it is also possible to argue that women are 'different' so as to strive after equality as a political aim: women are better managers so they should enjoy positive discrimination in order to achieve a more equal ratio of female and male managers.

3. Besides the lack of clarity of meaning of the concepts 'difference' and 'equality' themselves (see point 1), people appear also to have different (implicit and explicit) assumptions about the origins and the nature of 'difference' and 'equality'.[28] There appears to be a difference of opinion on the question of whether sexual differences have a social rather than a natural or 'essential' origin.[29]

In the so-called equality tradition, 'equality' is considered essential (women and men are essentially equal) and 'difference' is seen as social (manifesting itself in hierarchical inequality). However, in the difference tradition the meaning of both concepts is reversed: 'difference' is conceived as essential (essential otherness) and 'equality' is social (equality is a social good that can be achieved through egalitarian politics). Equality and difference, therefore, appear to have different meanings in the two theoretic traditions in which they figure.

As Costera Meijer rightly says, in social and juridical measures to promote equality between the sexes, the point of departure is a difference. We are concerned here with the *social* meaning of difference: difference as hierarchical inequality. In the culture-critical position sketched by her, the point of departure is an *essential* difference, an essentially other femininity which should, however, be evaluated equally.[30]

4. The debate continually emphasizes that the concepts of difference and equality 'presuppose each other'.[31] On closer examination

this presupposition itself appears problematic. Does the assumption of *essential equality* presuppose a difference? Not an essential difference, as that would be a contradiction. At most one has to eliminate a social difference. Does striving after *social equality* presuppose a difference? This means nothing more profound than that without social inequality there would be no need to strive after social equality. Striving after social equality in no way presupposes an essential difference, only a social one.

Does the assumption of an *essential difference* presuppose equality? Essential equality drops out as a possibility. At most, the assumption of an essential otherness of women will sometimes *go together* with a striving after an equal social evaluation. That is, however, not the same as difference *presupposing* equality.[32]

In short, the proposition that 'equality and difference presuppose each other' creates more confusion than insight. In no way do the concepts necessarily presuppose each other. Nor are they by definition each other's opposites as we have already seen.

From the above it will be clear that the concepts 'difference' and 'equality' do not have fixed, given meanings but are 'constructed' in certain contexts. In this 'construction', the various possible meanings and functions of 'difference' and 'equality' are often not recognized. As a result, it is difficult to determine what the debate is actually about.

These conceptual obscurities also affect the other dilemma discussed earlier: the dilemma between 'sexual difference' and 'differences in femininity' as a central theme of women's studies. For those who see this as a dilemma, the situation is perhaps comparable to the 'perceptual incongruence' which occurs when looking at a picture of a vase which is also a woman's face: you see one or the other, but never the two at the same time. Yet this incongruence is only ostensible: the fact that x1,2,3,4 . . . through x10 differs in certain ways from y1,2,3,4 . . . through y10, does not mean that the 'x's cannot differ from each other (and that applies to the 'y's as well). Nor does it mean that it is impossible to study both kinds of differences.

To apply this to women's studies: the differentiation between a socially constructed female and male gender in no way excludes the recognition of differences between women or, if you prefer, many femininities. There is neither a logical nor a theoretic problem here.[33] To use Nancy Cott's words: 'Feminist stress on women's socially constructed "difference" from men can go along with recognition of diversity among women themselves, if we acknowledge the multifaceted entity – the patchwork quilt, so to speak – that is the group called women.'[34]

CONCLUSION

As long as obscurities in the meaning and application of the concepts difference and equality have not been resolved, there is no sense in talking about a dilemma. A further reason for not doing so is that even those who see a dilemma here argue that it is not useful to choose either one side or the other.[35] A dilemma which comes with a recommendation not to choose either of the two sides is not really a dilemma in the sense of the Webster definition given at the beginning of this article. The implication here is that the other, related dilemma – that of 'making visible the shifting meaning of the feminine' on the one hand and 'sexual difference as central focus' on the other[36] – cannot be considered a Real Dilemma which justifies capital letters.

Exclusive attention for 'women' and 'men' as opposite social categories, which we find in Marxist and psychoanalytical approaches and in approaches whose point of departure is a one-sided power relation, does not do justice to the diversity in gender relations. If one focuses exclusively on differences and diversity within the category 'women', as is sometimes the case in discourse analysis, one runs the risk of overlooking the systematic pattern of inequality in gender relations, and thus the fact that gender relations are fundamentally determined by power. The strength of one type of approach appears to be the other's weakness. By postulating a dilemma between the two, a false opposition is created, which in its turn evokes unnecessary new problems. Dualistic views and oppositions usually result in the emergence of a 'good' and a 'less good' or even 'bad' side, as can be demonstrated in the example of the sexes and probably in some formulations of the dilemmas discussed here. Such hierarchized oppositions do not usually produce much good, either in academic debates or in the reality of social and political intercourse. In my view, thinking in terms of 'either/or' (oppositions, dilemmas) where 'both' (differences) is also possible, carries the risk of intellectual ossification and isolation.[37]

It is probably salutary for contemporary feminists to follow the example of their American suffragette forebears: depending on how opportune it is, one might sometimes adhere to 'difference' and at others to 'equality'. That would appear even more justified as almost no one in contemporary feminism uses a 'given' femininity as point of departure, and nowadays one hardly ever hears anything about 'the female essence'. (This makes it even more remarkable that a lot of essential ghosts are still haunting us: just think how frequently recent feminist publications emphasize that femininity and gender are not 'given'.)

And as far as women's studies are concerned, wouldn't searching for specific theoretic approaches to specific, defined research subjects be more beneficial than prematurely setting against each other confusing container concepts such as 'difference' and 'equality'?

NOTES

This chapter was originally published as an article, 'De constructie van dilemma's in het feminisme', in *Tijdschrift voor Vrouwenstudies*, 34, 1988, vol. 9 no. 2, pp. 76–93.

1 See for example *Te Elfder Ure, 39, Dilemma's van het feminisme*, SUN, Nijmegen, 1986.
2 See the editorial of the *Tijdschrift voor Vrouwenstudies*, 24, 1985, p. 379.
3 A recent example of such a general theoretic approach can be found in N. Hartsock, *Money, Sex and Power*, Northeastern University Press, Boston, 1983. Hartsock attempts to develop a general feminist theory of 'gender and power'. One of the central themes of the symposium 'The gender of power' held in Leiden in September 1987 was the usefulness of such a general feminist power theory. The paper I presented to this symposium, 'Gender, power and feminist theory', attempts to describe why I doubt that usefulness. This paper will appear in M. Leijenaar, K. Davis and J. Oldersma (eds), *The Gender of Power*, Sage, London, 1991.
4 Primarily S. Firestone, *The Dialectic of Sex*, Morrow, New York, 1970.
5 See for example Z.R. Eisenstein (ed.) *Capitalist Patriarchy and the Case for Socialist Feminism*, Monthly Review Press, New York, 1979; in the Netherlands, e.g. *Te Elfder Ure, 20, Feminisme*, vol. 1, SUN, Nijmegen, 1975.
6 See for example H. Hartmann, 'The unhappy marriage between Marxism and feminism', *Capital and Class*, Summer, 1979, pp. 1–33.
7 See M. Aerts, 'Het raam van de studeerkamer' ('The study window'), in *Tijdschrift voor Vrouwenstudies*, 3, 1981, pp. 360–75. See also J. Outshoorn, 'Feminisme en marxisme: het relaas van een echtscheiding op zoek naar een omgangs-regeling' ('Feminism and Marxism: the story

of divorcees looking for access rights'), *Tijdschrift voor Vrouwenstudies*, vol. 3, 1981, pp. 339–60.

8 This is expressed for example in J. Mitchell, *Psychoanalysis and Feminism*, Allen Lane, London, 1974, and in J. Mitchell and J. Rose, *Feminine Sexuality. Jacques Lacan and the Ecole Freudienne*, Macmillan, London, 1982.

9 N. Chodorow, *The Reproduction of Mothering: Psychoanalysis and the Sociology of Gender*, University of California Press, Berkeley, 1978.

10 See J. Mitchell and A. Oakley (eds), *What is Feminism? A Reexamination*, Pantheon, New York, 1986.

11 See note 3. As space is limited here I can only give a very brief summary of Hartsock's theory. In doing so, I am definitely not doing her sufficient justice. However, my concern here is only to reflect the essence of her analysis as a general theoretic approach to gender relations.

12 N. Hartsock, op. cit., p. 233. It should be noted here that recently Nancy Hartsock appears to have reconsidered this opinion, as became apparent during 'The gender of power' symposium (see note 3).

13 N. Hartsock, op. cit., p. 178.

14 *Tijdschrift voor Vrouwenstudies*, 16, 1983.

15 R. Coward, 'Is er een algemene theorie van vrouwelijkheid mogelijk?' ('Is a general theory of women's studies possible?'), *Tijdschrift voor Vrouwenstudies*, vol. 4, 1987, pp. 529–44.

16 A. Sommer and M. Dornekater, 'De algemene Theorie van Vrouwelijkheid nader bezien' ('A further look at the general Theory of Femininity'), *Tijdschrift voor Vrouwenstudies*, vol. 4, 1983, pp. 551–2.

17 See the editorial of the *Tijdschrift voor Vrouwenstudies*, vol. 24, 1985, p. 379.

18 See for example A. Sommer, 'Het verschil en de gelijkheid. Inleiding bij de lezingen' ('Difference and equality. An introduction to the lectures'), *Tijdschrift voor Vrouwenstudies*, vol. 6, no. 4, 1985, pp. 382–95; M. Aerts' contribution to this book, Chapter 1, above.

19 See M. Aerts, Chapter 1, above.

20 p. 33 above.

21 pp. 32–33.

22 p. 40.

23 p. 40.

24 A. Wilden, *System and Structure. Essays on Communication and Exchange*, Tavistock, London, 1972, pp. 169 and 174. Moreover, Wilden considers 'distinctions' as a sub-category of 'differences', namely as digital – as distinct from analogous – 'differences'. For an interesting exposition on 'difference', see also G. Bateson, *Mind and Nature. A Necessary Unity*, Dutton, New York, 1979.

25 In this tendency to 'binary thinking' – often seen as a fundamental characteristic of human cognition – deeply rooted social prejudices are frequently expressed which in their turn reflect prevailing power relations. The oppositions can be considered as ideological justification of those power relations. See Wilden, op. cit., p. 219.

26 In a recent article, C.J.M. Schuyt makes similar distinctions: equality

as descriptive term, equality as norm, equality as political or social ideal, natural equality and artificial equality. See C.J.M. Schuyt, 'Maatschappelijke ongelijkheid, een sociologische interpretatie' ('Social inequality, a sociological interpretation'), in *Maatschappelijke onge-lijkheid: de overheid een zorg?* (Social inequality: does the government care?), Nederlands Gespreks Centrum, Veen, Utrecht, 1987, p. 45.

J. Huisman also observes various levels in which the concepts 'difference' and 'equality' can be applied. See J. Huisman, 'The "family of women": A linguistic analysis of the feminist discourse on femininity, equality and difference', in D. Brouwer and D. de Haan (eds), *Women's Language, Socialization and Self-image*, Foris, Dordrecht, 1987.

27 N. Cott, 'Feminist theory and feminist movements: The past before us', in J. Mitchell and A. Oakley (eds), op. cit., pp. 49–63.

28 In her article 'The concept of "difference"' (*Feminist Review*, 26, 1987, pp. 29–41), Michèle Barrett goes into the different ways in which 'difference' is conceptualized within women's studies. As she talks more about the different theoreticizations of 'difference' than about the different ways in which the concept 'difference' functions in the debate, I will leave aside her – otherwise interesting – argument.

29 Obviously, this distinction itself is not undisputed. So it is extremely unlikely that empirically or theoretically convincing criteria will ever be found to distinguish 'nature' and 'culture'. However, in the framework of this article it would be going too far to go into this problem.

30 For further illustrations, see: A. Sommer, op. cit., p. 385; M. Aerts, Chapter 1, above; I. Costera Meijer, Chapter 2, above.

31 See A. Sommer, op. cit., p. 382; M. Aerts, Chapter 1, p. 00; I. Costera Meijer, Chapter 2., p. 00. See also S. Grotenhuis, 'Over geleerde vrouwen en geleerde feministen' ('On learned women and learned feminists'), *Tijdschrift voor Vrouwenstudies*, vol. 4, 1985, p. 395.

32 I have discussed here only a few of the possible combinations of meanings and functions of 'difference' and 'equality'. However, those combinations not discussed are also problematic.

33 See also J. Scott, 'Deconstructing equality-versus-difference: or, the uses of poststructuralist theory for feminism', in *Feminist Studies*, vol. 14, 1988, pp. 33–65. This article (in which Scott develops a similar argument) only reached me after my own paper went to press.

34 N. Cott in Mitchell and Oakley op. cit., pp. 59–60.

35 See M. Aerts, Chapter 1, above.

36 See I. Costera Meijer, Chapter 2 above.

37 See Wilden, who believes that cultures in which 'differences' are systematically transformed into 'oppositions' are ultimately doomed. Wilden, op. cit., p. 219.

Part II

NEW PERSPECTIVES IN HISTORICAL RESEARCH

INTRODUCTION

Following a general feeling of dissatisfaction with the oppression–liberation model current in the early 1980s, Dutch women's studies historians have, over the past ten years, adopted several new approaches. It became clear that the lives and experiences of women were too complex to encapsulate in a simple one-dimensional concept of oppression. Women certainly suffered hardship and bitterness as factory workers, wives, or mothers. However, a focus on sexual (and economic) oppression seemed to serve our need for identification rather than to offer a fair account of the lives of women. The reality of lives proved to be much more diverse, and their relationships much more differentiated than a simple polarized scheme could cope with. In the discussions that followed, the work of Michelle Rosaldo was very influential.[1] Universalistic terms and explanations were put aside and a new, more open perspective on history was sought. Concepts such as private and public lost their unambiguous and fixed meanings. Instead, research focused on the different meanings these concepts could acquire in different contexts.

The great popularity of the 'women's culture' approach was another characteristic feature of Dutch historical research in the 1980s. Carroll Smith-Rosenberg's now classic article entitled 'The female world of love and rituals: relations of women in nineteenth-century America',[2] functioned as an important source of inspiration. Her reconstruction of the intimate relationships between women opened up a new field of research focusing on the more private, hidden parts of women's history. This new interest in 'women's culture' also stimulated the use of new sources such as (auto)biographies, letters, and journals, and effectively changed the role of these 'ego documents'. They were no longer pieces of evidence used only to reconstruct a personal reality. Instead, these documents were interpreted as micro-histories reflecting our common past. This new approach made the distinction between historical and literary texts rather fluid, and strengthened the links between history and literature.

A third major influence in the Netherlands was the work of Joan W. Scott. In 1983, she criticized the 'her-story' approach as separatist, and advocated rewriting 'general' history from a feminist point of view.[3] This plea started a lively discussion among women historians on the value of the different approaches. A few years later, her proposal to use gender as an analytic category in historical research combined with the use of post-structuralist theory, was incorporated into this discussion.[4] Now, at the beginning of the 1990s, Scott is without doubt the most influential theoretician in historical women's studies in the Netherlands. The questions Scott raises on the relationship between gender and women's history, between women's history and mainstream/malestream historiography, and the relationship between gender history, post-structuralism and politics, can be regarded as the fundamental questions on the research agenda in the coming decade.

The three articles included here reflect developments in historical research in the Netherlands over the past decades.

Hélène Vossen's and Marjan Schwegman's contributions touch on the question of difference and equality, which can be seen as the central theme in Dutch women's studies in the 1980s (see Part I). Both try to answer this question by analysing the exact meaning of *which* difference and equality one is striving after in various contexts. Vossen analyses the production of sex differences in the Catholic 'Life Schools' after the Second World War. She traces the way definitions of masculinity and femininity were developed by the leading ideologists of these schools, and describes the opposition they faced from orthodox Catholic groups who still held polarized ideas on sexual differences. Through her reconstruction of the multiplicity, ambivalences and paradoxes contained in the historical texts and sources, Vossen also changes the image of the 1950s. Although usually seen as a dogmatic and conservative period, Vossen demonstrates that the roots of many radical future developments lay there.

In her article on the nineteenth-century Italian feminist Gualberta Alaide Beccari, Schwegman scrutinizes the meaning of terms such as 'moral revolution' and 'difference and equality' in the context of nineteenth-century Italy. Her research shows that the contemporary moral reform movement, which can easily appear a reactionary movement when looked at from a late twentieth-century perspective, in fact strove after a cultural revolution with liberating implications. Schwegman's article also raises the question of the feminist researcher's involvement in her subject. If the familiar ways of interpretation are no longer available because the researcher is seeking a more unprejudiced and open-minded approach to history, how should she deal with the 'strangeness' and the 'otherness' in history?

Marianne Beelaerts' contribution focuses on a Dutch novel published in 1915 by 'Ada Gerlo', the pseudonym of Annie Salomons. Gerlo presents her novel as 'memoirs', in other words as a personal history, and Beelaerts interprets its approach to literature, reality and dream. Although the book was criticized by contemporaries and later literary researchers from a realist perspective, Beelaerts' interpretation makes possible a coherent reconstruction of the fundamental problem described in the novel - how to combine the independence of a life as an intellectual woman with love and marriage.

NOTES

1 Michelle Z. Rosaldo, 'The use and abuse of anthropology: reflections on feminism and cross-cultural understanding', in *Signs* , vol. 5, no. 3 (Spring), 1980, pp. 385–417.
2 In *Signs: Journal of Women in Culture and Society* (1975) vol. 1, no. 1, pp. 1–29, translated in *Tweede Jaarboek voor Vrouwengeschiedenis* [Women's History Yearbook], vol. 2, SUN, Nijmegen 1981.
3 See: 'Survey article: women in history II. The modern period', in *Past and Present*, vol. 101, 1983. Translated in *Vijfde Jaarboek voor Vrouwengeschiedenis* [Women's History Yearbook], vol. 5, SUN, Nijmegen 1984.
4 See: J. W. Scott, *Gender and the Politics of History*, Columbia University Press, New York, 1988. And a review article on the work of Scott by J. van Eijt and H. Vossen 'Het verschil als actor in de geschiedenis? [The difference as an actor in history], pp. 299–312, in *Tijdschrift voor Vrouwenstudies*, vol. 11, 1990.

4

GUALBERTA ALAIDE BECCARI AND THE TEMPTING PERSPECTIVE OF THE MORAL REGENERATION OF HUMANITY (1868–1906)

Marjan Schwegman

MORALIZING FEMINISTS AND FEMINIST MORALS

Reading feminist writings from the second half of the nineteenth century is a fascinating but at the same time confusing occupation. Although these writings are more than accessible in that many of the problems discussed in them are still current today, when we examine the solutions they proposed it is almost like entering a different world. It is a world that has become foreign to us, and that we would prefer to leave as quickly as possible so we can focus on the familiar once again. Paradoxically, this one-sided focus on the recognizable elements of nineteenth-century feminism leads us to understand less and less of that same feminism. Concentration on the recognizable, the current, quickly tempts us to evaluate nineteenth-century ideas as if they were those of contemporary feminism. That can result in ahistorical, moralizing analyses in which the so-called 'limitations' of nineteenth-century feminism are the central theme. Examples of this kind of analysis can be found especially in the early works devoted to their predecessors by the generation of feminist historians in the 1970s.[1]

In very recent years, a change has become apparent in the way nineteenth-century feminism is approached. That change first occurred - as always – abroad, but now seems to have stirred the world of Dutch historians. In a recent article written as an introduction to the Dutch *Women's History Yearbook* devoted to the first feminist wave, Ulla Jansz and Tineke van Loosbroek argued that the time was ripe for breaking with the moralizing approach.[2] However, both this edition of the *Yearbook* and other contributions to feminist historiography show how problematic it is in practice to approach the history of feminism without prejudice or preconceptions. Thinking on the consequences of a breach with a historiography focused on 'ourselves' is still at a very early stage. Urgent, open questions are: how does the researcher cope with the 'foreign', 'the other' in history? Is there really life after the death of the moralizing approach?[3]

In this article I will enter the 'foreign' thinking of a nineteenth-century feminist – Gualberta Alaide Beccari. Some of the problems arising from my attempts to approach her thinking without prejudice will be discussed during this exploration.[4] However, I would like to look at one problem immediately and that is the question of the anachronistic use of certain concepts. This problem is linked to the desire to see the women's movement as comprising a number of clearly distinct and visible movements *from the very earliest beginnings.*

I will mention here only one of the best-known distinctions – the one which places 'rationalist' feminism opposite 'ethical' feminism. As such divisions are often made on the basis of terms – for example 'rationalist' and 'ethical' – which emerged *afterwards* to define or brand certain groups within feminism, this kind of classification can easily lead to ahistorical and moralizing analyses. Those researchers who use this kind of division as a point of departure have a tendency to indicate emphatically which movement should be considered the most feminist.[5] This prejudice impedes thorough research into the content of the various different strands of feminism. As a consequence, the – changing – meaning of a concept like 'equality', which forms the basis of 'rationalist' feminism, is not usually subjected to further examination. The same applies to the concept 'femininity', which is invariably mentioned in connection with 'ethical' feminism. In view of their use of the concepts of 'femininity' and 'equality', many nineteenth-century women appear to belong in both movements.[6] It would seem to me both useful and interesting to examine this (changing) meaning further before classifying these women in one or the other movement. In doing this kind of research, I would not assume that nineteenth-century feminists mean the same thing as contemporary feminists when they talk about 'femininity' and 'equality'. Instead, I would explore the feminist universe from the reverse point of departure.

The same applies to another element of nineteenth-century feminist discourse: the 'moral rebirth of humanity' formula often used by feminists of various plumage. It is a formula whose revolutionary implications have, in my view, been insufficiently recognized. Of course, the nineteenth-century struggle by feminists against the double standard has been described at length. But as the concept 'moral revolution' is now often associated with reactionary movements, there is little in-depth scrutiny of the meaning this concept had for feminists at that time. Those who strove after a moral regeneration of humanity (and these were not only feminists), had a coherent view of the development of society. However, this was a view whose inspiration was diametrically opposed to the then current social analyses inspired by materialism, such as Marxism. The nineteenth-century meaning of the concept 'moral' perhaps comes closest to what social science studies now indicate by the term 'cultural'. The moral reformers were looking for a kind of cultural revolution. That also applies to the feminist struggle against the double standard. In the striving after 'moral equality' of feminists, the stakes were nothing more or less than the creation of a counterculture in which women and the feminine were no longer excluded.

These feminist moral reformers were almost always inspired by religion. And the concept 'religion' can also lead easily to misunderstandings. It is quickly perceived as 'dominant institutionalized religious morals'. As a result, it is difficult to understand that religion can also serve as a basis for radical analyses of power relations between the sexes.[7] To illustrate the point, I will focus on an Italian feminist: Gualberta Alaide Beccari. She was one of those religiously inspired moral reformers whose ideas present the modern researcher with problems because of the confusion surrounding concepts such as 'equality', 'femininity', 'morals' and 'religious'. Depending on how these terms are interpreted, Gualberta's design for a New Humanity can be read as a design in which the difference between the sexes is central, or as a design which is a typical example of 'equality thinking'. However, I will show that it can also be read as a design in which the concepts 'femininity' and 'equality' are not mutually exclusive.

GUALBERTA ALAIDE BECCARI AND THE MAZZINIAN VISION OF THE NEW HUMANITY

Gualberta Alaide Beccari was born in the northern Italian town of Padua in 1842. Her parents were not wealthy, but came from good, partly aristocratic families. Both were ardent adherents of Giuseppe Mazzini. Mazzini belonged to the group of Italian intellectuals who had given their attention to the problem of Italian unity during the so-called Risorgimento.[8] The basis of what is called his 'creed' can be called 'enlightened religiosity'. He believed in a natural order inspired by God; the creed comprised a number of universal principles which formed the cornerstones for an ideal society: the principle of Love, to which Sacrifice, Suffering and Solidarity were irrevocably linked, and the principle of Equality of all people. For centuries, circumstances had prevented the rise of the ideal, 'true' society, but the fact that increasingly more peoples were preparing to liberate themselves from their oppressors had convinced Mazzini that the birth of the New Humanity was not only inevitable but also imminent. Mazzini's vision of the future embraced a world in which free peoples lived in harmony with each other; a world in which no absolute or part dictators could exist, in which feudal and clerical privileges were abolished, and in which people were reborn as free and moral because they were shaped by a New Education based on the already mentioned godly principles, and because each of them had finally acquired the rights which had been denied to them for centuries. One of these rights was universal suffrage. Mazzini had focused all his energies, especially after 1830, on the realization of one part of this sweeping ideal: the establishment of a democratic Italian republic.

Mazzini was Gualberta's great example and inspiration. To her – and not only to her – he was a divine herald, an apostle of the New Age and the New Humanity. The fact that, unlike most of his contemporaries, Mazzini saw equality of all people as precisely that and not just equality of all *men*, was of great importance to Gualberta. He may have believed in the existence of a 'masculine' and a 'feminine' nature, but he did not consider the 'feminine' nature inferior to the 'masculine'. In his view, men and women had equal responsibility in the creation of a New Italy. And the emergence of that New Italy would automatically put an end to the social inequality of men and women.[9]

Raised in this spirit, Gualberta long believed it was sufficient to put all her efforts into realizing the Mazzinian ideal that would end the social inequality between men and women she so deplored. But her optimism was shattered when her army-administrator father became ill and she took his place. The people around her reacted with surprise, ridicule and insults. As they were her parents' 'comrades', Gualberta concluded that quite a lot would have to change in what she called the 'morals of the Italians' before there could be any question of social equality between men and women. This realization laid the foundations for the idea of a revolution from which humanity, including the Italian part of it, would emerge as morally reborn in this sense too.[10]

Gualberta elaborated this idea systematically for the first time in *La Donna* (The Woman). This magazine had been started by her in 1868 and she remained its editor during the whole of its existence (1868–1891). The first signs of organized feminism emerged in Italy during this period. However, in the initial years of *La Donna*'s existence there was definitely no question of an organized movement. This was the period when feminist thinking was taking shape. *La Donna* was the first Italian women's magazine which demanded full equality of men and women before the law. It was also the first women's magazine in Italy and Europe which only published contributions from women. Gualberta justified this exclusivity as follows: if women really wanted to prove they were in no way inferior to men, then they had to carry on the fight for what Gualberta called the elevation of the female sex under their own steam.

Gualberta was not alone in her preoccupation with the moral transformation of the Italians. This question was the theme of a lively debate among many prominent figures in the Italian intelligentsia in newly unified Italy. My impression is that this debate was carried on more intensively in Italy than in other countries.[11] The youthful character of the Italian state made this discussion very important for its new citizens.[12] On the one hand, the young monarchy's new, virginal character seemed to offer unlimited opportunities for the implementation of radical changes. On the other, that same virginal state also caused concern. There was consensus that the unity of the Italians was a fact in a political sense, but they were nowhere near a unified morality. The priority was now to start the 'moral reconstruction' of the Italian people. In this debate, Italy – fondly called 'Italietta' by some – was represented as a wild, naughty child which had to be raised into a solid, disciplined adult. This is why the intellectual elite showed such a great interest in educational problems of all kinds during and after the Risorgimento. A growing interest in everything which had to do with children went hand in hand with this development. It is no coincidence that two of the most famous and most successful Italian children's books – *Cuore* (Heart) by Edmondo De Amicis (1886) and *Le avventure di Pinocchio* (The adventures of Pinocchio) by Carlo Collodi (1883) – appeared in this period.

Both books can be read as stories in which the moral conditioning of children is the central theme. According to Alberto Asor Rosa, both, and especially Collodi's story, can also be read on a different level: he believes Pinocchio's history symbolizes the painful process of 'Italietta's' maturing.[13] Of course, he does not go into the fact that 'Italietta' is represented by a male in this book (which is rather curious as grammatically Italietta is feminine). But Pinocchio's sex is no coincidence. The debate on the moral transformation of Italy was dominated by men and 'masculinity', but that won't come as a surprise to anyone. Gualberta introduced the woman and the 'feminine' into this debate via *La Donna* and other magazines, and through children's stories in which the education of *girls* was the central theme, preparing them for their role as the New Woman, a woman who was the (moral) equal of the man. Or wasn't she? What meaning did Gualberta give to 'sexual difference' and 'sexual equality'?

THE NEW WOMAN[14]

Gualberta believed it was women and not men who should be at the centre of the moral revolution. *They* were the moulders of the New Morality and it was on them that the birth of the New Humanity depended. In other words, they were the Mothers of the New Humanity. However, according to Gualberta, the great majority of women were not capable of fulfilling this important task satisfactorily. Women had first to be transformed into New Women. This process could take place with the help of the already mentioned New Education. To achieve this, society should make men and women equal before the law, so that women would have the opportunity of developing into New Women and would then be able to function as such in society. New Women should not limit their salutary, morally transforming work to the family. They should go out into the – public – fields of Art, Science, Charity, Politics and paid Employment as apostles of Truth.

From this sketch of the main points in Gualberta's programme, it will immediately be clear that the relationship 'sexual equality'/

'sexual difference' is a complicated one.[15] If we take into account the revolutionary implications of the 'moral regeneration of humanity' formula, then this programme can be read as a blueprint for a counterculture which is permeated by a fierce desire for the breaking open, the total shattering of a suffocating system of what she saw as false conventions, norms and values. The great but equally confusing challenge posed by her programme was that it invited women to cross demarcation lines between the sexes which had previously been considered inviolable, so that these would fade and even cease to exist.[16] This is most visible in Gualberta's urging of women to strike out into fields which had always been dominated by men – both literally and figuratively. Sex should no longer determine which activities were allowed. Gualberta introduced a new, moral criterion: just as men, women also had the right and the duty to develop activities both inside and outside the home, as long as these activities promoted the formation of a New Morality. The occupations allowed and encouraged included writing, politics, functions in *all* forms of education, and the professions such as law, medicine and pharmacy. Taking up occupations of this kind would automatically mean women would conquer new, public places, such as the street, the conference room, the school, the university. And these wouldn't be at the expense of the family. According to Gualberta, it was a misconception to think the proper performance of household duties required the continual presence of the woman.

Here we see one of the liberating promises the concept 'moral regeneration of humanity' could contain for nineteenth-century feminists. By putting the development of a New Morality first and foremost, Gualberta had come to a description of the concept 'duty', which meant a radical breakdown of old, sex-specific patterns. It was no longer important to determine who performed which activities, but to determine what was a 'morality-shaping' activity and what was not. Once the nature of an activity had been determined, it could then be performed by both men and women.

For the majority of Gualberta's contemporaries, this was a very disturbing vision of the future. Attacks on *La Donna* clearly exhibit great fear of a world in which 'sex' is no longer one of the most important structural principles.[17] This fear – expressed in the (familiar) accusation that Gualberta was a 'donna–uomo' (man–woman) and in other ways – was not only caused by her proposals to (at least partially) abolish the existing sexual division of tasks. Perhaps even more disturbing was that Gualberta's design appeared to suggest that there would be no question of unchangeable gender identities in the New World. In other words: Gualberta's programme also expressed a desire to break open the current 'masculine/feminine' dichotomy.

At first sight, the opposite appears to be the case. Gualberta's programme seems to indicate that women would become captives of a new, 'super-feminine' model: that of the New Woman who would have to be the Mother of the New Humanity. However, if the concept 'moral' is seen in the 'Beccarian' meaning, a totally different reading is possible. Such a reading makes clear that in Gualberta's programme the category 'femininity' had become irrelevant. According to Gualberta, the New Human Being's identity was based on a number of *universally* applicable moral principles, and not on the contingency of someone's sex. Here too, the perspective of the moral revolution offered Gualberta the opportunity of liberating herself and other women from limitations which were based on sexual difference. However, she never argues *explicitly* that the 'moral equality' she is striving for can indeed be considered the kind of equality which would exclude the dichotomy 'masculine/feminine'. In other words, is my (present-day) interpretation of the concept 'moral equality' thorough enough? We must now subject Gualberta's programme to further analysis.

LOVE AND (DISTURBED) HARMONY

Her point of departure was Mazzinian: like him, she believed that the universal, moral principles according to which humanity should be formed were contained in what she called divine nature. In essence, they could be reduced to a single principle – the principle of love. This was the kind of love Christ had taught from the cross. Love which is the basis of unity and solidarity of all people. Love whose greatest expression was sacrifice for others. However, Gualberta immediately added here that self-effacement in favour of others should never lead to forgetting that God lay at the core of *everyone's* being. For this reason, one should not accept humiliation, and should never allow slavery.

A further universal principle was harmony, which was closely interwoven with love. 'Heart' and 'reason' were irrevocably linked with each other and had to be developed harmoniously in every human being. Reason should be the heart's guide. Without the light shed by reason, the heart would wander and as a result pure feelings would become 'false'. And without the heart's warmth, human beings developed into sceptical, atheistic creatures.

Not only had the heart and reason to be in balance. The same applied to the 'physical' and the 'moral'. Again, it is important here to keep firmly in mind the meaning Gualberta gave to these concepts. The fact that she gave two different meanings to the paired concepts 'physical/moral', although without indicating this explicitly, is both intriguing and confusing. One meaning is borrowed from medical science and the other is taken from Mazzini's teachings. On 'beauty' she wrote something like this (I say 'something' here because a translation is an interpretation): 'The more explicit moral beauty becomes, the more it will add to outward appearance so that the true type of beauty will be revealed to us . . . an unnameable "something" of which we can nevertheless all conjure up some kind of image.'[18]

In this Mazzinian interpretation the body, the exterior, is the material expression of the divine in human beings. If the divine is allowed to develop purely, then human appearance will become increasingly more beautiful. Thus, in this sense, beauty has a supernatural essence and is independent of 'earthly' ideals. A very different attitude to the connection between the 'physical' and the 'moral' is expressed in Gualberta's numerous writings on the beneficial effects of physical exercises for women. In these writings, she states that physical exercises are essential for a balanced development of the human being: if the body is more active, people will also become more active in intellectual and moral life. Moreover, physical exercise had a special meaning for women: it would remove the difference in physical strength between men and women. According to Gualberta, that difference only existed because women's physical education had always been neglected. As a result, women had not only become physically weaker, but morally weaker also. Physical exercise would transform fragile, unconfident women into New Women who would radiate outward strength and self-confidence.[19] This is reminiscent of contemporary medical science. In contrast to Gualberta's Mazzinian interpretation, she presents here the relationship between the 'physical' and the 'moral' as one which can be defined in scientific terms. 'Morality' was an organic part of the body in the medico-scientific sense. The body was seen as a machine with all kinds of functions. If the body was to function properly, it was necessary to develop the various parts to the same extent and to stimulate them equally, so that a functional balance arose.

This medico-scientific interpretation of the link between the 'physical' and the 'moral' emerges especially in Gualberta's writings on illness. She presented illness as the result of disturbed balance between the body as a whole and one of its parts – 'morality'. However, following Mazzini, she also represents illness as a result of a disturbed communication between divine nature and the human heart. The heart is not presented here as an organic part of the body, but as the seat of 'morality'. According to this approach, someone becomes ill when true morality cannot pass freely from God to the heart.[20] Why was that communication disturbed so frequently? Gualberta sought an explanation in the history of humanity. Neither men nor women had been able to live according to the true morality. Misled by the Catholic Church especially, they had adopted 'false' principles as guidelines and as a result had become 'false', deformed or sick human beings. This deformation process, however, had followed different lines for men and women. Women's deformation was primarily due to the egotism and blind lust for power of man. He had prevented her from fully developing her intellectual abilities, which were equal to those of men. Deprived of the light of truth, she had become easy prey for false ideals. She had been degraded to a dependent, egocentric, superstitious, insincere, superficial, vain woman – a woman whose falseness was also reflected in her outward appearance. She did not emanate strength, purity and liveliness, but apathy, insecurity and insincerity, because her face was masked by a thick layer of paint, and her body contorted by misshapen garments. In contrast, the man was primarily the victim of a one-sided development of his reason. As a result, all too often he had a tendency to scepticism, preventing him from believing in true morality.

In a unified Italy – a state whose judicial foundations would be in accordance with the true laws of the divine nature – men and women would finally be able to win their true identity. However, it was the *woman* who had to shepherd the man through this process, through this moral revolution. The question is why Gualberta let the success of the moral revolution depend on women. And there is a more pressing question. Why would women appear to retain their leading 'moral forming' role when the moral rebirth of humanity was achieved? Nothing in Gualberta's programme indicates that women would ever lose their moral advantage. Apparently, women always had a moral advantage over men, even when the latter had become

New Men. In other words, the question is how do we reconcile this remaining sexual difference with the emphasis Gualberta places on 'equality'?

EQUALITY AND DIFFERENCE

The multiple meaning Gualberta gave to the concept 'equality' makes it problematic. On the one hand, it had a rationalistic charge: Gualberta emphasized more than once – and sometimes applied scientific arguments – that men and women possessed equal intellectual capacities and were also potentially equal in physical strength. But aside from that, she was primarily concerned with 'moral equality'. By that she meant that in principle the divine was present in every human being. However, this equality did not necessarily exclude a fundamental sexual difference. According to her, women had a more intimate and pure contact with the divine than men. Gualberta's explanation is ambiguous: on the one hand, she argued that the intellectual underdevelopment of women caused by historical circumstances had a positive consequence in that women had been more successful than men in preserving contact with divine nature and its inherent moral principles. The seeds of the New Human Being which everyone carried could, therefore, be brought to fruition more easily in women than in men. As a result, it was women, New Women, who could repair the disturbed communications between God and the heart of humanity by saturating *all* areas of social life with the new Morality.

On the other hand, she several times emphasized that a woman was 'instinctively religious'. Woman was, therefore, more receptive to the divine. And as a result, only *women* could open the eyes of others to the divine – adults who were blind to it and children who still had to be moulded. By projecting the divine themselves, primarily by loving unselfishly, women could bring others into contact with the divine in themselves.

Before a programme like Gualberta's is dismissed as odd or singular, I would like to note here the context in which such theories as hers were formulated. This was a period in which theorists such as Lombroso, Sergi, Ferri and others (and Weiniger and Moebius in a later period) were representing woman as a creature whose very nature excluded the possession of moral consciousness. No moral value was attributed even to the ability to bear children: the fact that a woman could become a mother demonstrated even more clearly her essentially *bestial* nature.[21] Bearing this in mind, it is probably not a complete coincidence that Gualberta and others presented women as 'queens of morality'.

EPILOGUE

On 24 September 1906, Gualberta Alaide Beccari died in Bologna. She was buried very late the same evening. The cart which bore her body to the churchyard made its way through the silent, almost deserted city streets, followed by only one carriage. Gualberta was a victim of diphtheria. Fear of infection meant few dared go near her body. The disease had taken its toll within hours; 'and that was', wrote one of her closest friends, 'truly fortunate, because she was so quickly stupefied that happily she did not notice the presence of the priest who had been called instead of a doctor by the people in the house . . .'.[22]

This image of Gualberta's end differs greatly from the picture which has come to dominate the (scarce) historiography. In the latter, 'official' version, the accent lies on sacrifice. Gualberta's infection with the fatal disease is described in pathetic terms. She had embraced and comforted a neighbour child suffering from diphtheria, with no thought to the danger of infection. Shortly after the child died, Gualberta herself became ill.[23]

Gualberta would probably have been content with the triumph of this latter image. Over the years, her writings on the construction of the New Humanity and her presentation of her own life had fused into a rhetorical exposition on the New Woman with the theme of sacrifice at its core. Increasingly, Gualberta's New Woman had assumed the form of a woman who suffers for *others*, for the New Humanity. Only a Suffering Woman is one with the divine. It is primarily this exaltation of a specific kind of suffering – expressed by Gualberta by the term '*martirio*' (martyrdom) – which makes hers a world which is foreign to me. In order to write history in which the foreign or strange is approached without prejudice or preconceptions, the researcher has to take into account such differences. But what then? How does the foreign acquire a place in historiography? There is life after the death of moralizing historiography, but I'm still wondering what that life looks like.

NOTES

This chapter was originally published as an article, 'Gualberta Alaide Beccari en het lokkende perspektief van de morele wedergeboorte der mensheid (1868–1906)', in *Tijdschrift voor Vrouwenstudies*, 28, vol. 7, no. 4, pp. 484–99.

1 I will mention here only a few Dutch examples: A. van Baalen, M. Ekelschot, *Geschiedenis van de vrouwentoekomst* (History of women's future), De Bonte Was, Amsterdam, 1980; M. Elias, 'De eerste feministische golf' ('The first feminist wave'), in A. Holtrop (ed.), *Vrouwen rond de eeuwwisseling* (Women at the turn of the century), De Arbeidenspens, Amsterdam, 1979, pp. 7–35; E. Sijses, 'Moederschap en de eerste feministische golf' ('Motherhood and the first feminist wave'), in *Tijdschrift voor Vrouwenstudies* 7, vol. 2, no. 3, 1981, pp. 417–31.

2 U. Jansz and T. van Loosbroek, 'Nieuwe literatuur over de eerste feministische golf' ('New literature on the first feminist wave'), in *Zesde Jaarboek voor Vrouwengeschiedenis* (Sixth Women's History Yearbook), SUN, Nijmegen, 1985, pp. 10–30.

3 For an interesting discussion on this and many other kinds of problems, see the intriguing book *Het vrouwelijke georganiseerd* (The feminine organized), Vakgroep Vrouwenstudies i.o., Fakulteit Sociale Wetenschappen, Universiteit van Amsterdam, 1986. It is intriguing because in it a number of historians and social scientists reflect publicly on problems which most researchers only consider in the privacy of their own homes.

4 One of the problems I will pass over here is the fact that I am working with texts in a foreign language, which nevertheless was quite a considerable problem.

5 M. Mossink offers examples of such ahistorical approaches in 'Tweeërlei strooming? "Etisch" en "rationalistisch" feminisme tijdens de eerste golf in Nederland' ('Dual movement? "Ethical" and "rationalist" feminism during the first wave in the Netherlands'), in *Socialisties Feministiese Teksten*, vol. 9, 1986, pp. 104–21.

6 Ibid. See also the final report 'Equality and Difference' on a seminar I conducted in 1984 whose subject was the Dutch feminist discussion on 'feminine nature' in the period 1870–1920, Subfakulteit Geschiedenis, Rijksuniversiteit Leiden (Dept of History, University of Leiden). Since the publication of this article (1986), the insight that equality and difference do not exclude each other in nineteenth-century feminist thinking has been postulated by a number of historians. See, for example, N. Cott, 'Feminist theory and feminist movements: the past before us', in J. Mitchell and A. Oakley (eds), *What is Feminism? A Re-examination*, Pantheon, New York, 1986, pp. 49–63.

7 For an example of an article in which the treatment of the concepts 'moral' and 'religious' is slipshod, see T. de Bie and W. Fritschy, 'De "wereld" van Reveilvrouwen, hun liefdadige activiteiten en het ontstaan van het feminism in Nederland' ('The "world" of revivalist women, their charitable activities and the origins of feminism in the Netherlands'), in *Zesde Jaarboek*, op. cit., pp. 30–59.

8 The literal meaning of this word is 'regeneration'. It is used to indicate the process of the rise of national consciousness in the Italian people.
9 See especially G. Mazzini, *I doveri dell'uomo* (The duties of man), Florence, 1943, p. 68.
10 Autobiographical note by Beccari, in Giulia Cavallari Cantalamessa, 'Alcune lettere di Adelaide Cairoli' ('Selected letters of Adelaide Cairoli'), in *Miscellanea di studi storici in onore di Antonio Manno* (Miscellaneous historical studies in honour of Antonio Manno), Part II, Turin, 1912, pp. 528–9.
11 Around the same period a section of the intelligentsia elsewhere also emphasized the desirability of an 'increase of morals'. For an interesting statement on the moral revolution from Wilhelmina Drucker, see F. Dieteren, 'De geestelijke eenzaamheid van een radicaalfeministe. Wilhelmina Druckers ontwikkeling tussen 1885 en 1898' ('The mental isolation of a radical feminist. Wilhelmina Drucker's development between 1885 and 1898'), in *Zesde Jaarboek*, p. 90, note 47.
12 A. Asor Rosa, 'La cultura' ('Culture'), in *Storia d'Italia*, Part IV, 2, Einaudi, Turin, 1975, especially pp. 823–40.
13 Ibid., pp. 925–40.
14 Gualberta's New Woman takes shape especially in the first eighteen months of *La Donna*.
15 This complexity is insufficiently emphasized in the few works in which Beccari's work is discussed. See, for example, B. Pisa, *Venticinque anni di emancipazionismo femminile in Italia* (Twenty-five years of women's emancipation in Italy), Quaderni della FIAP 42, Rome, 1983.
16 The same applied to borders between different classes. Due to lack of space, I will have to pass over this aspect.
17 See, primarily for the tone, M. Mannucci, 'Polemica sulla emancipazione delle donne' ('Polemic on the emancipation of women'), in *La famiglia*, vol. 1, no. 46, 1869, p. 190.
18 *La Donna*, vol. 2, no. 2, 1869, p. 246.
19 Ibid., vol. 2, no. 59, 1869, p. 234.
20 This kind of statement is interesting because Gualberta herself suffered from a mysterious nervous complaint for most of her life. For more on this illness, see my biography of Beccari, in which the history of the illness occupies a central place: *Feminisme als boetedoening. Biografie van de italiaanse schrijfster en feministe Gualberta Alaide Beccari (1842–1906)* (Feminism as a penance. A biography of the Italian authoress and feminist Gualberta Alaide Beccari), Nijgh & Van Ditmar, The Hague, 1991.
21 See, among others, A. Rossi-Doria, 'Nuova destra e movimento delle donne' ('The new right and the women's movement'), in *Memoria. Rivista di storia delle donne*, no. 11–12, 1984, pp. 152–63.
22 Letter from Giacinta Pezzana to Giorgina Saffi dated 27 September 1906, Bologna Archiginnasio, Archivio Saffi, sez. II, cart. 11. Gualberta hated priests because of her Mazzinian, and therefore anti-clerical, background.
23 See for example I. M. Scodnik, *Una martire. Gualberta Alaide Beccari* (A martyr. Gualberta Alaide Beccari), Florence, 1908.

5

PRODUCTIONS OF SEXUAL DIFFERENCES IN CATHOLIC 'LIFE SCHOOLS', 1947–1968

On firm convictions and doubts

Hélène Vossen[1]

Education researchers question the ways in which education contributes to the reproduction of inequality.[2] Feminists allege that schooling contributes to inequality and they advocate the examination of how sexual differences are produced through education. One problem is that, to many people, striving after equality means that women have a lot to catch up with, or, in other words, they must adjust to a male norm. On the other hand, maintenance of the differences – traditionally known as 'feminine values' – can mean a maintenance of existing power relations. A similar dilemma is posed within socio-educational research in relation to different classes and ethnic groups. This concerns climbing the social ladder by conforming to prevalent norms or maintaining cultural differences.[3] In contrast, in 'Meisjesonderwijs of onderwijs voor meisjes' ('Girls' education or education for girls'), Saskia Grotenhuis and Monique Volman argue that we shouldn't be thinking in terms of a choice between these two, but should be looking for other options: at which differences or equality are actually worth striving for.[4] Grotenhuis and Volman advocate research into the way production of sexual differences occurs within specific kinds of education, so that it becomes clear to what extent their content, design and culture is beneficial for the development of women. According to these researchers, revealing how sexual differences acquire meaning in specific contexts (training courses, etc. are meant here) can prevent the determination of new unequivocal meanings of femininity and masculinity.[5]

To find an answer to the strategic questions, it is important to discover how sex differences are partly produced by education. In this article I will be analysing how the concepts 'femininity' and 'masculinity' acquired meaning in Catholic 'Life Schools'.[6] I will demonstrate that in the period 1947–1968 shifts in the meaning of these concepts took place and there was a continuing conflict over the acceptance of one specific meaning of these concepts as the 'true' one. I will be examining definitions both of femininity and of masculinity as they were formulated officially by the life schools' national management organization,[7] and how meanings of femininity and masculinity were expressed in the educational aim and curriculum.[8]

With this article, I also hope to make a contribution to a different representation of the Catholic segment of the population after the Second World War. In the literature, the Catholic segment is often represented as a monolith and attention is focused primarily on organizational aspects. However, too little emphasis is placed on the fact that this segment consisted of different factions, some more conservative, others more progressive, which were frequently engaged in fierce conflicts. The more 'enlightened' faction within the life schools' national management organization ultimately gained most influence. From the beginning of the 1950s it contributed to the changes which would take place in the 1960s.

In this article, I will limit myself to examining two important aspects of the context in which these shifts took place. The reason progressive forces had more chance of putting forward their ideas in the 1950s and 1960s was due to the changes which took place in socio-economic, political and ideological thinking. As a result, the representation of the position of women, and the position itself, also changed. In the first decade after the Second World War, for instance, it was still taboo for Catholic married women to work outside the home. Attitudes to this changed slowly, partly as a result of structural labour shortages following continually expanding industrialization.[9]

A second point I would like to note here is the increasing influence of science and the process of professionalization. At the end of the 1940s, a conflict developed in the Catholic sector between theology and science, especially between theology and psychology.[10] The validation of ideas on the nature of woman (and man) was referred to less and less in terms of a natural order ordained by God, in which women and men were allocated specific roles and tasks, and the use of moral examples, such as those of Mary and Joseph, began to decline.

In contrast, science was increasingly brought in to justify notions of 'real' femininity, masculinity and sexual differences. The conflict between theology and psychology also took place within the life schools. Expert laity increasingly took over the positions once occupied by clergy. In many ways, the scientists functioned as the new clergy.

Finally, I would like to make some observations on the method I employed in this section of my research.[11] In 'Just the same or just different?', Mieke Aerts points out that the sexual difference is developed primarily by the regulation of the 'feminine'.[12] This would appear to be the case here, too. There is a lot more discussion on (the essence of) the feminine than on (the essence of) the masculine. I think this is due to the acceptance of man's position as more self-evident and therefore less open to discussion. I have indicated that, in contrast, the position of women was more subject to change. What people meant by 'masculine' was seldom defined. If such definition did occur, it was primarily to indicate the difference with the feminine. Discovering what people in this period meant by masculinity and how that difference was defined, requires a different reading. Selma Leydesdorff follows Gianna Pomata in advocating the study of the masculine/feminine opposition in places where it is not made explicit.[13] She states that many texts frequently refer to it implicitly – as is repeatedly the case in the documentation on the life schools. People are eager to expound what femininity is. It's a matter of great concern, not least to men, to do so. What masculinity means appears to be of less interest.

The determination of what femininity means or what the 'real' woman should look like does not only occur by setting femininity against 'real' masculinity (and vice versa), but also by conceiving other forms of femininity as deviations. The definition of the 'real' woman was also developed through the separation of 'real' femininity from what was seen as unfeminine, hyper-feminine or masculine.[14]

Irene Costera Meijer also suggests this in her article 'Real women and superwomen'. She writes: 'In my view, what a "real" woman is, or should be – in short, the concept "woman" – acquires shape and meaning largely through continually articulating deviations.' She believes the sexuality attributed to women who deviate from the norm plays a great role here: 'Woman is not so much . . . defined by indicating the sexual desires and behaviour attributed to her, which deviate from those of Man. More important for the classification in feminine and non-feminine is perhaps the designation of differences between women (colour, class, sexual preference, etc.) in terms of sexual deviation.'[15]

THE FIRST SCHOOLS[16]

The first Catholic life school for girls, the Mater Amabilis School (MAS), and the first equivalent for boys, the Pater Fortis School, were established in Maastricht in the extreme south of the Netherlands, just after the Second World War. They were so successful, many Catholics elsewhere in the Netherlands followed the initiative and set up similar schools. These were schools for young working people who had four hours of lessons every week. Initially, the Mater Amabilis School was intended for girls of 17 and over. In 1952, however, the life schools' national management organization also developed a course for 14 to 17-year-olds: 'The Mater Amabilis School Youth Course'. The Pater Fortis School for boys of 17 and older quickly turned out to be a failure. This institution then concentrated on the 14 to 17 age group. Mater Amabilis education was turned into Training for Young Adults in 1968. The Catholic youth course of the Mater Amabilis School merged with the Catholic life school for boys and with protestant-Christian and general training in 1970. The name was then also changed to Education for Working Youth.[17]

Mater Amabilis

The woman ideologist behind the foundation of the first Mater Amabilis School, the educationist M.S. Schouwenaars, saw the task of the MAS as developing the 'eternal feminine characteristics' which were in danger of being eroded by the type of work done by girls in factories and offices. For four hours every week she attempted to prepare young working girls for their future role as wives and mothers. This is apparent both from the aims and curriculum of the MAS and from Schouwenaars' definition of femininity.

According to Schouwenaars, femininity is largely the same as maternity. All 'real' girls were said to long for marriage, procreation and motherhood. But Schouwenaars did distinguish between natural and spiritual motherhood. The latter could be achieved by women in convents or within the social professions. Besides maternity, women had two other dominant characteristics: the pursuit of beauty and a desire

Figure 5.1   Learning to wash the baby as an aspect of child education
in the Mater Amabilis School

to please. Their desire to please meant that they wanted to please others.
Before puberty this was related to general matters, but in adolescence
it was aimed at achieving marriage. We should note here that this was
not a negatively charged term.[18] The name of the school refers to Mary,
the Holy Mother, and also expresses the ideal of amiability.

Pater Fortis

The ideas of the founder of the Pater Fortis School, Chaplain E.
Beel, are also apparent in the name he gave to his institute, its aims
and curriculum. Pater Fortis means strong father or man. Beel is
referring here to Saint Joseph, Mary's husband. In Beel's view,
an amiable mother was incomplete without a strong father and
dutiful husband at her side. His education programme was aimed
at educating boys to be good heads of family, exemplary fathers
and husbands. In addition, it was also to mould them into reliable
workers and solid citizens. In contrast to Schouwenaars, Beel did
not validate his ideas by referring to essential male characteristics.
Certain notions were implicit in his thinking but he felt no need to
express these in explicit terms. He considered them self-evident.

CONFLICTING IDEAS

The names of these schools soon came under attack from a group of progressive Catholics who used, among others, the influential Dutch magazine on youth affairs, *Dux*, as their mouthpiece. The philosopher H. Ruygers summarized the criticism of the name Pater Fortis in *Dux* in 1954:

> By posing Pater Fortis as counterpart of Mater Amabilis the meaning of the last word acquires an unacceptable implication: opposite the tough, masculine father is the charming, amiable wife and mother. This imposes on the Life Schools cultural ideals which belong to a past age. They are trying to shape girls according to Victorian ideals of womanhood – soft, sweet, timid, modest, tender, sentimental, given to weeping, and oh, so attractive as toys for the hard, tough, possibly chivalrous, domineering, resolute, patriarchal male figure.

Ruygers saw this as a 'worn out polarity'.[19] The life school for boys should not be a copy of the MAS: 'To girls, maternalness and even possible motherhood, appears a useful, and in fact appropriate and appealing central focus in education. To boys, the image of a strong man may be appealing, but the paternal instinct only awakens after the birth of the first child.'[20] The editors of *Dux* stressed their complete agreement with the arguments Ruygers had advanced. And partly as a result of this criticism, the schools' national management organization, which had been set up in the meantime, changed the name into 'Catholic Life School for Young Workers'.

The editors of *Dux* had criticized the name Mater Amabilis and its ideological background as early as 1951. Their main objection was that the amiability ideal in particular could be misinterpreted. Amiability should not be seen as an ultimate goal, not as a 'purely superficial characteristic', and it should mean more than only wanting to please others.[21] Amiability should be created by an inner harmony with self, God and other people. To avoid conflicts with the founders of the schools, the editors of Dux formulated their criticism very carefully, but it is clear that the 'desire to please' formulated by Schouwenaars was a particular thorn in their flesh.

A second point of criticism was Schouwenaars' emphasis on marriage and motherhood. Girls who did not marry might feel disgruntled and begin to see spiritual motherhood as a surrogate, whereas there were other ways of giving meaning to the unmarried state.[22] However, the national organization established in 1950 did not change the name. It was already a household word and the committee was afraid of offending the founders of the first school in Maastricht, who enjoyed widespread popularity elsewhere in the country.

From this criticism it would appear that these progressive Catholics had different views on masculinity and femininity from those held by the founders of the first schools. The progressives were in the majority on the national management committee where it appeared that they also had very different views on other subjects which the founders of the first schools saw in a more conservative light.[23] I will only discuss here those differences between the committee and the 'first founders' when they touch on notions of masculinity and femininity.

The progressive Catholics' ideas were based to a great extent on the thinking of a well-known Catholic psychologist F.J.J. Buytendijk who had published a book in 1951 called *De Vrouw. Haar natuur, verschijning en bestaan* (The woman. Her nature, person and existence).[24] This work also contained indirect views on masculinity. Buytendijk belonged to the group of progressive Catholics which also included the management committee of the life schools and the editors of *Dux*. The most important ideologist on the boys' schools within the management committee was the Jesuit N. Perquin, a prominent educationist within the Catholic sector and director of the Hoogveld Institute, which carried out a substantial amount of research on the lives of Catholic working-class youth. The psychologist H.M. Dresen-Coenders, one of the editors of *Dux* as well as a researcher on working youth through the Hoogveld Institute, was the most important ideologist behind the girls' schools. Both Dresen-Coenders and Perquin wrote numerous articles in *Dux*, whose editor-in-chief was H.M.M. Fortmann. All three belonged to an influential network of progressive Catholics.

THE NATIONAL MANAGEMENT COMMITTEE'S VIEWS

Educational objective

In his handbook for education training courses, *Paedagogiek. Bezinning op het opvoedkundig verschijnsel* (Pedagogy. Reflection on the educational phenomenon), first published in 1949,

Perquin states that the aim of education is to provide assistance in attaining maturity. In 1952, he defined maturity as follows: 'We speak of maturity when true independence has been achieved and man is capable of formulating a personal opinion, when he can enter into relationships unselfishly with other people, and when he has also accepted those values which demand independence and commitment.'[25] Both Dresen-Coenders and Fortmann were in complete agreement with this definition. In 1954, they added the following clarification: 'Maturity is not only independence and the ability to bear responsibility . . . . Its essence lies much deeper: in the profundity of real surrender, in the ability to love.'[26] Perquin agreed with this interpretation and referred to it in the third edition (1956) of *Paedagogiek*.[27] Both the MAS national organization and the life schools for boys included this aim of 'assisting in attaining maturity' in their curricula.

Buytendijk's woman

Buytendijk's book *The Woman* was very influential.[28] It was frequently referred to in life school documents. From interviews with former MAS national committee members, staff and teachers it is apparent that almost all had read it. First, I will give a brief overview of his ideas on masculinity and femininity as these must be considered part of the ideology behind this group of progressive Catholics.

According to Buytendijk, femininity meant 'being in the world as a caring being'. In contrast, masculinity was 'being in the world as a working being'. Boys' nature was more expansive, conquering and aggressive. They tried to overcome obstacles and to get to grips with the world. The nature of girls was more adaptable, compliant, more willing to adjust or, as he calls it, 'a dwelling upon things', 'a being at one with the self'.[29]

However, these characteristics should not be taken as absolutes. Masculinity and femininity were characteristics which could occur in both men and women. Each person should develop both, although to a greater or lesser extent. A man who lacked some feminine tenderness or the ability to 'dwell' on things would be lacking in humanity. Maternalness and tenderness manifested themselves in both the male and female. Maternalness, says Buytendijk, can be translated as 'tender love', and a man also needs that in his 'make-up'.

'The man needs maternalness so that he does not become too exclusively male.' A fulfilling womanly existence demands elements of the
masculine form of existence, such as objectivity and detachment: 'A
woman who is too maternal is not a good mother and a woman who
is too feminine is as incapable of love as an excessively masculine
man.' Both should try to achieve full humanity.[30]

Buytendijk's argument comprises no few ambivalences. On the
one hand, he states for example that much of what is considered
masculine or feminine is determined by culture. On the other, he
distinguishes different basic structures – masculine and feminine,
working and caring. However, he did not see these different basic
structures as necessarily determining vocation: 'Nature determines
nothing, prescribes nothing and does not proclaim vocations.'[31] In
this sense, his view was progressive in Catholic circles. His book can
be seen as a plea against the immediate condemnation of women who
chose a life other than the traditional one. But he does not agree with
people who think men and women are equal. Simone de Beauvoir is
the main target of his criticism and he reproves her for formulating
an ideal of equality which implies that woman can only become
human if she conforms to the masculine. In his argument against de
Beauvoir he stresses the different basic structures of the man and the
woman and the resulting, more obvious choice of different ways of
living, in other words working and caring.

Caring beings

As already indicated, Buytendijk's definition of femininity as 'living
in the world as a caring being' was frequently quoted in the MAS,
especially in the 1950s. The message was that the mature woman
could best experience her responsibility in responsible caring.
Dresen-Coenders added that 'wholeness and concern for others'
were the special characteristics which enabled a woman to do so.[32]
But she also believed women could give meaning to the unmarried
state in other ways. Like Buytendijk, she thought the definitions
of femininity and masculinity given above should not be seen as
absolutes. Thus, she created space for women who wanted to be
active in other areas. There is, however, little trace of this thinking in
the early MAS curriculum. Schouwenaars' study programme had by
this time been approved by government and had been incorporated
into the Industrial Education Act for girls. It was aimed primarily at

preparing for life as housewife, mother and wife.[33] It was not until the end of 1950s that Schouwenaars' thinking came under direct attack, and the MAS national organization carried out changes in the curriculum. There was slightly less emphasis on the family and slightly more on society. This coincided with a general call for an 'own contribution' from women in all areas of society.

The MAS Youth Course curriculum had been developed by the national management organization itself. It was also aimed at preparation for motherhood and the housewife's existence. In comparison with the MAS, recreation played a greater role here. Furthermore, its aim was to ease pupils through the transition from school to work.[34]

The concept of 'own contribution'

Writers in the *Journal for Mater Amabilis Schools* and other progressive Catholic publications increasingly pointed out the fact that society was becoming more and more complex and confusing, and that technology and mechanization had penetrated every sector, resulting in a dehumanization of society. Women should provide a counterbalance to this development. In 1962, the psychologist H. Penders, who was on the MAS national staff, summarized these arguments as follows:

> What is at issue here . . . is nothing less than a *humaniza-tion* [my italics, H.V.] of existing relationships . . . . It is of immense importance that the woman, with her characteristic focus on life and the personal, with her primary attention for the whole and the concrete, should participate as intensely as possible in all areas of human existence.[35]

In the 1960s, women were expected to make their own specific contribution to maintaining quality of life in an increasingly technologized society. This contribution should be made primarily on a personal level and in areas of human relationships because women had more competence in these fields. Feminine warmth to counterbalance (cold) male society? The ideal image propagated by the MAS in the 1960s was that of the practical, nimble housewife who ran her business (the home) efficiently and had time to spare for her husband and children, and – when the kids were older – for a job outside the home. But the question was, according to

Figure 5.2   A lesson on spending the family budget in an economic way
in the Mater Amabilis School

psychologist and MAS-staffer Celeste Herberichs, whether women
could combine their work at home with an outside job without the
family suffering:

> Nor should girls' education focus on career and society
> resulting in the neglect of the very essential and demanding
> tasks of wife, housewife and mother . . . . Consideration for
> human relationships, interest in the personal, the ability to
> create atmosphere, attention to detail, none of these are matters
> which can be brushed aside as old-fashioned . . . . The women
> who have succeeded in combining their double orientation into
> one whole are few and far between.[36]

And that brings us back to the MAS ideal in the 1960s: training girls
for a task in two worlds.

As spokesperson for the national organization, Herberichs'
numerous articles in the *Journal for Mater Amabilis Schools*
advocated the breaking down of the taboos on married women's
work outside the home, which were still the norm in Catholic
circles then, and for the development of sound professional training
programmes for girls.

The MAS curriculum shows that in the 1960s there was thought for the world outside the home and that the servility ideal was less prominent. But it also demonstrates that preparation for a family was still fairly central to MAS programmes.

Working beings

What is striking is that there was a lot of talk about the 'essence of woman', but very little about the 'essence of man', evident already from the comparison of Schouwenaars' and Beel's ideas. No book appeared on the nature or essence of men. Buytendijk only mentions masculine basic structures when he uses them to clarify differences with those of women. The source material shows clearly that the people who ran the life schools for boys shared Buytendijk's views. However, they saw no need to refer continually to his definition of masculinity as 'being in the world as a working being', or to validate this view.

Yet we do find implicit expressions of notions on masculinity, for example when the definition of maturity is discussed or when we examine more closely Perquin's view of working youth. An important element of the definition of maturity was the ability to surrender, and to love. Mature surrender, Dresen-Coenders and Fortmann argued, was not a sign of weakness, but a sign of strength.[37] They felt the need to emphasize this with regard to men, because surrender was associated primarily with femininity. But they did not think it necessary to remark on this when the same educational ideal was related to femininity.

When discussing the behaviour of skilled workers, Perquin repeatedly referred to their assertiveness and urge to achieve, of which he strongly disapproved. The life school's task, among other things, was 'to remove the overevaluation of assertivity and achievement, so that there would be space for softer feelings . . . for social duties and for human relations'.[38] The life schools should only appoint teachers who themselves had attained this kind of maturity. They should act as examples for the boys who attended the schools and they should provide security, safety and love.[39]

Just as in the notions of Ruygers mentioned above, the hard, tough and proud male image loses its validity and has to make way for a new ideal image in which the courage to enter into relationships, the ability to make commitments, and to love profoundly were the most important elements. According to Perquin, the aim of the life schools was the promotion of growth to maturity in physical, mental and emotional senses. The emotional aspect was especially stressed. This attitude also indicates his rejection of the 'too masculine male' (just as Buytendijk does).

Yet Perquin does not go so far as to strive after equality. He saw great differences in aptitude, again referring to Buytendijk. In 1960 he spoke out emphatically against 'treating the sexes as equals': 'Following the striving after equality, it is as if numerous girls are confused about their identity. Men and women are equivalent, not equal.'[40] Ten years later, in 1970, he still held the same opinion, and added: 'There are people who with heroic devotion are occupied in creating the dullest world imaginable, namely a world in which there is no difference between men and women.'[41]

There are some ambivalences in Perquin's ideas, too. On the one hand, he resisted the idea that men and women were equal. However, just as Buytendijk and Ruygers, he was completely opposed to the outdated polarity between the sexes as an absolute. Like Buytendijk and Dresen-Coenders, he feared the masculine would be the norm in the equality ideal and that women would have to conform to it.

Perquin's educational ideal remained current until 1970 when the life schools for boys were abolished. Occasional criticism arose only towards the end of the 1960s. For example, in 1968 Herberichs wrote:

> The atmosphere in which life schools carry out their educational tasks sometimes evokes associations with a rather biased, *overly concerned maternalness* [my italics, H.V.]. Just take the example of discussions on the controversy surrounding vocational education. It seems as though people see the achievements considered essential in training programmes today as disastrous for the development of personality in young people. These have to be supervised continually in everything they do and protected against all kinds of influences from the big, bad world outside . . . . They'll never have it so good as in the cosy, safe life school.[42]

There appears to have been no response to Herberichs' criticism – at least I could find nothing in the archives.

The curriculum designed by Perquin was aimed primarily at the transition from school to work. In addition, the boys were taught to spend any free time in useful ways and they were prepared for their role as solid citizens. How to socialize with girls was still part of the curriculum. Perquin had scrapped the preparation for fatherhood which had been included in the initial programmes for the first Pater Fortis School.[43]

DIFFERENCES BETWEEN MEN AND BETWEEN WOMEN

The majority of MAS pupils came from the 'lower' socio-economic classes. These pupils had different ideas on 'being a woman' from those of the national organization and the MAS teachers, who generally came from 'higher' social classes and characterized these girls as unfeminine, masculine or hyper-feminine. This last occurred primarily because of their 'deviant' sexual behaviour. An examination of what they considered *unfeminine* also tells us a lot about their ideas on 'real' femininity. I have already raised this point in the introduction to this article. In my view, references both to men and to other women play a major role in determining what a 'real' woman is. The same applies to the establishment of what masculinity means, or what a 'real' man looks like, although I found no evidence in the sources of differences between men expressed in terms of sexual deviation. It was stated, however, that just like girls, boys from 'lower' social classes often lacked the ability to recognize 'objective' values and detachment. They were said to be too subjective and egocentric.[44] The skilled working-class boys especially had too much assertiveness and too great an urge to achieve. All of this showed only a quasi-maturity. How differences between men were articulated requires more research. The same applies to the question of how sex and class differences were interrelated. It is striking, for example, that when Buytendijk was talking about women in more general terms he stated that the fulfilled feminine existence also required elements such as 'objectivity and detachment'. If both women and young people from the 'lower' social classes had not developed these dimensions sufficiently, who had?

My research shows that differences between women were indeed partly designated by referring to them in terms of sexual deviations. *The way in which* leading MAS ideologists judged working-class girls' sexual behaviour changed during the course of time. Schouwenaars rejected their sexual behaviour on moral grounds: she thought they were all morally sick.[45] Dresen-Coenders expressed her disapproval in more psychological terms. She saw a disturbance in their physical and spiritual harmony. The vital-emotive, erotic and physical were too dominant, which was most visible in the factory girls.[46] Terms such as 'immoral' and 'degenerate' were replaced by 'primitive personality' and 'quasi-maturity'. In both of these, this concerned to some extent the relationship of these girls to sexual and physical matters which was seen as problematic. A series of personality types was developed based on a 'real' maturity scale; factory girls were at the bottom end.[47] What was considered 'real' maturity in women was in fact almost synonymous with 'real' femininity. It should be noted here that the definition of maturity was based partly on research on young people (especially working-class young people) who were not yet mature or 'quasi-mature', in other words through research on deviations.[48]

TO CONCLUDE

This historical analysis demonstrates that the terms masculinity and femininity are not unequivocal, but are fleshed out in various ways depending on context and time. Educators do not merely pass over knowledge to others. Education does not only *reproduce* inequality, it also *produces* specific sexual differences although these differ depending on type of school. The sexual differences were not self-evident, but the subject of discussion and argument which was also going on in other areas. We should note here that pupils did not automatically accept the notions put forward by their teachers. The question of how receptive the students were to the transfer of norms, and whether, how and to what extent these were integrated into their ideas on what 'real' masculinity and femininity should be, still has to be answered. This answer would require a different kind of analysis: interviews with former pupils could be of great help.

While shifts were occurring in ideals of femininity and masculinity, the same was also happening to the idealized polarity between the sexes. Its absolute character disappeared with the course of time. As a result, *doubt* made its entrance and certainty on the 'correct polarity' was lost.[49] The latter is especially apparent from the ambivalences in statements on masculinity and femininity made by the already mentioned group of progressive Catholics, and by Buytendijk, Dresen-Coenders, Fortmann and Perquin in particular. On the one hand, Buytendijk stressed that so-called feminine and masculine characteristics were determined culturally. On the other, he argued that basic structures or aptitudes of men and women were different. These Catholics were more inclined to the view that men and women were equivalent but not equal, not the same but different. But how different was a question which was answered increasingly by less unequivocal replies. Buytendijk emphasized explicitly that masculine and feminine traits occurred, and should occur, in both men and women, although to a different extent. A fulfilling human existence required both elements of objectivity and detachment as well as commitment and tenderness. An excessive assertiveness and urge to achieve in men should make way for softer emotions. In place of the somewhat unequivocal views of Schouwenaars and Beel on masculinity and femininity, the progressive Catholics saw (and they were almost unanimous in this) personalities of a much more pluriform kind.

Yet, according to them, men and women were not equal. They were as frightened of the world without difference sketched by Ruygers as they were of the 'outdated polarity'. I have already indicated that Buytendijk criticized Simone de Beauvoir because, in her plea for equality, she wanted women to conform to male norms. When de Beauvoir's work was 'rediscovered' in the late 1960s, Dresen-Coenders once again raised this argument.[50] The idea that the masculine would become the norm held little attraction for them. From Buytendijk's notions on how men and women should be if they were to attain *fulfilled humanity*, from the definition of maturity formulated by Perquin, Dresen-Coenders and Fortmann, and their pleas for a *humanization of society*, it appears that they saw more in what we would now probably call a feminization of social relations.[51]

This article has also demonstrated that the Catholic segment in the post-war period consisted of different factions. The changes which took place in the 1960s did not come out of nowhere, but were partly engineered by a network of progressive groups. An important role was played by the group which had gathered around the magazine *Dux*, the staff of the Hoogveld Institute and the Catholic life schools' national management committee. Another important centre of progressive Catholicism was the Catholic Central Association for Mental Health in which Buytendijk and Fortmann played a prominent role. Ruygers and Dresen-Coenders were also involved in this association. All were psychologists with the exception of Ruygers who was a philosopher.[52]

Within the life schools we see a shift from a moralizing approach (with Mary and Joseph as examples of 'good' women and men) to a psychological approach. Dymphie van Berkel views the psychologization of education as one of the disintegration phenomena of the Catholic segment because it meant 'the clergy had finally lost their grip on education'.[53]

This view implies that psychologization automatically means secularization and that scientists are laity not clergy.[54] The rise of expert laypeople was indeed unstoppable but my research shows that a number of laypeople propagated a modern approach to education but presented it as a Catholic approach. The fact that in the course of the 1960s these progressive Catholics, the MAS committee members among them, could not say what was Catholic about their approach does not detract from the original intention. That intention is apparent from Dresen-Coenders' statement that in some cases the emancipation process would not have 'swung towards a total break with Catholicism' if conservative forces had not held back the progressives for so long.[55]

Van Berkel's general statement on the psychologization of education fails to take into account the important role played by women such as Dresen-Coenders and Herberichs in the conflict among Catholics on the true definition of femininity and masculinity. My research shows that in their pleas for a humanization of society , and by giving shape and content to the meaning of femininity, progressive Catholics attributed specific competence to women. Women such as Dresen-Coenders personify the modern Catholic woman which she herself helped to create.

NOTES

1 This chapter is a revised version of the paper I presented to the Third International Interdisciplinary Congress on Women, 'Women's Worlds, Visions and Revisions', in Dublin, July 1987. I would like to thank Liesbeth Bervoets, Jac Bosmans, Marjan Schwegman and Hennie Siebelt for their comments on this version, which is part of a larger dissertation on sexual and denominational segregation in youth education in the period 1947–1973.

2 For example, see A.A. Wesselingh, *Onderwijs en reproduktie van maatschappelijke ongelijkheid 1975–1985* (Education and the reproduction of social inequality, 1975–1985), Diss, Nijmegen, 1985; J.L. Peschar and A.A. Wesselingh (eds), *Onderwijssociologie. Een Inleiding* (Educational sociology. An Introduction), Wolfers-Noordhoff BV, Groningen, 1986.

3 See among others: Y. Leeman, 'Onderwijs en etnische verhoudingen'

(Education and ethnic relations), in J.L. Peschar and A.A. Wesselingh, op. cit., pp. 427–8.

4 S. Grotenhuis and M. Volman, 'Meisjesonderwijs of onderwijs voor meisjes' (Education for girls), in *Pedagogische Studieen*, vol. 63, no. 7/8, pp. 326–36 (esp. pp. 333, 334).

5 Ibid.

6 These were youth education centres set up in the Netherlands specifically for working teenagers by the Catholic Church just after the Second World War.

7 The MAS national management organization included both committee and staff who worked together very closely. This national umbrella organization developed the ideas mentioned here and financed and controlled the schools.

8 I will not be examining the special pedagogic-didactic methods which were developed in these schools. See H. Vossen, 'De kunst om aan te sluiten. Nieuwe leermethoden in de levenscholen voor jongens en meisjes 1946–1960' ('The art of fitting in. New teaching methods in the life schools for boys and girls, 1946–1960'), in G. ten Dam, M. Schoenmacker and J. Sibbes (eds), *De-konstruktie van vrouwelijk leren* (Deconstruction of female learning), Zomeruniversiteit Vrouwenstudies, Groningen, 1986.

9 My undergraduate thesis goes into this in depth. See H. Vossen, 'Huishoudonderwijs als een vorm van gezinspolitiek. Huishoudonderwijs en Mater Amabilis scholen tussen 1945 en 1960 en de voorgeschiedenis' ('Domestic education as a form of family politics. Domestic education and Mater Amabilis schools between 1945 and 1960, and earlier'), Catholic University Nijmegen, pp. 78–82 and p. 90.

10 W. Berger and J. Janssen talk in this connection about 'the fight for a fitting distance', which raged between 1950 and 1970. See W. Berger and J. Janssen, 'De katholieken en hun psychologie' ('The Catholics and their psychology'), in A. Weiler (ed.), *De identiteit van katholieke wetenschapsmensen* (The identity of Catholic scientists), Baarn, 1980, pp. 26–8. How this was expressed in the MAS is described in H. Vossen, 'Van katholiek meisjesonderwijs naar algemeen vormingswerk. Ontstaan en ontwikkeling van de Mater Amabilis School (MAS), 1947–1968' ('From Catholic girls' education to general training. Origins and development of the Mater Amabilis School (MAS), 1947-1968'), in *Jaarboek Katholiek Documentatiecentrum* 1985, Nijmegen, 1986, p. 93.

11 At the time this article was written I was inspired by post-structuralist theory and the debate on the interrelation between difference and equality, which in 1987 had been going on in the Netherlands for some years. I have not clarified this further because it was well known in women's studies circles in this country. For the method of post-structuralist theory, please see Joan W. Scott, 'Deconstructing equality-versus-difference: or, the use of post-structuralist theory for feminism', in *Feminist Studies*, vol. 14, no. 1, 1988 and published in Dutch translation in *Jaarboek voor Vrouwengeschiedenis* (Women's History Yearbook), vol. 10, 1989. Scott explains the terms language,

discourse, difference and deconstruction and shows how they can be productive for historical and other research. She also provides a further lucid exposition in *Gender and the Politics of History*, Columbia University Press, New York, 1988, which was reviewed by Jose Eyt and myself in the *Tijdschrift voor Vrouwenstudies*, vol. 10, no. 3, 1990.

12 M. Aerts, chapter 1 above, p. 28.

13 S. Leydesdorff, 'Wij en de geschiedenis' (History and us), in *Te Elfder Ure*, vol. 29, no. 39, 1986, p. 147.

14 See H. Vossen, 'Vrouwelijkheid in de Mater Amabilis School 1947–1968' ('Femininity in the Mater Amabilis School'), in G. ten Dam *et al.* (eds), *Leren* [Learning] (Summer University publication), Zomeruniversiteit Vrouwenstudies, Groningen, 1987, pp. 101–11. In this article I look into the interrelation between class and sexual differences.

15 I. Costera Meijer, 'Echte vrouwen en supervrouwen. Feminisme en homosexualiteit 1972–1975' ('Genuine women or superwomen. Feminism and homosexuality'), in *Te Elfder Ure*, vol. 29, no. 39, 1986, p. 60; see also M. Barrett and M. McIntosh, 'Etnocentrisme en socialisties-feministiese theorie', in *Tijdschrift voor Vrouwenstudies* 24, vol. 6, no. 4, 1985, p. 490.

16 The origins and development of the MAS are described in H. Vossen, 'Van katholiek meisjesonderwijs . . .', op. cit., pp. 81–130. The origins and development of the Pater Fortis School until 1955 is traced in H. Vossen, 'De Mater Amabilis en Pater Fortis School 1947–1955. Het ontstaan van een nieuw schooltype in Maastricht en de navolging ervan elders in Nederland' ('The origins of a new type of school in Maastricht and its imitation elsewhere in the Netherlands'), in *Sociaal Historisch Jaarboek voor Limburg*, vol. 32, Assen/Maastricht, 1987. Detailed source notes can be found in these publications. See also J. Perry and H. Vossen, 'Old problems, new solutions. Working-class youth culture and some efforts to change it, 1945–1955', in: L. Heerma van Voss and F. Holthoon (eds), *Working-class and Popular Culture: Papers Presented to the Fifth British–Dutch Conference on Labour History*, Stichting Beheer IISG, Amsterdam, 1988, pp. 209–27.

17 Until 1971, employers were not obliged to allow young employees to attend the courses. The life schools were unique to the Netherlands. In contrast to part-time education or day-release programmes in other countries such as the UK, they did not provide vocational training; the emphasis was on character formation.

18 Schouwenaars' ideas are described extensively in H. Vossen, 'De eerste jaren van de Mater Amabilis School. Meisjesonderwijs en gezinspolitiek' ('The first years of the Mater Amabilis School. Girls' education and family policy'), in *Comenius 17*, vol. 5, no. 1, 1985, pp. 31–48.

19 H. Ruygers, 'Gespreken met lezers (1). Pater Fortis Scholen?' ('Conversations with readers. Pater Fortis Schools'), in *Dux*, vol. 21, no. 3, 1954, p. 205.

20 Ibid.

21 Postscript from the editors on an article by M.C. Schouwenaars, in *Dux*, vol. 18, nr. 1, 1951, pp. 30–34.

22 Ibid.

23 See H. Vossen, 'Van katholiek meisjesonderwijs . . .', op. cit., and H. Vossen, 'De Mater Amabilis en Pater Fortis School 1947–1955', op. cit.
24 Het Spectrum, Utrecht/Antwerp, 1951.
25 N. Perquin, *Paedagogiek. Bezinning op het opvoedkundig verschijnsel* (Pedagogy. Reflection on the educational phenomenon), J.J. Romen en Zonen, Roermond/Maaseik, 1952, p. 77. (The influence of this book in both Belgium and the Netherlands is apparent from the fact that it was reprinted nine times between 1949 and 1967.)
26 H.M. Dresen-Coenders and H.M.M. Fortmann, 'Ontwikkelingstypen op weg naar volwassenheid' ('Types of development towards maturity'), in H.M. Dresen-Coenders *et al, Bijdragen over het rapport van het Mgr. Hoogveldinstituut, Moderne Jeugd op weg naar Volwassenheid* (Contributions to the Mgr. Hoogveld Institute Report, Modern Youth on the way to Maturity), 1955, pp. 115–16. The articles in this book appeared earlier in *Dux*, this particular text was published in 1954.
27 N. Perquin, *Paedagogiek*, op. cit., 3rd edn, 1956, p. 80. Perquin notes that his definition of maturity was influenced by the results of the research carried out by the Hoogveld Institute on Catholic working youth. The collection of articles mentioned in note 26 is a summary of the results of this report.
28 *De Vrouw. Haar natuur, verschijning en bestaan* (The woman. Her nature, person and existence), op. cit. This book was also well known in non-Catholic circles. It was often used as a reference, and was quoted in numerous government papers. It was reprinted eighteen times between 1951 and 1975 and a total of 110,500 copies were printed. The greatest number for one year was sold in 1958/59 (30,000). See 'Conversation between H. Vossen and R. van der Hoeden', *Het Spectrum*, 21 August 1987.
29 F.J.J. Buytendijk, op. cit., pp. 128–9 and pp. 279–99.
30 Ibid, pp. 335, 336.
31 Ibid., pp. 323–5. H.M.M. Fortmann's article on the book contains the same ambivalences. See 'Mannen en vrouwen, jongens en meisjes' ('Men and women, boys and girls'), in *Dux*, vol. 20, no. 2, 1953, pp. 61–91.
32 These two characteristics were, according to Dresen-Coenders, closely linked: 'In general, the man is more business oriented than the woman and is more able to separate work and home life, or at least he is more able to see both on separate levels. In general, the woman is more people oriented, and if she gives herself up to something, she will be more inclined to do so with her whole being.' See H.M. Dresen-Coenders, 'Iets over de psychologie van het fabrieksmeisje' ('Notes on the psychology of the factory girl'), in *Dux*, vol. 15, no. 10, 1947–48, p. 259.
33 Subjects included cookery, needlework and child care. For an exposition on the curriculum, see H. Vossen, 'Van katholiek meisjesonderwijs . . .', op. cit.
34 Ibid.
35 H. Penders, 'Ontwikkelingen in de opvattingen over de arbeid van de gehuwde vrouw in het katholieke volksdeel' ('Developments in

notions on married woman's labour in the Catholic segment of the population'), in: F.J.J. Buytendijk *et al.*, *De niet-aanwezige huisvrouw. Beschouwingen over de buitenshuis werkende gehuwde vrouw* (The absent housewife. Reflections on the working married woman), Paul Brand, Hilversum/Antwerp, 1962, p. 50.

36 C. Herberichs, 'Vormingswerk voor werkende meisjes boven de 17 jaar' ('Education for working girls of 17 and older'), in H. Cremers *et al.*, *Vorming Werkende Jongeren* (Educating Working Youth), Utrecht, 1965, p. 59.

37 H.M. Dresen-Coenders and H.M.M. Fortmann, op. cit., p. 116: 'But now the question arises: are surrender and openness not weaknesses? Are they compatible with the expansiveness of an adult male, his businesslike attitude, his masterfulness, "his labour" and his searching?'

38 N. Perquin, *Een levensschool voor de jeugd in de bedrijven* (A life school for youth in industry), J.B. Wolters, Groningen, 1958, p. 37.

39 Ibid., p. 141 and pp. 162–3.

40 N. Perquin, 'Jeugd in de wereld van heden' ('Youth in today's world'), in Documentatie Raad van de Jeugdvorming. Archief Nationale Stichting voor Mater Amabilis Scholen [Board for Youth Education Documentation. National Foundation for MAS], box 686–7, Catholic Documentation Centre, Nijmegen. Perquin emphasizes the equivalence of men and women, which is progress compared to Beel's notions (and those of many others) in which the husband, as head of the family, is placed in a hierarchical relationship to his wife.

41 N. Perquin, 'Jeugd in de samenleving van nu' ('Youth in society today'), in *Impuls*, vol. 3, no. 9, 1971, p. 282.

42 C. Herberichs, 'Indrukken van een congres' ('Impressions from a congress'), in *Dux*, vol. 35, no. 8/9, 1968, p. 394.

43 For an exposition on the teaching programme, see H. Vossen, 'De Mater Amabilis en Pater Fortis School 1947–1955', op. cit.

44 H.M. Dresen-Coenders et al., op cit. See also J. Perry, H. Vossen, 'Old problems, new solutions . . .', pp. 214–17.

45 H. Vossen, 'De eerste jaren . . .', op. cit., p. 38.

46 A. van Drenth, 'Het massameisje' ('The mass girl'), in *Comenius*, vol. 5, no. 17, 1985, pp. 19–28.

47 Ibid., pp. 27–8, and H.M. Dresen-Coenders and H.M.M. Fortmann, op. cit., pp. 118–23. Dresen-Coenders quickly dropped the term 'primitive' because she thought it incorrect. Unpublished interview with H.M. Dresen-Coenders, 30 April 1985.

48 See Perquin, *Paedagogiek*.

49 F. Buers also points out that within progressive Catholic circles doubt was seen explicitly as 'a healthy matter'. He researched *G3*, the magazine for Catholic conscripts. See '*G3* en "Waalheuvel". Werken aan een vernieuwing van het katholieke geloof in de periode 1951–1965' ('*G3* and "Waalheuvel". Working on a renewal of the Catholic faith in the period 1951–1965') (undergraduate thesis), Beek-Ubbergen, 1986, p. 47; and interview with Dresen-Coenders.

50 H.M. Dresen-Coenders, 'Naar aanleiding van de zoveelste publikatie

over de vrouw' ('In response to the umpteenth publication on women'), in *Dux*, vol. 35, p. 3, 1968, p. 142.

51 The fact that in the humanization of society a major role was ascribed to women is also apparent from F.J.J. Buytendijk, S.J.B.J. Trimbos and A. de Waal, *Vorming tot vrouw* (Educating women), Het Spectrum, Utrecht/Antwerp, 1967. See especially pp. 28, 43 and 50.

52 I have not mentioned all of the progressive groups here (see note 49). I would also like to note that these 'enlightened' Catholics based their ideas primarily on personalism. The Italo-German, Catholic personalist Romano Guardini's ideas were very influential. See H. Vossen, 'Van katholiek meisjesonderwijs . . .', op. cit., p. 109.

53 D. van Berkel, 'Dit moederhart! Wie zal het beschrijven? Een analyse van "Huwelijk en Huisgezin", tijdschrift voor katholieke vaders en moeders' ('This mother's heart! Who will describe it? An analysis of "Marriage and family", magazine for Catholic fathers and mothers'), in R. Buikema *et al.*, *Liefhebben* (Loving), ZUV, Zomer Universiteit, Groningen, 1987, p. 50.

54 Perquin and Fortmann, for example, were both clergymen and scientists. Perquin fought for the acceptance of pedagogy as an independent science, separate from theology. More conservative Catholics saw pedagogy as 'applied' theology, or as 'theology's serving girl'. See interview with Dresen-Coenders, op. cit.

55 Ibid., and letter from Dresen-Coenders to the author, 13 August 1987. See also N. Perquin, *Herinnering en overpeinzing* (Memories and reflections), J.J. Romen en Zonen, Roermond, 1969, p. 177. He writes: 'Now it has erupted, that thing which they tried to prevent . . . . And who is to blame?' According to Perquin, the orthodox Catholics had arrested 'normal, healthy development'.

6

THE YOUNG, INTELLIGENT WOMAN

Marianne Beelaerts

From the time women were admitted to universities, it appeared that studying presented women with specific problems. How did the new life as a student relate to the old life as protected and dependent daughter and especially to the future life as wife and mother? In 1915, Annie Salomons published an autobiographical novel on this problem under the pseudonym Ada Gerlo. *Herinneringen van een onafhankelijke vrouw* (Memoirs of an Independent Woman) describes the dualism of an educated woman's life at the beginning of this century.

That this dualism has still not been resolved is illustrated by a paper published by educationists in 1982.[1] It sketches the dual future perspective of women as a problem in girls' education. 'How sacrifice can be combined with independence is a girl's dilemma. Future perspectives based on the double orientations towards independence and the nurturing role of mother and wife are still ambivalent.' Annie Salomons would have recognized this ambivalence; she recorded it in novel form more than seventy-five years ago.

Memoirs was a 1915 equivalent of a best-seller. An initial 10,000 copies were printed and the book then went through reprint after reprint and even had to be chained to the shelf at Leiden's library as copies were always being stolen. It was reprinted for the seventeenth time recently by the *Wereldbibliotheek* (World Library). Ada Gerlo's first book had been equally popular. When *Een meisje-studentje* (A Girl Student) appeared some years earlier, it generated a polemic on the image of the female student it provided. Annie Sillevis[2] penned a pamphlet against *A Girl Student* in an attempt to show there were numerous serious female students whose time wasn't filled with tea parties and excursions. This polemic was part of a discussion which had been going on for some time on the pros and cons of a university education for women. When Annie Salomons was writing, it was not uncommon for the Dean to include his opposition to female students in his opening speech of the academic year. Scientific research was carried out to support this view. Using question-naires, the problems of female students were charted, and doctors examined changes in women's bodily functions which were seen as a consequence of studying. So it is not surprising that a novel on the life of a female student written by someone with first-hand knowledge would be received with great interest in university circles.

Just as in *A Girl Student*, the main character in *Memoirs of an Independent Woman* is a female student. But the emphasis in the second book is very different. *Memoirs* is no chronologically told story focused on the novelty of a student's life, but a review of the problems encountered by a now graduate and independent woman in her relationships with men. Annie Salomons certainly uses her second book to participate in the debate on women students, but in *Memoirs* she approaches this discussion in a much more com-prehensive way than she had done in the first. The older woman questions the impersonality of learning, the desirability of marriage, the possibility of having children. She chooses the life of a single woman at a time when this was a condition that was looked on with pity. Like further education for women, marriage was also the subject of a fierce debate at the beginning of this century. Voices were raised comparing marriage to slavery. For example, in 1899 Cornelie Huygens argued that marriage was not much more than 'a relationship in which the man possessed the woman as private property, and is thus an excrescence of the capitalist system. Marriage is the worst folly into which a person can fall.'[3] Mathilde Wibaut, Betsy Perk, Mina Krusemann and Wilhelmina Drucker also wrote militant texts on the same subject.[4]

In this context, *Memoirs of an Independent Woman* could be characterized as reactionary. Annie Romein-Verschoor classifies *Memoirs* as a 'lady's novel' in her classic thesis on Dutch women novelists after 1880.[5] She argues that Salomons 'spells out the hor-rors of a single existence and idealizes marriage and motherhood'. Romein attributes the high sales and popularity to the realism with which 'this kind of book reflected the longing for emotions and originality, and the narrow sphere of interest of one social group'.

Annie Romein was not the first to discuss the book's popularity.

In a review published in the August 1915 issue of *De Nieuwe Amsterdammer* (The new Amsterdammer) when the book had just appeared, the authoritative literary critic Frans Coenen raised a number of objections to the book: 'It was suspected that the I-character here has much in common with the author herself, and some see this as an insurmountable objection . . . . People felt, rightly or wrongly, that it contained self-endearment and self-pity, and that is always irritating.' In fact, both of these evaluations neglect the text's structure; they do not see its form. In Romein's case, the focus is on the 'interests' of the 'social group reflected' in the text, and in Coenen's review the similarity to the 'author herself'. Thus, the text becomes a vehicle or a mirror for (already known) reality. How the text as text functions is not examined.

In this article, I would like to focus on the text's structure by examining the way tension between love and education, between independence and dependence is developed. This tension concerns the conflict between the narrated experiences and accepted norms of femininity, but also between fantasy and reality. How the writer structures this field of tension is the question I would like to discuss here. I will be examining memoirs as a method of narration with emphasis on the role played by time, perspective and observations on writing. In addition, the interrelationship of the various story lines will be looked at briefly. By examining *Memoirs* in this way, a picture of the problems of independence emerges which is considerably less cut and dried than that of the older reviews cited above.

MEMOIRS AS A NARRATIVE FORM

The title page of *Memoirs of an Independent Woman* immediately indicates what kind of text this is. The book comprises memoirs, a review of events and occurrences from her own past, written by an older woman. What form is given to these memoirs, and from what point of view is she remembering? What role is played by time? Time plays a role in all memoirs, but the way it is used can differ greatly. The simplest method is a chronological construction of memories, but using flashforwards or flashbacks offers a way of linking up various events. They can thus acquire different perspectives; a dual point of view – that of the main character in the situation which is being recounted, and that of the narrator who is looking back on the event. Examining what happens to the time intervals can make clear

Figure 6.1 Portrait of Annie Salomons c. 1905

how these two points of view are related to each other in *Memoirs of an Independent Woman*.

The first few lines of chapter one immediately describe the time that is being remembered: 'It was in my first year as a student that I learnt to know hunger.' These events occurred at some time in the narrator's past. We know no more about her than that she herself is the main character in these memoirs. She uses the past tense to describe the past while sometimes turning to the present tense for small hints on the actual time gap which has to be bridged between the time of narration and the student days, such as in this paragraph: 'I remember everything about those months with a marvellous clarity; I can still smell the bitter scent of withered, damp leaves; I remember a tenuous, translucent mist shrouded the old tower; I remember the blouse I wore that morning . . . .' The importance of that past event is emphasized by a jump in time. The

Figure 6.2 Portrait of Annie Salomons in 1915

memories of it are just as strong years later. At the same time, there is a moment of distance, and something about the present is said by recalling the past. The greater part of chapter one is told in the past tense and in chronological order.

Only after forty pages does the narrator's present begin to play a definite role. The older Ada Gerlo who is recalling times past then comes together with the 18-year-old Ada and in two pages the great difference between both versions of the same person becomes apparent. Up to page forty we follow the adventures of a young, idealistic woman who throws herself into a new life and her first love affair. She is impressed by philosophy and literature, and she is pleased her allowance is sufficient to help out her financially distressed new boyfriend. Then the narration changes to the present tense and the narrator takes over: 'A tenderness swells in my heart, and perhaps there is a trace of sentimentality; it is as though I were writing about a younger sister, a sweet, young sister who died prematurely. I close my tired eyes and I see how I must have stood there that evening . . . .' And later: 'I have become old, sensible, practical, critical; and I think: what was the greatest, or even the most important thing about being an impoverished student?'

The difference between both becomes even more clear in the following, rather artificial passage in which the older Ada thinks about the recriminations the younger could level against her older self:

> And it is as if my long-gone self, as if that child with her eyes full of dreams lifted to the stars, answers me: Oh, of course, everything could have been different, the whole thing could have passed without any romance whatsoever . . . if I hadn't been at the gateway to life, my heart awakening and longing to make the great sacrifice.

Apparently, Ada has changed in the period between her student days and the moment of narration. At first, she was optimistic and romantic, now she is older, tired and sensible. How we should see this change in the main character is answered gradually in the course of the memoirs; the Ada Gerlo in the story does not remain the same person. Her points of view change through the influence of her experience.

Thus, *Memoirs* consists of two layers: the narrator's layer, the thirtyish Ada, who recalls memories and sometimes intervenes using the present tense: and the layer of narrated events, in chapter one an 18-year-old Ada, in the past tense. The time being recounted changes continually. The young Ada grows older and her opinions and character change in the course of time. But the point of view on which the narrative is based remains the same. In chapter one it is described as old, tired and sensible. This is fleshed out in the course of the book, but it does not change. At the end, the Ada Gerlo who has been written about has become the Ada who writes. In the final chapter, their opinions are almost the same. The conversations, events and considerations in the intervening chapters have thus bridged the difference between the two versions of the same person.

Time is well organized and straightforward from beginning to end. Each of the four chapters covers a single period of around a year and each describes one love affair. In this sense and in contrast to what we expect from memoirs, the book has a fairly tight structure. Links are made between the various periods described using flashforwards and flashbacks. Chapter two is somewhat different from the other three chapters as the love affair it describes is not hers but that of a friend. Ada's role here is that of an eye-witness narrator. The other three chapters concern three periods in the main character's life: the student days of the 18-year-old in chapter one, the independent period of the 21-year-old woman in chapter three, and finally, in the last chapter, the time of the 30-year-old lonely writer. In both chapters one and three, the memories are interrupted occasionally for comparisons with the narrator's circumstances or comments from her point of view. In contrast, in chapter four her bitterness and cynicism are frequently set against the earlier faith in the future, the idealism and the capacity to love without expecting anything in return. This again emphasizes the horrors of an existence as an older, single writer, while the naive youth and earlier dreams are idealized. So there is something to Romein's claim about this book when she says that the horrors of being alone are spelled out. But her subsequent remark, that it idealizes marriage and motherhood, is incorrect. Through the use of flashforwards and flashbacks there is rather an idealization of the past. Happiness is found in youth's first love. Hope evaporates in subsequent years giving the memoirs a touch of melancholy.

Thus, the use of time in *Memoirs* is important for the understanding of the view on independence. But Ada Gerlo is not only narrator of and main character in the memories, she also reviews poems and novels and becomes a writer herself. In the sections devoted to reading and writing, she expresses explicit opinions on literature. These opinions offer indications of the way *Memoirs* itself can be read as literature.

Shifts in time also play a role in these opinions on literature. At the beginning of the book, the 18-year-old Ada has different preferences and opinions from those of her older self. As a young girl, her opinions are limited to the books she reads, but in later life she reviews texts, developing her own ideas on writing. In her first year, Ada reads *fin-de-siècle* and earlier nineteenth-century literature. She admires books by Flaubert, Baudelaire, Gorter,[6] Couperus,[7] Streuvels[8] and Shelley. Her boyfriend lends her Spinoza, but she can't understand much of it and prefers Nietzsche's paradoxes. She loves the poems of Kloos[9]: 'very far and very beautiful'. However, too great an appeal to emotion evokes indignation: 'I stated that I found Werner and Marlitt's books the most immoral imaginable because they falsify life and turn emotion into a morbid fever.' She is not so much concerned with strong or lofty feelings. She advocates authenticity: 'I became enthused by the thought of the much-scorned Zola who was not perhaps noble, but was in any case real and honest.' This quotation comes from the second half of *Memoirs*, when Kloos' poetry has lost its place at the top of her list of preferences.

As the 30-year-old narrator, Ada comments on this first preference as early as chapter one. At 18 she did not know what the 30-year-old would think: 'I was still too idealistic and too eager to fill my life with beautiful thoughts and noble feelings to have a taste for light-hearted stories woven together with melancholy and cynicism.' And this one sentence casually encapsulates the essence of *Memoirs* – a light-hearted story woven from melancholy and cynicism. That is what it is all about for the writer. From her reaction to the letters of her lover Joost in chapter three, it becomes apparent that her preference has little to do with what is normally considered realism. Joost lacks the emotion and vision which could give colour and meaning to what is written: 'He only knew one way to write, just as he only knew one way to tell; jumping around from people to facts, but with a lot of positive knowledge, a lot of interest in concrete matters, and an unlimited amount of *joie de vivre*. His interests appeared to me banal.'

So the narrator searches for her own opinions on literature. She rejects exaggerated romance and vulgar realism. She loves Kloos, Zola and Nietzsche. In her own work she combines light-hearted stories with an atmosphere of melancholy and cynicism. The book's final lines clarify her view of literature. They indicate which meaning attaches to memories when hope for a better future has vanished. Memoirs and literature more or less coincide. At the end of the book Ada has regained her freedom after a failed engagement. She remains alone: 'grateful for the free possession of my dreams. . . . From that moment I knew that my innermost life could only be "memories".' While the narrator's life is bitter and tarnished, the 'innermost life' survives only in memories. In view of these final lines the book's title could have been translated into: 'dreams and ideals of an independent woman'. The difference between dream and reality, between literature and life give tragedy to both. In *Memoirs* melancholy and cynicism stand alongside ideals and dreams.

ELEMENTS OF THE STORIES

The changes that the main character undergoes and that turn her into a cynical, melancholic writer cannot be understood without knowing the events which caused them. The explanation for these changes lies in the structure of the action. First, I will give a short overview of the events which take place in the four chapters, and then I will examine how these elements differ from each other. Primarily I will be discussing chapters one and four as these differ most.

In chapter one, 18-year-old Ada leaves home to live a student life in digs. Friends visit and she falls in love with one of them, a thin, quiet boy called Ru who, after a while, just stops coming. Her desire for Ru prompts her to visit him. When it turns out that lack of money is the reason he stayed away, Ada tries to help him. Ru needs a substantial sum every month; Ada just manages to prevent his suicide because of lack of money. In Ru she finds a spiritual teacher, both in terms of learning and in terms of suffering and love, which are at least equally important. Ada has to go home for a few days to get back her strength, and on her return she finds Ru has left because of illness. Some days later she sees the announcement of his death in the newspaper.

The other chapters also centre around love affairs, and all of these also finish badly after a period of happiness. The main character in chapter two is Lotte, a good friend of Ada. Wil, a sensitive, artistic boy is in love with Lotte, but she cannot respond because she knows she will disappoint Wil's wonderful dreams. She tries to leave him his illusions. That is how she comes to marry a businessman and start a family. In the meantime, Wil has come to an unfortunate end. He becomes engaged to someone else and later kills himself. In contrast to the men Ada meets, Wil loves Lotte unconditionally. Lotte, however, sees much more quickly than Ada – who needs the rest of the book to understand this – that one cannot experience perfect happiness in love. That is why she attempts to maintain the beautiful dreams. But in spite of this, their story also comes to a miserable end. The distance between dream and reality is unbridgeable.

As a 21-year-old, Ada, on a holiday, is young and happy once again. She meets Joost in Italy and he captures her heart with his boyish charm. However, once back in the Netherlands the problems start. Joost realizes Ada is a learned woman who has a mind of her own. Joost cannot handle her independence and breaks off the relationship.

In the final chapter, Ada is no longer popular and optimistic. She is alone and feels as if she's missing out on something. When Gerard, an old, faithful friend who understands her position offers to marry her, she jumps at the chance. Gerard is a down-to-earth businessman even when it comes to love and children. His spiritual poverty causes great irritation. And just as Ada seems about to become a 'normal' woman, more and more irritations impede the marriage. During a short trip with a friend she decides to regain her freedom.

The second chapter is rather at odds with the others because the main character is not Ada but a friend. In a sense, Lotte's story reflects the events in the rest of the book. But Lotte chooses a solution which Ada does not try. Lotte marries and is resigned to the limitations of a marriage of convenience so that she can keep pure her ideals of love. Ada, on the other hand, attempts to experience that love but finally comes to the same conclusion: happiness can only be experienced in dreams. The chapter on Lotte again emphasizes that there is no way out for a young, intelligent woman: whatever she chooses, whether she marries and puts aside her ideals, or tries to experience love, she will in any case emerge with empty hands. Reality is simply not a dream. The action in the other chapters is fairly simple; there are few elements to be taken into account. The number of characters is limited, the action is simple and the goals which motivate the action are clearly made explicit.

Chapters one and four differ in almost all ways. In the first place, the main character has undergone a complete change. Her partner in chapter one is also a great deal more attractive than the Gerard in chapter four. Ru is wise, inspired, well-read and artistically gifted. In comparison, the faithful, modest, sensible Gerard fades into the background. In chapter one, Ada herself initiates the action. She wants to become wise and happy, she longs for Ru's company and she wants to do everything she can for him. Her visits to him are well motivated. In chapter four, in contrast, Ada sees no way out. Following pitying reactions from others, she opens up to Gerard. The action comes from him. She allows the engagement to more or less just happen. She accepts Gerard because she wants children and she wants to be rid of her loneliness. Her motives have little to do with love for Gerard. The relationships are broken off in both the first and last chapters, although Ada's role is very different. In chapter one, Ru dies quite suddenly. In the last chapter, the end is really the only time Ada herself intervenes once again. She leaves Gerard and accepts her loneliness. Besides these contrasts, there are also similarities between the stories at the beginning and end of the book; both end badly, and no blame attaches to Ada. There is a question of fate in chapter one. Ru had been spiritually strong, but financial problems had weakened his physical constitution. He could not stay alive. Ada does not mourn him long. In chapter four Ada is once again the victim of fate. There is simply no 'Mr Right' available for her. Marriage and loneliness are both negative options. She is an inwardly divided child of her time.

Thus, events change Ada as time goes by, and her independence also changes. This one concept, independence, is made up of diverse aspects and its meaning shifts in the course of the book. In the following section I will try to discover which meanings this concept acquires in *Memoirs*.

DILEMMAS AROUND INDEPENDENCE

The main character's independence causes problems with love. In which ways is Ada Gerlo different from other women? How does she perceive her independence, and what causes her problems with men? Is independence a woman's strength or is it a burden? Does love win, or is the mind or art the victor? These are questions which require further attention.

In chapter one, the situation is relatively simple. In the subsequent chapters, independence causes more and more problems. Ada's introduction to an independent life in chapter one is the result of a new life as a student. Emerging from the protected world of her youth, the main character finds her first freedom to do what she wants – as long as she does not give her family and landlady cause for concern. Her chosen subject and the new room of her own provide opportunities for friendship, literature and a pleasant independent life. Her love and caring for Ru fit into this new life perfectly. She admires his wisdom and can learn from him. Her sacrifice to help him demonstrates her spirit. She is proud of the fact she has a secret which distinguishes her from other female students. Through her love, she finds in Ru the spiritual guidance she needs in order further to educate herself. There is as yet no conflict between love and independence. Both her need to admire a man, and her unorthodox behaviour and interest in intellectual matters are advantageous to her. If Ru had not suddenly died, there would have been no problems with independence and the book could have finished with chapter one. When this first lover has gone, independence turns out to have its drawbacks. The new holiday friend in chapter three makes that patently obvious when the two return home. Although he is deeply infatuated, he cannot cope with Ada's intellectual learning:

> I knew you studied, but . . . how does a nice girl usually do that? It's the current fashion, like keeping small dogs or like philanthropy or social work. No one thinks it anything very special . . . . But everyone had heard of you, and everyone knew you were an exceptional girl; 'eccentric' was what most said, with a whole set of friends and an iron heart, a kind of virago who knew everything except how to kiss . . . . Sorry Ada; but it's all so dreadful . . . .

Joost's reaction hits her hard. Ada begins to doubt the things she has come to take for granted in her independent life. She is prepared to conform to Joost's norms. In the self-examination which is necessary before she comes to that decision, she expresses her doubts on the value of her intellectual development:

> I began to doubt everything I had always considered indisputable. Were art and science truly so important in a human life, and was it really the case that ideas superseded reality? Was it not one-sided to be interested only in literature and music and painting and philology? Had I been right in giving in to my predilection for the vague, the intangible; was it noble to want to know about intellectual life only in the narrow sense, and to dismiss as inferior everything the mind was able to achieve for the common good?

In this relationship, her intellectual values and independence come into conflict with her desire for the charm and protection of a man. But to Joost what is perhaps even worse than her superior intellectual development is her strange behaviour at times when art or study are not at issue. The fact that she carries her own suitcases and looks after her own money is perhaps eccentric, but her independence only disturbs the relationship between man and woman irretrievably when Ada comes to his room alone and finally gives him a first kiss in Brussels. This kind of independence embarrasses him deeply. And when Ada almost begs him not to control himself, the relationship is broken off. The tragedy here is that this relationship has taught Ada just how traditional her desires are. In spite of her independence, she is searching 'as a woman for a lord and master, for powerful arms which can carry me; a will which is above my will . . . .' Ada is surprised at her traditional feelings, but she is still too modern for Joost. He looks for and finds a less eccentric woman.

Thus, in this relationship, independence emerges as a problem. While on holiday, Ada behaves as a 'normal' woman and it turns out she wants nothing more than an old-fashioned, forceful man. But she can no longer deny her independence. She may still have the desires of a traditional woman, but her behaviour does not fit in with that image and her intellectual development is not attractive to the old-fashioned Joost.

After the intellectual, free and jolly independence of chapter one, the more down-to-earth independence of chapter three leads to problems. Finally, in chapter four the situation becomes rather hopeless. Loneliness begins to dominate. Studying, which in chapter one is mentioned merely as a precondition for an independent life, must now replace love:

> I had my work; and I worked with flat, zestless industry, which sees no end, and dares not hope for change. I conscientiously criticized my muddled texts, but I had long given up any conviction that I was doing anything useful or important.

Through the passage of time she is now seen as one of a kind – the image of the proud, independent woman has made way for that of the old maid whom real life passes by. She lives amidst women like her. Every trace of idealism and self-glorification has now disappeared from the descriptions. Her women friends are drawn with acidity:

> If the three of us went to a concert and I saw their equally elderly backs as we sidled into our row . . . then I was overcome by a melancholy which knew no respite. And later, as I stood among the crowds drunk on the music, pitiful through having to fight for my coat, and I then watched them pin under their chins white wool scarves they had crocheted for each other – then I was again torn by disgust . . . which made me explode unreasonably as we walked home through quiet streets, like seamstresses in a row.

The joy of an independent life has disappeared. Living without love and intellectual exaltation is a heavy burden after a series of unpalatable affairs has shown that love usually does not last. Ada is in a bind. Her experiences through the course of time have made her disillusioned and demanding, while most of the men in her milieu are now married. She no longer expects to find a man who will love her independence and whom she can admire.

Towards the end of the book the problems of independence are introduced with increasing frequency and more explicitly. In comparison with the emptiness of an academic's existence, that of a young mother seems so much happier. Although for them

> nothing was of greater importance than making porridge or finding a sock, and their brains were not capable of any serious, concentrated rational work ... this is their whole world: life; yet these women can look at life wide-eyed, serene and confident, in ways I had never seen a scientist or someone with book wisdom do.

She no longer knows whether 'the mind is a curse or a blessing'. She attempts to make a calm marriage with a childhood friend and set up her own household. But Gerard's admiration for her work and her studying leads to misunderstandings about love and living together. The engagement degenerates into irritation.

Her independence leads to contradictions. At the end of her engagement, Ada summarizes her dilemma once more and searches for its cause in the time in which she lives:

> I would have preferred to live in the time when the woman was still undivided and could surrender to the stronger [sex] without inner dissension. Or I would have wished to have progressed further in my self-fulfilment, and to have rid myself of the tendency to reject new rights, to be again tyrant and slave instead of equal. ... And still I must not violate my personality and attempt to make myself conform to an obsolete ideal in order to reach the end more easily.

So, in the end, the marriage does not take place and Ada regains her independence. Although she bravely chooses for her own destiny, the unequivocalness in her life as independent woman is not solved. As a woman, she deviates too much from other women. She will not accept a marriage based on misunderstanding, as her artistic friend Lotte did, and she cannot find the man she can admire the way her jolly female classmates have done. However, without a man she is unhappy.

The men who admire her looks or want to protect her are irritated by her erudition and her independence. The men who respect her intellectual qualities are impeded by anxiety and expectancy in eroticism and love. However, the desire of the independent woman is dual: she wants to act independently and she is in search of guidance, she wants to be admired for her erudition and be surpassed in wisdom, she wants to sacrifice herself and be protected. There is no solution to this duality. The problems are merely illuminated from various angles.

CONCLUSION

In each of the four chapters an attempt is made to link the woman and lover to the artist and academic. None of the affairs end happily. There is no solution. In this sense, one could say the book has no moral, as it does no more than pose the problem (four times in different ways). How to combine love and independence remains a problem. For the main character, either her independence spoils a beautiful love affair (in chapter three), or lack of love spoils the advantages of independence (chapter four). This duality can only be overcome in the dream of memory. What is impossible in reality can be possible in literature. The ending of the book offers only that consolation, the consolation of a fantasy world.

In chapter one, when the memories begin with the first experiences as a student and the initial introduction to love, the events and the reactions to them are the least realistic. The story is improbable. It is a beautiful dream offered us by a narrator looking back on the past. The hindsight of a changing main character/narrator gives the opening of the book a melancholy, romantic charge. The simultaneous presence of two personages makes possible the evaluation of the same situation from both perspectives. These perspectives are to some extent each other's opposites. In the course of the text it becomes clear how both relate to each other, and how the earlier idealism has changed into the narrator's point of view.

Through the main character's experience and the reactions her increasing independence evokes, the problems around her independence become increasingly greater. She has been presented with all kinds of options, but love and learning could not be combined in any of them. Her eccentric attitude comes into conflict with her desire to be conquered and protected. Despite the amount of variation norms of femininity may admit, they have no place for this independence. The main character has a little of everything, but does not fit into any type. She differs from the protected girl at home, or the fanatical language student. She does not want to imitate the free woman, or the uneducated housewife, or the self-effacing mother. She is a conflict in herself, and the men she meets accept only one side of her. Her partners are looking for either the intelligent, artistic woman (Ru and Gerard) or the dependent girl (Joost). They are either modern and do not know what to do with traditional feminine aspects, or they are old-fashioned and cannot cope with independence.

Although there are short periods of happiness in all the affairs, it becomes increasingly clear why these relationships cannot last. Reality is limited and imperfect. The resulting feelings of disappointment seek refuge in dreams. What is impossible in reality becomes possible there. Dreams and memories are literature's domains. Through the main character, Ada can retain her ideals although the older narrator knows that in reality they cannot be maintained. That about sums up the end of *Memoirs of an Independent Woman*. No escape is possible, except in literature. This hypothesis is brought to life through the diverse facets of the main character, and the reflective sections in between. In reality, a woman's ideals of love and learning lead to insoluble dilemmas. Only in literature can they perhaps coexist. If this forms the core of *Memoirs*, then Annie Romein's perception of the novel or Frans Coenen's criticism of the book's qualities are not very convincing. Annie Romein was indignant about the glorification of marriage and motherhood. Frans Coenen noted the writer's self-glorification and self-pity. Both based their opinions on isolated statements in the text.

It is by no means difficult to find positive statements on motherhood and marriage – chapter four is full of them. Nor is it hard to cite quotes by the older narrator on the beauty and intelligence of her younger self, or bitter comments full of self-pity on her loneliness now she is older. But these comments form only part of a larger whole. The pursuit of motherhood quickly leads to hypocrisy and the loss of independence. The main character finally refrains from marriage in an attempt to retain at least some of her dignity. Nor is it the case that the interests of one social group are being reflected here, as Annie Romein states. This book is more concerned with the contrast between ideals and reality, leading to a duality which cannot be solved. There is no question of a clearly reflected group interest; at most we are dealing with the conflicting interests of one person.

Perhaps this situation is typical of a new group, but even in that light Annie Romein's reading is still one-sided. Like Annie Romein, Frans Coenen based his critical review on the realism in *Memoirs*. I hope it has become clear that the *Memoirs* of Ada Gerlo have a different function. They belong rather to the sphere of dreams, literature, fantasy and romance. The *Memoirs* are fictitious histories. Too great an emphasis on the question of similarity between the main character and the writer distracts from the book's construction. Ada Gerlo is a fictional character. She exists only as the narrator of a text and as a character in that text. To what extent Ada Gerlo resembles a certain Annie Salomons from Rotterdam is not essential for any evaluation of the book. Even if the problems described in the book are immediately recognizable, it is still worth examining how they have been treated in story form. Both critical reviews of the book placed too much emphasis on what was already known. That is the disadvantage of a realistic approach to literary criticism. It ignores how the text functions as text.

Obviously, more than enough objections can be found to *Memoirs*. The characterization lacks subtlety. The death of a lover twice in one book is really more ridiculous than moving or convincing. The images of masculinity and femininity, except that of the main character, are shallow and uncomplicated. The flight into literature and the mixture of sentimentality and cynicism will not appeal to every reader. But the problems of independence and the gradual loss of possible solutions to them is brought to life in a cohesive way and this only becomes clear when the structure of *Memoirs of an Independent Woman* is examined. The way dilemmas on love and independence are given shape makes this book interesting – even today.

NOTES

This chapter was originally published as an article, 'De problemen van de jonge intelligente vrouw', in *Tijdschrift voor Vrouwenstudies*, 30, 1987, vol. 8, no. 2, pp. 171–89.
  1 'Meisjespedagogiek' ('Girls' pedagogy'), Internal Paper, University of Amsterdam, 1982.
  2 A contemporary of Annie Salomons and also a student at Leiden University.
  3 Cited in A. Holtrop (ed.), *Vrouwen rond de eeuwwisseling* (Women at the turn of the century), De Arbeidenspers, Amsterdam, 1979, p. 108.

4 All of these women were active in the women's movement at the turn of the century.
5 A. Romein-Verschoor, *De Nederlandse romanschrijfster na 1880* (The Dutch woman novelist after 1880), Thesis, Leiden, 1935; reprinted SUN, Nijmegen, 1977.
6 Herman Gorter (1864–1927), one of the most important poets of the Dutch literary movement known as the Tachtigers (literally 'Eighty-ers'), an influential literary school.
7 Louise Marie Anne Couperus (1863–1923), decadent Dutch novelist influenced by naturalism.
8 Stijn Streuvels (1871–1969), Flemish novelist influenced by the Tachtigers and naturalism.
9 Wilhelm Johan Theodoor Kloos (1859–1938), well-known Dutch poet, leader of the movement known as the Tachtigers and influenced by Keats and Shelley among others. Kloos placed great emphasis on pure beauty and considered poetry the most individual expression of the most individual emotion.

Part III
THE BODY

INTRODUCTION

No subject in the history of feminism and women's studies has given rise to so much controversy as the body. Many feminists refuse to explain women's position in society by referring to their bodies; biology is not destiny. Feminism should therefore strive to eradicate the meaning of bodily difference. Others localize femininity in the body; they claim the female body is a source of social change, and take the body as a starting point for further theorizing.

Early second-wave feminists such as Simone de Beauvoir often sided with the first position. In her classic bestseller *The Second Sex*, de Beauvoir pointed out the way 'woman' was turned into 'The Other' of the masculine subject. In Germany, Alice Schwarzer wrote another bestselling book, although from a different theoretic point of departure. In *Der 'Kleine Unterschied' und seine groszen Folgen. Frauen über sich. Beginn einer Befreiung* (The small difference and the big consequences. Women on women, the beginning of a liberation), she showed that the enormous social inequality between the sexes was caused by bodily differences almost trivial in themselves.[1]

This position was theorized a few years later by Gayle Rubin in terms of a division between 'sex' and 'gender'. 'Sex' referred to the biological and therefore fixed and universal difference between the sexes, whereas 'gender' referred to the variable meaning which a culture attaches to this minor biological difference. So while 'sex' was a given, 'gender' was a changeable variable, and should therefore be the focus of feminists' attention. In other words, social inequality resulting from the meaning attached to the body, and not the body itself, should be analysed.

At the other end of the spectrum of feminist positions on the politics of the body, were those who argued that in fact this strategy of reducing the meaning of the body led to conforming to

125 .

masculine norms. This position was most clearly defined in France, as a direct critique of de Beauvoir's work, by the so-called *écriture féminine*, a school of thought whose most important exponents were Irigaray, Cixous and Kristeva. They argued that de Beauvoir's plea for equality was based on an eradication of the body and consequently of the feminine. According to *écriture féminine*, it was no accident that western thought and western culture excluded both the feminine and the body; these exclusions presuppose each other. Feminists should take the body as a source of social change because of this collusion.

Both positions have been criticized for conceptualizing the body as a pre-social entity. Rubin's division of sex and gender, implying a notion of a universal and unchangeable 'sex', presupposes the existence of a natural body, untouched by cultural meanings. *Ecriture féminine* assumes an authentic force to be present in the female body by assigning the body the role of source of social change.

The criticism of a pre-social body was elaborated by Brown and Adams, among others.[2] They argued that the notion of a natural body is counter-productive, whatever the theoretic position. There is no natural body; the concept of the natural is itself a cultural notion. They criticize *écriture féminine* for, among other things, defining the body as part of the 'natural', outside the realm of culture. Yet the body is culturally constructed, not least by the category 'nature'.

Their criticism, of course, implies that the sex–gender distinction, as made by Rubin, cannot be maintained: there is no biologically given, natural 'fact' of bodily sexual difference which can be transformed into meaning by culture. The denaturalization of the body as theorized by Brown and Adams, and also by many other scholars outside women's studies, resulted in a lot of social, philosophical and historical studies on the body. The body then became a social category instead of a biological one. This implies that biology should be restricted to the study of the biological, natural body, while the humanities focus on the social body. However, neither the humanities nor most women's studies scholars want to become involved in biological thinking which is assumed to be sexist and racist.

In this section, Annemarie Mol questions this opposition. She argues that the claim that women's biology should not be their destiny made feminists suspicious of biological theories and explanations, especially when applied in social theory, because this would imply 'biologism'. Mol shows that biological and social sciences cannot be separated, and she shows to what extent they are interconnected, for example through shared metaphors and by their commitment to common techniques. Explanations of inequality using sociological models are therefore not necessarily less sexist than those using biological models. The tension between refusing to explain women's position in society by referring to their bodies and the claim that the female body can be a source of social change, is especially obvious in feminist debates on sexuality. Strategies against both feminine sexuality's oppression through sexual violence and the development of a feminine sexuality different from male sexuality, are included. Evelien Tonkens' and Monique Volman's contribution analyses the Dutch sexuality debate in the 1980s, demonstrating the limiting implications of both positions.

In the Netherlands as elsewhere, the feminist struggle against sexual violence has been phrased largely in terms of protection of the body's integrity. Prevention programmes against incest for example have been created as a result. Saskia Grotenhuis critically analyses one such programme, claiming that a focus on the integrity of the body can lead paradoxically to an intrusion into a child's privacy.

NOTES

1 Alice Schwarzer, *Der 'Kleine Unterschied' und seine groszen Folgen. Frauen über sich, Beginn einer Befreiung* (The small difference and the big consequences. Women on women, the beginning of a liberation), S. Fischer, Frankfurt am Main, 1975.
2 B. Brown and P. Adams, 'The feminine body and feminist politics', in *m/f*, no. 3, 1979, pp. 35–50.

7

'LET THE BODY TALK', OR CAN CHILDREN LEARN TO PROTECT THEMSELVES AGAINST INCEST?

Saskia Grotenhuis

Chorus:
My body's nobody's body but mine
you run your own body, let me run mine

My body jumps and runs all around
flies through the air, or crawls on the ground
your body loves to pedal a bike
our bodies do whatever they like

When I am touched, I know how I feel
my feelings are mine, my feelings are real
Chorus

Sometimes its hard to say no and be strong
when the no feelings come, then I know something's wrong
my body's mine from my head to my toe
please leave me alone when you hear me say no

My body's mine to be used as I choose
Not to be threatened, forced or abused
Chorus

Don't hit me or kick me, don't push or shove
Don't squeeze me too hard when you show me your love
secrets are fun when they're filled with surprise
but not when they hurt us with tricks, threats and lies

This is my body, it's one of a kind
I've got to take care of this body of mine
Chorus[1]

'Tell the children that talking about sexual abuse is necessary so that you can protect yourself against it. Make a comparison with road safety lessons.'[2] Just as you cannot start teaching road safety precautions early enough by instilling in children the rules they should obey to ensure their own safety, they should also learn at a very young age that their bodies could be in danger of abuse and that they can protect themselves against it. The prevention programme for primary schools, 'Feeling Yes, Feeling No' is a learning programme complete with exercises to train the children in behaviour which will increase their safety. The difference between lessons on road safety and lessons on sexual abuse is that in the latter the main theme is not rules which have to be obeyed, but learning to talk about feelings.

In recent years, talking about child sexual abuse has led to a recognition of its existence, which in turn has made talking about it possible. The courage of the first speakers (women who had been sexually abused as children by relatives and family friends) created a climate in which other victims could (finally) tell their stories. As a result, they could start the process of dealing with the abuse and the traumas which it almost invariably produced. They joined battle against a long-concealed problem, against denial and trivialization of sexual abuse perpetrated (almost exclusively) by men against (their) children: girls, and to a lesser extent boys.

In addition to support for victims (the development of aid programmes, therapies and tracing victims), there is also a search for preventative measures whose aim is to make children more resistant to sexual abuse. On the one hand, the goal is to support and encourage children who are suffering from abuse in their search for help. On the other hand, the aim is to teach children to recognize attempts at sexual abuse so that these can be prevented or stopped in the initial phases. 'Mijn lijf is van mij' ('My Body's Mine') is the first educational film on this subject which has been adapted for Dutch primary education and is available to schools.[3] The film raises a number of questions on the possibilities of similar preventative measures in this area, for this age-group (young children) and in this form (learning programmes, projects and so on).

MY BODY'S MINE

The educational material comprises two video films, one for children of primary-school age and one for parents and teachers. The teaching package also contains written material which 'is considered essential for the success of this program'. Originally a Canadian programme, the package has been adapted for Dutch primary education 'following numerous requests'.[4]

The film consists of three 15–minute parts. Three adults (two women and a man) act out short scenes which involve all kinds of child sexual abuse. They act out the scenes in front of a class of boys and girls aged between 8 and 10 years old, and then the scenes are discussed with these children. The whole programme is systematically and didactically structured. Each part has a clearly described aim, and the textbook contains exercises so that the pupils can absorb the aims. These aims are described in the learning material as follows:

– in part 1 they learn how to distinguish different kinds of feelings and to express them ('yes feeling' and 'no feeling');
– in part 2 they learn what is considered 'sexual abuse' and they practice the 'three questions for strangers'[5] which they have to learn to ask themselves in situations of potential danger;
– at the end of part 3, the children have the skills to ask for help and they can judge whether the help they are offered is adequate.

(p.17)

The first thing that strikes one is the programme's aims. It sets out not only to give educational information, but also to provide a training programme. By means of all kinds of exercises, children have to learn to express themselves in difficult situations. If the instructions are followed, then children will have acquired specific skills at the end of the programme. There is also a further condition which has to be met if the programme is to be successful. This concerns 'the attitude of the school as a whole': all members of the school team have to co-operate 'unanimously'. This communal preparation has the advantage 'that everyone becomes aware to an almost equal extent of the problems that go hand in hand with sexual abuse' (p. 11). This presupposes a single correct definition of, and attitude towards, the problem. Prevention and discussion seem to preclude each other.

The English title of the film, 'Feeling Yes, Feeling No', and the Dutch title, 'My Body's Mine', together summarize the programme's point of departure – learning to recognize and express yes or no feelings about all kinds of touching of certain parts of your body.

TWO SCENES FROM THE FILM FOR CHILDREN

These are the first and last scenes from the film. The song is sung in between every act.

Part 1: first scene

After the first verse and chorus, the actors say to the children in the classroom:

> We like that song because what it says is true – my body's my own, and hers is hers, and yours is yours (twice), and no one knows your body or your feelings better than you do. Today we're going to talk about our bodies. Our bodies can do and feel different things, like touch. There are all kinds of touches between people. You can [this is acted out] hold someone's hand. Pat them on the back. Scratch heads. Tickle. Hug. [It is clear that these are all pleasant touches or feelings, as the actors laugh and smile.] When our body is touched, it tells us how it feels. If we like it, we get the yes-feeling. But if we don't like it, we get the no-feeling. Only our own body can tell us how we feel, a yes-feeling or a no-feeling.

child:	I get the no-feeling when my stepfather[6] is kidding around and hangs me upside down by my feet.
child:	A no-feeling is when someone touches you and you don't feel comfortable with it.
child:	I get the yes-feeling when we go swimming and you run up from behind and splash water.
child:	The yes-feeling is like when you're happy about something.
child:	It's like shaking your hair, or something like that.
actors:	What can we do when we get a yes-feeling or a no-feeling. Let's watch a scene between two friends, Barbara and Fran. Watch for a time when Barbara's touched by

131

Fran in a way that gives her either a yes-feeling or a
no-feeling.

[Fran combs Barbara's hair.]

Fran: Oh Barbie, you've got such lovely hair, so nice and short.
            Do you think I should get mine cut?
Barbara: Oh, no way. You should let it grow.
Fran: Okay.
Barbara: Mmmm, that feels great, keep brushing.
Fran: Hey, you know what my mom says? If you brush your
            hair a hundred times a day it gets real shiny.
Barbara: Really?
Fran: Yeah, do you want me to?
Barbara: Oh, yes.

[All of this with a lot of grins and beaming, almost beatific smiles.]

Fran: One, two, three, four, five, hey, quit squirming around.
Barbara: Well, I'm trying to sit still but you're pulling so hard.
Fran: Well, look I'm going to have to start over again, I lost
            count. Baby. [she starts brushing again but vigorously]
Barbara: [pushes her hands into her hair] Fran, you're giving me
            a headache.
Fran: Well you asked me to do it, stupid.
Barbara: You don't even know what you're doing, jerk.
Fran: [very indignant] Oooo.

The third actor joins them and asks:

            How do you feel, Barbara?
Barbara: Hurt.
Brian: And you Fran?
Fran: Bad.
Brian: [to the children] Did anyone see a time when Barbara
            was touched in a way that gave her a yes-feeling?
child: Yes.
Brian: How did Barbara let Fran know she had the yes-
            feeling?
child: She said so.
Brian: She said so? [looks round the class]
child: She was asking for more.
Brian: And did you see a time when Barbara got the no-feeling?

child: Yes.
Brian: How did she let Fran know she had the no-feeling?
child: She said Fran was giving her a headache.
Brian: Yes.
child: She was moving restlessly, trying to get away from the
            brush.
Brian: Yeah, she tried to get away from the brush.
child: She said she didn't even know what she was doing.
Brian: She said she didn't know what she was doing, yes?
child: Yes.
Brian: Did anyone hear her say 'Stop, don't do that any more?'
            Did she tell her how she felt?
child: Yes.
Brian: So . . . in some way she tried to say no. When we have
            the no-feeling, it's very important that we let the other
            person know how we feel. I think of it as having a
            great big NO inside me that's just dying to get out.
            Let's look at the scene again [and very emphatically to
            Barbara]: when you get the no-feeling then let it out
            and say NO.

[The scene is repeated and when the brushing starts to hurt Barbara
holds her head and looks at Fran]

Barbara: NO! [Fran stops brushing and looks at Barbara question-
            ingly] It hurts too much.
Fran: Oh, sorry. It's probably this brush, the bristles are too
            hard. I'll do it softer.

[Then she begins brushing gently and both smile and grin. When
Barbara is asked how she feels, she's ecstatic]

Barbara: I've got the yes-feeling!

Concluding commentary: When we have the yes-feeling, we can say
yes. When we have the no-feeling, we can say no. We can tell other
people how we feel about the way they touch us.

    When I am touched, I know how I feel
    my feelings are mine, my feelings are real
    Chorus

                        * * *

Part 3: final scene

(This part concerns sexual abuse by relatives, friends and people known to the child. In the first part situations are acted out in which the children get help from adults whom they have told about the problem. This next section is introduced as follows: 'Unfortunately, adults can't always give you the help you need. Let's see how Barbara tried to get help with her problem.')

Barbara: My mom and dad got divorced a couple of years ago. It was real hard and mom was always worried about money and bills, and things like that. Then my mom's brother, Uncle Phil, moved in with us. Things were better. He takes us to movies and things like that. My mom's a lot happier. And I was at first, too. But then he started coming into my room at night and touching me all over my body. I don't like it. I said no but he said if I didn't let him he wouldn't help us out any more. I want it to stop. I'm going to tell my mom.

(Mom doesn't believe her: 'How dare you say that about Uncle Phil. If he could hear you, he'd be real mad, you've been dreaming, etc.' The mother tries to smooth over the situation by suggesting a fun outing – a movie, new clothes. Then Barbara tries to tell her soccer coach, but he advises her to ignore Uncle Phil and get into her soccer practice: 'You're a real great athlete.' She tells a friend's mother, but she says it wouldn't be happening if Barbara hadn't asked for it. Finally, she goes to her teacher.)

Barbara: Can I talk to you?
teacher: Sure you can. Is there anything wrong?
Barbara: Well, it's kind of hard to talk about it, but my uncle is sexually assaulting me. I don't want to cause any trouble or anything, but he keeps coming into my room at night and touching me where I don't want to be touched. I said no, but he won't listen to me. And my mom won't believe me.
teacher: It's okay, I believe you.
Barbara: My friend's mother says I must be doing something, but I don't know what I'm doing to make this happen.
teacher: Honey, you're not doing anything wrong. It's not your fault. He's doing something wrong, and what

he's doing is against the law. First, we should tell the school counsellor.

Barbara: (frightened) Why do we have to tell anybody else, my coach says I should just ignore it and it'll go away.

teacher: No honey, this is not just going to go away. You know, you're not the only person to have been sexually assaulted. The school counsellor knows someone who has helped lots of kids this has happened to. So okay if we tell him?

Barbara: I guess that would be okay.

teacher: Barb, it took lots of courage for you to come and talk to me and I'm so proud of you for not giving up.

Barbara: Really? [tentative smile]

teacher: Do you feel better?

Barbara: Yes, I feel a lot better. Thanks.

(The actors then discuss with the class what would have happened if Barbara had given up trying to find help. Everyone agrees that it would have continued and that you should never stop trying to get help.)

Concluding commentary: Keep telling people until someone believes you. It may not be easy for Barbara and her family, but she's going to get help. It's going to stop. We think she's on the right track. We hope you always get the help you need the first time you ask for it. But remember: not all adults can help you with your problems. In fact, it was an adult who caused this problem in the first place. So if you need help, keep asking adults you trust until you find someone who says: 'I will help you with your problem', and does. Let's sing the song.

THE CHILD(LIKE) BODY

Children playing in a playground (an image that recurs regularly in the film, especially when the song is sung) makes clear that a child's body is meant for playing. You use it to run, jump, and so on. In short, you are supposed to have fun with your body, preferably with other kids. To many adults and educationists, the playing body is probably the most unproblematic image of a child's body. And there are clearly very good reasons for making this the first image in the film and the first verse of the song.[7] References to children's bodies as lustful or exciting, playing with themselves or with each other, hardly exist. For adults, these kinds of activities and concepts are quickly seen in terms of sexuality, and that is considered a reality for children only when they reach puberty. In the film there are in fact two kinds of bodies – those of children and those of adults.[8] The former are asexual and the latter are sexual. In this article I would like to show that this representation plays an important role in the way adults try to encourage children to recognize and verbalize their feelings about others touching their bodies, and to make them responsible for their own bodies in the prevention of sexual abuse.

The fact that children's bodies are not unproblematic but can be threatened is expressed in the film's Dutch title – 'My Body's Mine'. This clearly implies that it could also *not* be your own, or at some point control over your body could be taken away. You have to take possession of your body. On the one hand, it is of course an inalienable possession; it's yours and you know it best. On the other hand, you have to get to know it, you have to take control of it, and you have to become responsible for it. The film teaches children to protect their own bodies and thus to help prevent sexual abuse. This learning is no transfer of knowledge but an exercise in becoming aware of the knowledge that your body already has. You have to know what your body is feeling and to say what it feels. You cannot learn what you feel, you yourself know that best, but the film shows how you must express those feelings in words.

THE BODY AS EXPRESSIVE FEELING

A child's body is introduced as something which can do things and with which things can be done – it can be touched in various ways. Touching is immediately registered by the body in yes and no feelings. The body tells us how we are feeling. Fortunately, the body's language is very simple. There are only two kinds of feelings – yes and no feelings – which coincide with right and wrong touching. Although there is a possibility that one feeling can change into another, you can only have one feeling: a positive or a negative feeling.

> Every child has a 'little voice inside them' and the loudness of
> that voice depends on how well it is developed and whether

it is listened to. That applies not only to children, but also to parents, teachers and other adults.

(p.25)

This programme develops that little voice in children and teaches them to listen to it. And there is no doubt about the importance and effectiveness of this:

A child's safety increases as its ability to clearly express feelings is enhanced. A child who is equipped with the ability to tell others how she/he feels runs less risk of being sexually abused.

(p.29)

Of course, this does not mean that you can control whether others (adults) will listen, but it is a 'very important' beginning. Moreover, the film aimed at parents and teachers also has a message for adults – listen to the child and believe what he/she says.

According to Valerie Walkerdine, this 'tell it like it is' aim is characteristic of the educational climate at the end of the 1960s and during the 1970s. It was preceded by a belief in experimental and natural development in which 'talking was subsumed to doing'. She argues that this changed: 'Talk became an aspect of freedom, of the facilitation of language, which unfolded almost of its own accord in the right conditions.'[9] Walkerdine discerns two consequences of this development. Firstly, it appears as if language is natural when regulation is not present, and secondly, that not talking becomes pathologized:

Thus texts had to build upon natural language and 'tell it like it is'. Like natural reason, natural language was allowed, permitted, desperately facilitated. It is therefore very difficult to understand such practices as regulative. Regulation has gone underground.[10]

Just how real this pathologization of silence is in incest is apparent from the problems exhibited recently by social services and prevention work in which silence is often seen as 'an indicator of'. But though the title of one of the first publications on incest, 'The sentence for silence is life', makes perfectly clear just how essential talking is for victims of incest, I do not believe that 'obligatory' talks about the feelings which every 'arbitrary' touch can produce is validated in the framework of preventative activities.

And certainly not when the way in which this talking is done becomes fixed.

A RIGHT WAY TO TALK ABOUT
THE BODY/FEELINGS

In the hair-combing scene, Barbara's ouches and wriggling away from the brush were not sufficient. According to the children, she made her 'no-feeling' very clear, but in the discussion afterwards it appeared that ouches and wriggling are only an attempt at saying no. She should have said a very clear NO, a NO that had to be expressed.

According to the textbook, this can also be practised. Through body language, 'the way I show others what I feel inside' (p. 29), saying no can be accompanied by the right expressions, vocal intonations, and so on.

Body language	'I mean NO'	'I mean YES'
posture	shoulders straight	shoulders straight
facial expression	straight face	smile
eye contact	straight look	looking
head	shaking head	nodding head
hands	hands by sides	moving, open
words	no!	yes!
tone	hard and low	soft and clear
vocal sound	clearly audible	loud and clear
repeat	say again: no!	say again: yes!

The reward for the right no is great. In the second scene of the first part, Fran is on a bus. A strange man sits beside her and puts his arm around her shoulder. Fran looks shocked, but does not know what to do. In the discussion of the scene she says that at first she thought it was an accident, but she later realized he had done it on purpose. That's when she got her no-feeling, but she did not dare say no. When the scene is repeated she does say no, looking the man straight in the face. The man is shocked, immediately removes his arm and gets up. When Fran is asked how she feels, she replies, smiling: 'Great.'

Apart from the fact that to me it seems wrong to establish a way of talking or acting as right/best, it is questionable whether this advice, which in fact comes down to always showing open resistance, is best in all circumstances. It may be that this emphatic NO causes a lot of commotion (or worse) on the bus, which can be extremely unpleasant for a child (and for an adult) and difficult to cope with.

THE MYTH OF NOT BEING ABLE OR NOT DARING TO SAY NO

Should children have to learn to know their own yes and no feelings? Should they have to learn to express them, or should adults learn to listen to children? And if adults do not listen or when a situation arises in which children cannot or may not say what they think, is the problem that children cannot express themselves, or are unable to do it clearly enough?

The suggestion that children cannot express their feelings, or cannot do so clearly enough, is especially problematic in the case of sexual abuse. Nel Drayer's research showed that 'the vast majority of abused women (84%) did in some way or other resist the abuse'.[11] This finding is an important argument against suggestions that children themselves give rise to or in any case were not averse to it.

The film is based on the idea that children either do not know or dare not express what they feel. Saying NO is especially problematic for them. And that is why they have to learn how to do it. But not every no is good. The film teaches children that to be effective, NO has to be said in a specific way. One girl in the film has really done her homework: 'You shouldn't say "No, I don't want that" [she says this very calmly, without any head movements], you have to say: "NO, I DON'T WANT THAT" [she now stresses every word and emphasizes this with clear head movements, looking directly into the camera]'. This forceful NO is central to almost every scene. In the scene which shows a girl meeting an exhibitionist in the schoolyard, we see her in a state of shock, immediately telling her teacher. She looks at the teacher, clearly pleased with herself and full of expectation, and says 'but I looked him straight in the face and said NO in a very loud voice'. The teacher answers: 'good for you, well done, I'm pleased you knew exactly what to do.'

The next scene attempts to show children that these situations are not their fault, whether they are able to say NO clearly or not. A girl (Barbara) is enticed away by a man in the park on the pretext of looking for his dog. In the class discussion on this scene, the children are asked whose fault it was that Barbara was molested. The answer was: Barbara's fault. She had not asked herself the 'three questions about strangers', she had gone with a strange man, and she had not told her father where she was going. This answer is immediately corrected by the adults: of course Barbara should not have gone with the man, but that does not mean it is her fault and that the man is allowed to molest her. He is never allowed to do that, it is forbidden. In view of the film's aims, learning to say NO, the children's reactions seem to me to be in total agreement with what is being taught, although it is contrary to the film's goal.

The fact that children have to learn to say No in a specific way, that they themselves can and have to play a role in the prevention and termination of sexual abuse, makes children responsible for what is done to them. This reasoning makes children guilty, or they will feel guilty, if they do not resist. The argument that the man who molested Barbara was doing something forbidden, and that he is at fault and not Barbara, does not detract from the fact that the film places responsibility on children.[12]

The myth of saying YES or NO also touches on the idea that there are only two sorts of feelings expressed by the body. There is no mention of a mixture of differing feelings. In addition to the feelings which a specific touch can evoke, there are also feelings of liking the person or not liking him/her, of dependence on the person concerned. The notion that the body has one feeling caused by one specific touch seems fundamentally opposed to all the research on sexual abuse which emphasizes the existence of contradictory feelings, often caused by the intermingling of different problems and situations. There is a question here of the same unequivocalness which is presupposed, or rather demanded, by the programme.

Not only is one specific way of saying NO presented as the most correct, but there is also one correct way of reacting to children who talk about their experiences of abuse. The instruction booklet gives 'the five right answers' which are not only to be learnt by the adults, but also by the children so that they will know how an adult is supposed to react to their story.[13]

PREVENTION AGAINST WHAT?

Imagine you are a child and you are presented with the following questions:

– what if a bigger kid says you have to give him/her your money, what would you do?

– what if your aunt Mildred wants to give you a big kiss, but you don't want her to?

– what if someone gives you money to buy a popsicle, what would you do?

In the context of a prevention programme on sexual abuse it is clear that all the questions refer to suspect situations and that you should answer no to all the questions. But why? In what context does the child ask for money, and how much older is he/she? Doesn't that influence your answer to the question? In the second question it is patently clear that you don't want to kiss Aunty, but who says you should and why? If we take the third question, then at first sight there appears to be no problem – I would say the answer is to go and buy an ice-cream as quickly as possible. But of course that is not the intention. Here too there are underlying questions such as who is giving you the money for the ice-cream and why? What do these questions actually have to do with sexual abuse? What threat is inherent in these 'what if' situations? In how far is it useful to teach children to link this kind of situation with sexual abuse? The reason for placing all these situations in the framework of sexual abuse is because prevention cannot begin young enough. And not only at the earliest possible age, but also in situations which in themselves have nothing to do with sexual abuse, but in the long term could potentially lead to sexual abuse, or to an inability to prevent it.

> An awful lot of prevention starts really early by giving children choices. And many of us fail to do that because we really want children to be well-liked and please adults. For instance often it'll be a little child's bedtime and we'll say: well, go on and kiss everyone good night. And the child looks around the room and she might see an aunty who smells of gin and tobacco, and yuk, she doesn't want to kiss this aunty, and yet to be sweet and cute and desirable and an okay-person, she does it anyway. And what she's really doing is denying her own feelings about not wanting to touch that person.
>
> (Quotation taken from the film for adults, and spoken by the expert in the parent discussion.)

In the first place, it is striking that tobacco or alcohol validates not wanting to kiss a person (aren't children allowed to simply dislike someone?), but more important is that children learn that every touch, every situation in which they can get something or can be asked for something, should be evaluated on its yes and no feelings. They learn to recognize that every situation which they do not want and which evokes a no-feeling is potentially a threat to their integrity and safety. The threat lies both in the specific occurrence itself, and in the possible extreme consequence – sexual abuse. Let's imagine Aunty again. The expert is right: everyone has had an aunt, uncle or grandmother whom you hated having to kiss. And it is also the case that many adults think children should kiss as a greeting or farewell, or thank-you, and rarely consider the idea that children may not like kissing that adult or perhaps just don't like kissing in general, and will not accept that from a child. It is important to impress upon adults that children should be able to decide whether or whom they want to kiss. But to perceive these situations in, and link them to, the framework of sexual abuse (prevention) is disproportionate.

Every unpleasant or undesired touch thus becomes a threat to the body, and is placed in a context of sexual abuse. My objection is that sexual abuse is seen as one whole, in which everything is equally terrible and dangerous. Sexual abuse=molestation=all kinds of touching of or looking at chest, vagina, bottom and penis (or having to look at or touch those parts of other people) which evoke a no-feeling. It is all 'forbidden', as is exhibitionism. Without saying that exhibitionism should be seen as the most ordinary thing in the world, it would seem to me of great importance to teach children to differentiate between non-threatening, more or less threatening and very threatening situations. If I then consider that all children probably show their vaginas or penises to each other at some point, then I wonder if it wouldn't be better to discuss exhibitionism in terms other than as a 'crime'.

The film is intended to teach children in clear terms what sexual abuse is, because 'children are often advised not to go with strangers, not to get into cars, not to take money or candy from them, but they are never told what the stranger wants in return for the money or the candy. They do not know what's in store for them' (from the film for parents and teachers). Part 2 goes into this as follows:

142

(class and actors)

Fran:	Does anyone know what sexual assault is?
child:	When they touch things you don't want them to.
Fran:	Right, when someone touches you where you don't want them to touch you.
child:	When someone makes you look at parts of their body.
Fran:	What kinds of parts of their body?
child:	Uh, do I have to say that? [laughs in embarrassment]
Fran:	Yes, it's embarrassing isn't it? Does anyone get embarrassed when they talk about that kind of thing? [various children nod hesitantly] Well, everybody does a bit, don't they? I get sort of embarrassed talking about those things, it's kind of embarrassing. But you know, it's really important to talk about our bodies and learn how to keep them safe. If you're a girl and someone touches you on your breasts, your vagina, or your bum and you get a no-feeling, then we call that sexual assault.
Brian:	If you're a boy, it's sexual assault when someone gives you a no-feeling by touching your penis or your bum.
Barbara:	Sexual assault is also when someone gives you the no-feeling by making you touch or look at those parts of their bodies, such as in the scene we watched with the man who exposed himself. Even though he didn't touch Fran, that is still sexual assault.

Although 'everybody gets a bit embarrassed by talking about these things', they are described in detail: for girls there are three and for boys two threatened bodily areas. If and when there is a question of a threat, then the body has a no-feeling. The film seeks clarity by calling specific parts of the body by their names as if children would not know them and would not know they could be touched.[14] However, there is no information whatsoever on what could potentially happen to 'those' parts of the body: no mention is made of erections, orgasms, sexual intercourse, etc. I wonder if it is possible to make clear the serious nature of the threat if there is no explanation of what sex is, that all touching of the body has to do with feelings of lust and is aimed at satisfying those feelings. Is the stroking of breasts, bottoms, vaginas or penises terrible in itself, or when and because it is aimed at all forms of adult sexuality, and carried out by an adult? Isn't it the use of a child's body as an adult body, for the satisfaction of an adult, that we want to protect children from? In addition, matters like coercion, the secrecy involved, that no one is allowed to know, and the 'emotional' abuse, which in fact by-passes the child by excluding his or her wishes and feelings, are equally serious. Not just the seeing or touching.

DIFFICULTIES AND LIMITATIONS OF INFORMATION ABOUT PREVENTION OF CHILD SEXUAL ABUSE

In contrast to what the film suggests, it is not altogether clear, in my view, how the problem should be approached and prevented. The 'therapy' of teaching children to recognize their yes and no body feelings and to express them in the 'correct' way, the lumping together of unpleasant touching, exhibitionism and molestation/rape and the hopelessly frumpish design make these films too much of an assertiveness training and too unappealing. Although the notion 'something is better than nothing' is very understandable, I find the thought that a lot of schools and institutions are probably using this material more alarming than reassuring. It doesn't take much imagination to come up with something better, both in terms of content and design. But before we can commission film or documentary makers to do a film of this kind,[15] we must address the question of the possibilities and limitations of information material for children on the prevention of sex abuse. The immense number of sexually abused children makes it essential to do everything possible to prevent this crime. But I doubt if the biggest problem is that children are not able to make clear what they do and do not want, and if we should be aiming to set up prevention programmes to teach them what they feel or how to express their (already existing) feelings.

In my view, information about what sexual abuse is should be clear and explicit, and should not avoid describing the sexual aspect of the abuse. Talking about touching and showing certain parts of the body which evoke a no-feeling is not telling the whole story. It remains a mystery why it is all so terrible. However, if doing this means children are given an extensive story on sex, eroticism, lust and so on, then I have my doubts too. How far should an area that is primarily a private matter for most adults (apart from the sex industry) become public terrain for children?[16] Is it possible to provide information in this area without 'bothering' children with the problems concerned with adult sexuality. The recognition that children have sexual and lustful bodies does not mean that that body should and can be made public, because we do not know what the body means to them. The recognition of that body means no more and no less than that children can discover that body on their own 'terms' either by themselves or with others in their own room or in corners of their schoolyards, without the presence of adults. In other words, how can we avoid moralistic teaching on this subject? It is one thing to differentiate according to the children's ages, say the highest or lowest class. But in my view the possibilities of providing information for all groups of children with a view to preventing sexual abuse are limited. How far is it possible to obviate all the objections to a film like 'My Body's Mine' in an official educational programme? Official programmes elevate learning to talk about this theme as something important. That this is important for victims of child sex abuse is clear to me, but to talk about it in public is another matter. This leads me to wonder whether there has been enough thought for the protection of victims of child sexual abuse who tell their story publicly in the classroom. Although the film does not encourage public confessions, learning to talk about all kinds of touching, and assertiveness exercises, could encourage a child to speak out in the classroom or in public elsewhere. Instead of trying to provoke this reaction, teachers and adults should be working to prevent it. Taking a teacher into your confidence is very different from putting sexual abuse 'into the group'. There could be negative as well as positive consequences, but in any case a child cannot foresee them. A culture which considers that speaking is positive and silence is negative is a dubious climate for prevention work on child sexual abuse.

In my view, the school's task in this matter cannot be other than limited: it should be aimed at providing information on the existence of child sexual abuse and on organizations such as Child-line and so on. Information material should be aimed primarily at describing what sexual abuse is. The last scene in the film could have worked well (although the teacher's reaction could have been less 'proud' of the fact that Barbara dared tell her, and the child less ecstatic about her 'great feeling' at having told the teacher). It shows various aspects of the problem: confusion (Uncle was so nice at first), fear (if I tell him he'll go away), disbelief (so not every adult you tell it to actually believes what you say and takes action), and it supports children in their continued search for help.

However, the main focus of information and prevention should be adults – teachers, social workers, care-givers. But the question also remains: prevention of what? If one explores the literature on prevention of and aid to the victims of child sexual abuse, one could find the extensiveness of the list of possible indicators of and risk factors for child sexual abuse is frightening rather than reassuring.[17] We have to ensure that child sexual abuse is recognized, but by the same token we have to prevent the line of thought that we can see it everywhere as long as we are attentive to it, and know exactly how we should look and listen.

NOTES

1 The Dutch adaptation of this song text is almost literal except for verses two and four: verse two in Dutch has become 'Touch me, oh yes, that feels very good; right in that place, yes that's the right place'. Verse four is 'Don't force me all the time even though I'm a kid, I'll choose for myself, what I think feels good'.

2 From 'Feeling Yes, Feeling No'. A Sexual Assault Program for Young Children, National Film Board of Canada, Montreal, 1985. The programme has been translated as 'Mijn Lijf is van mij' ('My Body's Mine'), Cinemien, Amsterdam, 1988. This quote is taken from the written lesson material, p. 30. There are in fact two films – a 45-minute programme for children and a 27-minute one for parents and teachers.

3 According to Cinemien a lot of copies of this film have been sold.

4 The film won awards at the Educational Film Festival at Oakland, California in 1985.

5 The three questions for strangers are: '1. Do I have a "yes-feeling" or a "no-feeling"? 2. If I do what the stranger asks, does anyone I trust know where I am? 3. If I do what the stranger asks will there be anyone to help me if I get in trouble? If the answers to one of these questions is "no", it means that I shouldn't do it. I should say "no" clearly and tell someone I trust what has happened' (p. 31).

6 This term is used frequently in the programme. Isn't it time we relegated this word to the realm of fairytales?

7 In view of the accompanying image, the text of the third verse is extremely unfortunate. We must assume that a very different kind of playing is meant here.

8 The children's genitals are never in camera. The child's body is represented as sexually neutral and in that sense both boys and girls are addressed in the same way, and both are also represented as potential victims. It is rather different for the adults because their sex is implicit in the sense that the perpetrator is always male (only once is it suggested that 'the stranger' could be a woman – she invites a child into her home for freshly baked chocolate-chip cookies). Although the

film also evokes questions on this point, I will pass over the sex of the body in this article. (One possible question is how far you can or should address young children in terms of their gender in educational projects on sex abuse. Does this imply that girls are addressed as potential victims and boys as potential perpetrators, and what would be the consequences of this?) The reason for passing over the point is not because (sexually abused) children's bodies are sexless, but because this point requires more research than was possible during the preparation of this article.

9 V. Walkerdine, 'On the regulation of speaking and silence: subjectivity, class and gender in contemporary schooling', in C. Steedman, C. Unwin and V. Walkerdine (eds), *Language, Gender and Childhood*, Routledge & Kegan Paul, London, 1985, p. 221.

10 Ibid., p. 212.

11 N. Drayer, *Een lege plek in mijn geheugen. Seksueel misbruik van meisjes door verwanten* (An empty space in my memory. Sexual abuse of girls by relatives), Ministry of Social Affairs and Employment, The Hague, 1988, p. 35.

12 The instruction booklet talks about the dilemma which is evoked by the programme's aim: 'teaching children a high level of responsibility for their health and welfare'. Even though you teach children this, 'then it does not mean nothing will ever happen to them: they cannot be made responsible for the behaviour of others' (p. 16). However, the idea that children are responsible for their own behaviour, for their own safety, is problematic (and certainly in the case of sexual abuse). After all, the problem is that the children are being made (partly) responsible for the abuse because they have not protected themselves against it adequately.

13 The five right answers are: 'I believe you; It is not your fault; I think it is terrible that this has happened to you; I'm glad you told me this; I am going to help you' (p. 58).

14 This appears more an impoverishment of a child's vocabulary than anything else, I'm afraid.

15 I am deliberately talking about the film/documentary makers here because I want to focus attention on design. For instance, why are there no competitions to generate scenarios for information programmes for children? Much of the information material we see seems to indicate that it is put together by social service people, policy makers and social scientists whose professionalism lies in a different field.

16 Just take one of the exercises for the older groups: 'The children are capable of keeping a diary on their personal thoughts and feelings. Duration: about 15 minutes a day on this. Materials: an exercise book and a pen for each child. Method: Tell the children you are starting something new. They will be given an exercise book in which for some time they can record their thoughts and feelings. Stipulate that no one can look at anyone else's book without permission. The children should write "My Diary" on the front. Discuss what kind of things the children should put down in their diaries' (p. 41). In addition, there are exercises such as: 'discuss an exercise using the question "what have you learned

THE BODY

about yourself?", and "what have you learned about the child you are paired with?"' (p.40).

17 A-M. den Haan, M. Kavelaars, *Preventie van seksueel misbruikte kinderen. Deel 1: De huidige stand van zaken onder een theoretisch zoeklicht* (Prevention of child sexual abuse. Part 1: The current state of affairs in a theoretic searchlight), Landelijk Ondersteuningspunt Preventie, Utrecht, October 1988; P. Windmeyer, *Voorlichting over seksueel misbruik aan kinderen door leerkrachten. Optimaliseren van de gebruikswaarde van het informatiepakket 'Voorlichting over seksueel misbruik aan kinderen'* (Information on child sex abuse by teachers. Optimalization of the user value of the information package 'Information on child sexual abuse'), Research report, Faculty of Pedagogy, University of Amsterdam, April 1987; H. Woelinga, M. van Staa, K. Eeland, *Hulpverlening aan seksueel misbruikte kinderen en hun gezin. Met moed, beleid en trouw.* (Help for sexually abused children and their families. With courage, policy and trust), VU-Uitgeverij, Amsterdam, 1989. An example: A working mother can be both a risk factor – the child is left alone too often – and a positive factor as she offers an identification option as an independent female person. And a child whose sleep is highly disturbed, or who exhibits excessive interest in its own or others' genitals or for sex in general (pp. 21 and 22) can also be an indication of sexual abuse.

8

WOMBS, PIGMENTATION AND PYRAMIDS

Should anti-racists and feminists try to confine 'biology' to its proper place?

Annemarie Mol[1]

In the old days, when there were housemaids, one rule predominated – they had to know their place. From the figurative place a housemaid occupied in the social pyramid everything else could be deduced – her literal place, for example, in the kitchen during the day and in the attic at night; the language she could and couldn't use in front of her mistress and the guests; and that she was to take her master's coat when he came home.

There aren't many housemaids left in the Netherlands these days. Moreover, it is no longer customary to discuss social relations in spatial terms. Today, we do not talk about the place people – should – take in respect to each other, but use a series of different terms. We can discuss people's roles, their reciprocal expectations and dependencies, or the conflicts and compromises between them. Yet, when we talk about relations between the sciences instead of relations between humans, it appears that the metaphor of the pyramid in which every entity has its proper place still persists.

Look at the way biology is discussed in anti-racist and feminist circles. In both circles there is resistance to biological explanations of social inequality; sociological explanations are preferred. Biology is accorded a circumscribed place – it can take up some matters but has to leave others alone. This is a strategy that is undoubtedly sensible in some cases, but not in general, as I will argue here.

TERRITORIAL DIVISIONS

Biological explanations for social inequality come in various guises. At the beginning of this century, for instance, the biological notion that some living creatures are superior while others are inferior was used to explain the social differences between 'negroes' and 'whites' in the United States. Negroes were supposed to be of a biologically inferior kind. They were less intelligent than whites because they represented a less developed stage in evolution. Proof of the difference in intelligence could be given by measuring the Intelligence Quotient of both groups with statistically reliable tests.

Biological notions were also used to explain why Dutch women in the 1950s cared for their children at home while their husbands went out to work. This explanation, however, was not couched in superior/inferior terms. Women nurtured not because they were inferior, but because they had a caring nature, which was rooted in their ability to bear children. This nature became apparent by means of long observations of mothering monkeys.

These different biological explanations led to comparable reactions. On the one hand there was criticism of the instruments of measurement that supported the claims. That black Americans scored lower on IQ tests than their pink compatriots was, according to the critics, due to the IQ tests used. These tests did not measure 'cleverness', but the ability to answer questions that derived from the interest spheres of 'white, middle-class males'. Proofs of the naturalness of maternal care were also dismissed. Monkey mothers in the bush treat their young differently from those in laboratory conditions, and moreover simple extrapolations from monkeys to humans cannot be justified.

Alternative explanations for the social inequalities concerned were subsequently derived from sociology. Black Americans' 'backwardness' was attributed to the circumstances in which they were raised. In the poor black neighbourhoods the intellectual stimulation of children was insufficient. The fact that mothers in the Netherlands took care of their children full-time without being paid was caused by the division between house and workplace, which began with the industrial revolution. This division implied that the person who stayed at home to look after the children could not work for money at the same time.

The attack on biology's claims to explain social inequalities did not entail a total ban on biology. A division of domains was advocated. Biology had to leave alone people's chances of social success, sociology was needed for that; but biology was allowed to give its opinion on the pigmentation of the human skin. Biology had to keep away from the upbringing of children because only the social sciences could hope to understand that, but it was allowed to talk about childbirth.[2] Special terms marked this division of domains. Biology could talk about people's 'nature', sociology discussed their 'nurture'. Biology was useful in mapping 'sex', while 'gender' belonged to the domain of sociology.[3] This division of domains implied that anti-racists and feminists imposed a spatial rule: biology had to know its place.

PROBLEMS

As a strategy the division of domains has a number of limitations. In the first place it is unclear where exactly to draw the boundaries between biology and sociology. It is, for instance, not evident that bearing children is a biological phenomenon, while their care is something social. In the Netherlands of the 1950s, it was not 'women' who bore children but married women. The unmarried mother was an exception: she must have had a difficult youth and she definitely needed a social worker. Who bears and who does not is, in short, socially organized. That organization changes: in the Netherlands of today, it is no longer scandalous to bear a child without being married, and in another thirty years there will probably be 'birth-mothers' in whom other women can have their eggs implanted for money.

Besides childbirth, many other matters that, in a division of domains, are allocated to biology vary according to more than simple biological factors. Human beings in rich regions grow taller than those in poor regions, the intestines of vegetarians function differently from those of carnivores, a shepherd's blood pressure is lower than that of a bus driver. All these phenomena cannot be explained without sociology. Conversely, the elements that are allocated to sociology are seldom purely 'social'. Who takes care of the children and who does not may be socially organized, but sociology does not hold a theory that is able to explain why children die if they are not fed. Anyone who thinks biology is irrelevant in the domain of child-care forgets that children must eat before anything else.[4]

The boundaries between the domains of study of biology and sociology cannot be drawn easily. There is a further problem. Anti-racists and feminists often appear to believe that social explanations of inequality will contribute to the abolition of that inequality. But that is anything but certain. Anyone who studies the American IQ debate carefully will begin to doubt it. This debate concerned the contribution of nature and nurture to intelligence, but it concerned even more the question of whether it made sense to educate black Americans. If stupidity was innate, schooling would be pointless, but if upbringing determined intelligence, then schooling would be useful. The advocates of schooling were not merely enlightened – they were under the impression that the American economy would soon need skilled labour. The opponents of schooling made a different estimation of the development of the economy. They were convinced that in the near future there would be a great shortage of unskilled labour. Advocates and opponents talked to each other in a common language, the language of 'social policy'. They both wanted an educational system that would help the economy to thrive. They shared the same goal – the stimulation of the economy – and each bent their arguments in such a way as to indicate that this goal could be achieved through their intervention.[5]

An analysis like this shows that an explanation of social differences in sociological terms does not automatically support the 'oppressed'. Industry can also thrive on it. It is even possible to deliver nothing but sociological explanations and still be markedly racist or sexist. As has been emphasized in recent years, modern Dutch racists have learned that biologizations are suspect. They do not say Moroccans are 'inferior' because there is something wrong with their innate natures. No: 'it is just that Moroccans have a different culture'. They do not stink, their food stinks. For organized racism in the Netherlands, which has the 'expulsion of strangers' as its aim, this emphasis on 'cultural differences' meets the needs quite nicely. Their 'own culture' is allocated its 'own place' – it belongs in 'the country of origin'. Moroccans are not inferior, no. But they belong in Morocco.

THE PYRAMID

Demarcating domains is a problematic strategy. The boundaries between the biological and the sociological domain are hard to plot. Moreover, social explanations of social inequality do not automatically yield the political gains anti-racists and feminists expect from them. Is it possible to overcome these problems by refining the strategy? I think it is not, as the problems go back to the very image of sciences and their mutual relations on which the strategy of dividing domains is based. According to this image sciences are compilations of theories, which refer to reality. That reality is layered: it can be divided into levels of successively greater complexity. Each science belongs to one of these levels and that determines the mutual relations between the sciences. Like the layers of reality, the sciences can be piled one on top of the other in a pyramid.

There is a view that holds that the science studying the smallest particles will ultimately be able to explain all of reality from the behaviour of those particles – if only it is allowed enough time for its calculations. Most of the current pyramid thinkers, however, consider the threshold between one level of reality and another as an unbridgeable, qualitative jump. Opinions on the nature of that qualitative jump differ. In recent years, a school of theorists has emerged which argues that coincidence is found at each level of reality and accounts for the organization of reality at that level. Thus explanations from lower levels become pointless.[6] Other objections to the 'reduction' of the complexity of higher levels to the simplicity of lower ones have been raised as well. The singularity of biology is defended with the argument that 'life' can never be understood in physical or chemical terms, because living creatures can fall ill and die.[7] And in countless variations it has been emphasized how 'man' escapes biology because of human consciousness or because of the unique character of human society.[8]

It is this pyramidal view of science that makes biological explanations of social inequality look like attempts to explain a complex social situation from the behaviour of its constituent parts, human bodies. It is the idea that sciences are piled one on top of the other in a pyramid which makes one want to warn biology against transgressing the threshold between 'life' and 'social life'. If biology does so all the same, it makes a formal error, which does not belong in a proper science.

There are, however, also other opinions on the sciences and their mutual relations. Firstly, it is possible to abandon the idea that reality – whether in layers or not – is ready and waiting to be known. The objects of the sciences were not there from the start, activity is required to demarcate them. To understand how 'trajectories', 'pigmentation', 'education' and so on, became objects of science, one needs to know the historical circumstances at the time of their demarcation. Secondly, it is possible to abandon the idea that the language in which sciences are couched is transparent. Instead of silently assuming that – scientific – language makes reality visible, research into the specific dynamics and history of languages is then required. And thirdly, it is possible to view sciences no longer as systems of theories, but as part and parcel of the techniques with which they are interwoven. Techniques do not refer, but intervene in reality and change it. Each of these steps stimulates the drawing of a different picture of the relations between biology and sociology, a picture that calls for a new anti-racist and feminist strategy.

THE DEMARCATION OF OBJECTS

If the demarcation of the objects of science is linked up with historical circumstances, then we do not need to reflect on the order of things to understand which subjects sciences talk about, but historical research. The fact that biology has 'bacteriology' as a sub-discipline, for example, is only explicable through a specific coincidence of circumstances at the end of the nineteenth century. In the course of a zealous struggle against epidemics at that time, the 'microbe' was demarcated as an object. This took place in a busy interchange between laboratory and farm. Living bacteria removed from sick cows were cultured in Petri dishes and thus made manipulable. Journalists looking out for sensation, farmers eager to have healthy stock, hygienists who wanted to protect the population from yet another outbreak of cholera, and the chemist Pasteur who tied up the ends, all did their bit.[9] If objects of sciences are demarcated in this way, it is no wonder that they cannot be arranged neatly in a pyramid! This idea could only exist thanks to the philosophers' habit of making models instead of writing history. How ever to pile up 'microbe', 'syphilis', 'reflex', 'institution', 'property' and 'affection' on top of each other, from small to large, from simple to complex? All these objects of science have been demarcated in different contexts, in reaction to different questions. That implies that there are no general rules regarding the question of their mutual relations. The relations between sciences are local phenomena, which can only be traced through historical research.

What does this mean for anti-racists and feminists who are concerned with biology and sociology? Instead of trying to confine each discipline to its proper place, they can try to find out where and when branches of science borrow each other's object demarcation and thus literally build on each other; and where and when sciences demarcate an object that bears no resemblance to the objects that have been outlined by a 'more basic' science. The intention of this endeavour is not to discover who keeps to the rules and who does not. Rather, this kind of research provides a better insight into the contents of the various branches of science.

Thus we find that a sociology that departs from the sex/gender distinction makes itself dependent on biology. The 'woman' whose 'gender-characteristics' are examined by such a sociology has, after all, a pre-established 'sex'. Before sociology begins to talk about the 'woman' who takes care of her children at home, biology has already determined something about her: she has a womb.[10] Not all of sociology departs from this kind of dependence. There are social theories around in which 'woman' equals 'wife/mother'. The professed lesbian is then simply a 'non-woman', whether she has a womb or not. The 'wife/mother', in her turn, remains a 'woman' even if energetic gynaecologists have removed her womb.[11] Whether a human being is a 'woman' or a 'non-woman' depends in this framework on her/his social relations to husband and children, and not on the biological possession of a womb. The demarcation of the object 'woman' is this social theory's own work, which entails a different content for the term 'woman'.

Sociology does not have to take biology as a foundation. But it can do so and in many ways. To build on another science does not need to be done in the familiar way. Look again at the example of modern racism. All human beings, or so a modern racist is willing to endorse, are biologically equal. They just have different cultures. Ties with a biology that talked about 'inferior' and 'superior' have been cut. Does that mean modern racism is independent of biology? Racisms that are formulated in merely 'sociological' terms can indeed be found. But anyone who has an eye for the fact that sciences can link up with each other in many ways will soon realize that a new co-operation has developed. That is the co-operation between cultural racism and socio-biology.

Socio-biology takes as its point of departure from laws that apply to all human beings. All human beings, it claims, strive after the same ideal: survival. Then it turns out that it is not the humans who want to survive, but their genes. These genes live in different individuals. And the closer their genetic relationship, the more genes individuals have in common. Thus, or so the argument goes, genes prompt people to be kind to those related to them and unkind to others. As people have regulated kinship within their own culture since time out of mind, their genes 'know' that they do not live in people of other cultures. That is why all human beings on this earth – and in this respect they are all equal – dislike people from other cultures. A reasoning like this implies that it is 'natural' for Londoners to try to get Pakistanis to leave the country. Moreover it places this kind of behaviour on the same level as the fight for independence Pakistanis waged against the English a few decades ago.[12]

Racism that elaborates on socio-biology is not necessarily more dangerous than mere cultural racism that does not mention genes but holds that cultures all 'belong' in a specific geographic location of their own. Nor is it less dangerous than racism that is cast in terms of 'superior' and 'inferior'. But it is different. There are differences between one way of discriminating and another.

THE POWER OF LANGUAGE

In the pyramid model, the relations between the sciences depend on the relations between their objects. Language is supposed only to reflect the reality of those objects. If language is seen not as a passive framework, but as an active mould, however, the relations between the sciences also depend on the relations between their languages.[13] Different sciences can share terms and themes. Models that emerge in one science can enter others and vice versa.

The example of the model of the struggle for survival is well known. At the end of the eighteenth century, Malthus developed a social theory in which human life is represented as a struggle for survival. Humans, according to Malthus, fight for their food; there is not enough for everyone. Malthus took this as a reason for advocating birth control. Darwin incorporated the model, which characterized the relations between individuals in a liberal society, into biology. In his work, the struggle for survival was turned into the mechanism behind the evolution of the entire animal and plant world. Darwin argued that the fittest survives. As a next step this idea was taken up by Spencer, who again incorporated it in a social theory and used it in his pleas against charity – which disturbs the social order by keeping the weak on their feet.[14]

The transfer of terms, model and metaphors from sociology

to biology and vice versa is yet again an interesting theme for anti-racists and feminists. What makes it interesting? Until now this transfer has primarily been looked at in order to keep 'organic' models out of sociology, where they are supposed to have reactionary implications. Sad examples of this can indeed be found. Take for instance the immunological model of the body. Immunology is the science of the body's resistance to alien entities and emerged at the turn of the century in an attempt to answer the question of how the body learns to fight microbes instead of succumbing to them. According to immunology, a body can distinguish between its own cells and substances and alien cells and substances. If it comes across something strange, the body begins to make antibodies in order to expel or destroy it. In the 1930s, this immunological model was transferred from the body to the nation.[15] A number of social theories stated that a nation, just like a body, had to protect itself against infection by strangers. These had to be wiped out as if they were microbes. The transfer of the immunological model to sociology thus resulted in a social theory that could legitimate the destruction of people marked down as 'strangers' – and was actually used to that end in Nazi Germany. That indeed is a sound reason to be suspicious of the transfer of biological models into social theories!

And yet, xenophobia is not inherent in the relocation of a model from biology, or even immunology, to sociology. The sociology of deviance that was current in the 1960s can serve as a counter-example. This sociology talked yet again about strangers, though this time the focus was not on 'people from outside', but on insiders who were not 'adjusted'. Deviants were people who behaved in a strange way, who 'acted weird'. Sociologists studied not only the behaviour of the deviants themselves, but also the way well-adjusted people interacted with them. They found that the adjusted stigmatized some people as strange, and subsequently expelled them. Here again, the immunological model of the relation between a body and alien elements was imported into a social theory. There is a radical difference, however: the sociologists involved were in no way attempting to legitimate the 'expulsion' of the deviants which they detected. On the contrary, the fact that society expels everything strange just like a body, was to them a reason for criticism. They criticized the intolerance of the adjusted worthy citizens and of 'western society' that could not abide anything out of the ordinary.

Thus, the use of biological models in sociology does not invariably have nasty political repercussions. In the recent past, the very same biological model, taken from immunology, first functioned as a legitimation for xenophobia and was subsequently used to defend people who 'behaved strangely'. For anti-racists and feminists, the importance of models that move between biology and sociology is therefore not that they indicate some formal error. Instead of a reason for general suspicion, they offer an opportunity to gain more insight into the contents of various sciences. The movement of a social theory becomes more comprehensible if the biological model that lies 'behind' it is brought to the fore – and vice versa.[16]

TECHNIQUES

Branches of science are tied up with different techniques. One of the many aspects of the relation between sciences is therefore the relation between the techniques with which they are interwoven. This relation is seldom unequivocal. At the beginning of this century, various branches of science were working together to control infectious diseases. Each of them had developed its own technique. The science of hygiene called on people to wash their hands, spit in spitoons and clean their houses. It wanted to control infectious diseases by preventing the microbes from moving from one body to another. The young science of immunology strove to combat infectious diseases by increasing the healthy body's resistance. It turned up with immunization programmes and nutritional guidelines. Sociologists, finally, discovered that it was the poor who suffered most from infectious diseases and so they advocated yet a different technique: they argued in favour of a more equal distribution of wealth. In short, hygiene, immunology and sociology developed remedies for the same disease, but they were different remedies. They worked together in fighting infections, but as soon as there was money to divide, each technique was proclaimed better than the others. Then they began fighting each other.

Anti-racists and feminists can learn a lot by analysing techniques. The way this or that branch of science intervenes in human lives doesn't always follow directly from the way it defines its objects and models its stories. What sciences 'say' does not automatically reveal what they 'do'. In the above example of infectious diseases, the intervention is in line with the stories. The techniques mentioned appear to be logical consequences of the theories of hygiene, immunology and sociology on respectively infection, susceptibility and the spread of disease through populations. The techniques 'work together' and 'fight' each other parallel to the way the theories do. Often, however, the link between a theory and the technique with which it is interwoven is more complex.

It would be nice to look at the relation between the disciplines of endocrinology and sociology of the family in the Netherlands of the 1950s. The way in which the object 'woman' was demarcated in both disciplines differs enormously. Endocrinology saw women as unstable hormonal creatures, whereas for the sociology of the family they were the warm, restful centre of family life. Yet both of these branches of science were interwoven with the technique of modern contraception, which transformed women's lives in the 1960s. It was the endocrinologists who developed 'the pill', making contraception more attractive because it no longer required the manipulation of forbidden parts of the body. In the meantime, sociologists were saying that birth control belonged to the modern way of life and moreover fostered mutual relations in the family. Contraception enabled father and mother to love each other without anxiety and to love their controlled number of children more intensely. This was good news for general practitioners who for years had refused to fit Dutch caps but were relatively fast in prescribing the pill.[17] Studies that focus on endocrinology's and sociology's respective demarcation of 'woman', discover an antagonistic relation between both branches of science. They both distinguish – discriminate – 'woman' in a different way. However, an examination of the technique of contraception, in which both endocrinology and sociology are interwoven, reveal co-operation. Each of the disciplines forms one of the links in the chain of events that got 'the Dutch woman' fixed up with the pill.

Thus, in this case, a biological and a sociological theory contributed to the design and establishment of one and the same technique. Does that imply it has to be a sexist technique? We haven't finished discussing the consequences of the introduction of the pill for women. Did the pill free married women from the burden of large numbers of children and by that means enable their emancipation – or at least the second feminist wave? Or did the pill poison their bodies and rob them of the right to refuse sex to their husbands? Did the pill redefine sex as part of a relationship rather than as something productive, so that homosexuality became a tolerable variant? Or did it rob lesbians of the secret pleasure that their sex wouldn't make them pregnant? In short, the question of whether the pill works to the advantage or disadvantage of women is not easy to answer. The more so when the pill is not only available over Dutch counters, but is also used for contraception and population control in large parts of the rest of the world.

WITHOUT SAFETY AND SECURITY

As soon as the pyramid model is abandoned, the relations between the sciences are no longer fixed in a natural order. All certainty about the 'proper place' in which a science belongs is lost. There is no longer an epistemology that knows the rules. It is pointless to confine biology in general terms to its proper place, because it is not clear where that place could be. If there is no fixed norm for a 'right' relation between biology and sociology, this has consequences for the way racism and sexism in science should be handled. We cannot continue to see racism and sexism as formal errors, as biology exceeding its boundaries. If a branch of sociology borrows object definitions from a biological branch, that does not necessarily have to be dangerous. If it makes its object definitions on its own, that is no guarantee of safety. Models that move from one science to another may carry evil implications along, but that is no law. Finally, there is no reason to mistrust techniques that are connected with biology more than techniques that have a rationale provided by some branch of sociology.

In short, racism and sexism in science are not a matter of a 'right' or a 'wrong' division between the domains of biology and sociology. As a result, they stop being two variations of the same problem. They are different problems whose specificity should be kept in mind. There are historic cross links, but there are also moments and situations that contain racism but no sexism and vice versa.[18] One could even wonder whether 'racism' and 'sexism' in science are distinct entities all through the diverse forms they can assume. Diverse forms of both racism and sexism have been considered in this article. They differ greatly: under the heading 'racism' we can list the idea that black Americans are of an 'inferior race', and the idea that Moroccans should leave the Netherlands because they 'belong' in Morocco. The first example is 'race'-ism in the strict sense of the word – it mentions 'human races' and even puts them in a hierarchy. The second example might also be called 'xenophobia'. There are differences between these two. At the same time the similarities are so great that within the framework of this article I have talked about them in the same breath. However, it seems to me such similarities do not come together into a list of essential characteristics by which every form of racism can be recognized. If we are to recognize racism or sexism, we must always look at the contents of stories, the effect of actions. What did theory so-and-so say about human behaviour and its origins? What did it say about the behaviour of genes, hormones, red blood cells? In which debate was it put forward and what was the stake in that debate? Which interventions were linked up with it?

A firm standard by which all the answers can be measured simply doesn't exist. We have no option but to get involved, and remain so, in discussions about the advantages and disadvantages that different object demarcations, models and techniques entail for different groups of people.

NOTES

This chapter was originally published as an article, 'Baarmoeders, pigment en pyramiden. Over de vraag of anti-racisten en feministen er goed aan doen de biologie haar plaats te wijzen', in *Tijdschrift voor Vrouwenstudies*, 35, 1988, pp. 276–89.

1 Thanks to the Groningen philosophy students of 1986–1987 who made the course 'Life and Social Life' worthwhile.

2 For a range of clear examples of the strategy of putting biology in its place, see the contributions to S. Rose (ed.), *Against Biological Determinism*, Allison & Busby, London, 1982.

3 In feminist circles this division of domains became known as the sex/gender distinction. See for this distinction G. Rubin, 'The traffic in women', in R. Reiter (ed.), *Toward an Anthropology of Women*, Monthly Review Press, New York/London, 1975. For a sound criticism, see T. Akkerman, 'Een algemene theorie van de helft van de wereld?' 'A general theory on half the world?', *Tijdschrift voor Vrouwenstudies*, 21, 1985, pp. 23–43.

4 For this reason some social scientists speak out from time to time in favour of more attention to 'the body'. See A. Verbij, 'Heeft links nog iets om het lijf?' ('Does the left have any body?') in *Psychologie & Maatschappij* 21, 1982, pp. 497–501; G. Hekma, 'Verzwegen zinnen. Een sociologie en geschiedenis van lichaam en lichamelijkheid' ('Suppressed senses. A sociology and history of body and corporality'), in *Skript*, vol. 9, no. 4, 1987–88, pp. 199–208.

5 For this analysis, see J. Harwood, 'Heredity, environment, and the legitimation of social policy', in B. Barnes, S. Shapin (eds), *Natural*

THE BODY

Order. *Historical Studies of Scientific Culture*, Sage Publications, Beverly Hills/London, 1979.

6 Coincidence is central to the order/chaos debate. The finding that the emergence of order out of chaos depends on coincidence at every level of reality induces the chemist Prigogine and the philosopher Stengers to oppose the idea that chemistry can be reduced to physics; the biologists Maturana and Varela use it as an argument against the idea that life can be understood in terms designed for the non-living; and sociologists like Dupuy and Roth use it to characterize social reality as something with its own liberties. For an overview, see J. Gleick, *Chaos. Making a New Science*, Viking, New York, 1987.

7 G. Canguilhem, *Le Normal et le pathologique*, PUF, Paris, 1966. (English translation: *On the Normal and the Pathological*, Reider, Dordrecht, 1978.)

8 For a number of classic examples, see T. Adorno, *Der Positivismusstreit in der deutsche Soziologie*, Suhrkamp, Frankfurt, 1969.

9 See for this B. Latour, *The Pasteurisation of France*, Harvard University Press, Cambridge, Mass., 1988. We should note that the 'microbe' was split in two in the 1920s when bacteria and viruses were attributed different characteristics.

10 This argument is used by O. Verhaar in 'Voor de wet is iedereen gelijk, ook voor de Wet Gelijke Behandeling' ('Everyone is equal before the law, even before the Equal Treatment Act'), in *Tijdschrift voor Vrouwenstudies* 32, 1987, pp. 448–61. Verhaar sharply criticizes the fact that the Dutch Equal Treatment Act departs from an anatomical definition of 'woman'. Note that determining the female sex by pointing out the womb is not 'biological' in general, but 'anatomical' in particular.

11 I. Costera Meijer (Chapter 2 above) signals 'mere sociological' demarcations of 'woman'. She argues in favour of a more frequent enquiry into 'woman/non-woman' distinctions and urges us to keep in mind that the meanings of 'woman' and 'non-woman' do not necessarily run parallel with those of 'non-man' and 'man'.

12 For this example, see M. Barker, *The New Racism*, Junction Books, London, 1982.

13 Individual sciences, of course, also look different when their languages are analysed. For an example, see D. Haraway, 'In the beginning was the word: the genesis of biological theory', in *Signs*, vol. 6, no. 3, 1981, pp. 469–81.

14 For this example, see R. Young, *Darwin's Metaphor. Nature's Place in Victorian Culture*, Cambridge University Press, Cambridge, 1985.

15 In Dutch – and German – there is a word that could be used at the time for both 'a people' and 'the nation': *volk*. That word figured in the social theories in question.

16 This also applies to the transfer of models among social sciences – see A. Mol, 'Eet mama ons op? en andere verhalen over moedertje staat' ('Will mama eat us? and other stories on Mother State'), in *Groniek 97*, 1987, pp. 9–25, in which the relations between theories on 'mother' and 'state' are examined; and to the transfer of models among the branches of biology – see D. Haraway, 'Animal sociology and a natural economy

162

of the body politic, Part I: A political physiology of dominance', in *Signs*, vol. 4, 1978, no. 11, pp. 21–36, in which she demonstrates how models from embryology end up in ethology.

17 For endocrinology, see E. Bransen, 'Wankele wezens. Het premenstrueel syndroom en de constructie van vrouwelijkheid' ('Unstable creatures. The premenstrual syndrome and the construction of femininity'), in *Tijdschrift voor Vrouwenstudies* 33, 1988, pp. 28–42. For Dutch sociologists on birth control, see M. de Boer and D. Bos, '". . . het gemiddeld kindertal verdient ongetwijfeld alle aandacht . . ." Sociologen over geboorte, bevolking en gezin' (". . . the average number of offspring undoubtedly deserves all our attention . . ." Sociologists on birth, population and family'), in *Ideeën en identiteiten. Facetten van de Nederlandse sociologie* (Ideas and identities. Facets of Dutch sociology), Siswo, Amsterdam, 1987. The enthusiasm of general practitioners for the pill cannot be explained entirely by the approval with which they quote sociologists of the family. Further research is required. Note that 'Dutch caps' in Dutch are called by a Latin name: 'pessarium'.

18 A good example of an article that analyses a specific interconnection is N. Leys Stepan, 'Race and gender. The role of analogy in science', in: *ISIS*, vol. 77, 1987, pp. 261–77. Stepan shows that in biology in the late nineteenth century analogous terms were used for the description of 'black men' and 'white women', which left 'black women' with a very singular series of characteristics.

9

... AND LUST FOR ALL!

The end of the sexuality debate in the women's movement?

Evelien Tonkens and Monique Volman[1]

It would appear that the discussion on sexuality within the women's movement has made way for other themes. If you use the feminist press as a thermometer for determining currently 'hot issues', then you will find it presents a totally different picture from a few years ago. The bad girls and the sad girls of 1982 are now all installed behind computers in sisterly fashion, and feminists today appear more involved in the pleasures and dangers of career strategies than in those of sexuality. General questions such as 'what aspects should a feminist strategy on sexuality comprise?' are no longer talking points. The struggle against sexual violence – one of the answers to that last question – has now joined the ranks of policy and research. Questions on what feminine sexuality is and should be are yesterday's news. Not long ago, the first ever 'darkroom' for women was opened at a well-known (women's) disco. However, rumour has it that this room's main use is not anonymous sex, but provides a place for intimate chats between bosom friends.

This appears to be a good moment to reassess the discussions of the past few years. What intrigues us is the fact that, in the space of a few years, the feminist standpoint on sexuality in the Dutch debate seems to have come full circle – an about-face that is usually analysed as a victory for liberal views over more moralistic attitudes.

In this article we would like to look at discussions on feminism and sexuality using texts generated by and in response to the Melkweg Women's Festivals held in Amsterdam in 1982 and 1985. We will be examining whether there has in fact been an about-face from moralism to liberalism during those years. We will also argue that there could be a continuation of moralism centring on the dilemma that, on the one hand, 'liberalists' are not supposed to define feminine sexuality, but on the other have to define it.

MELKWEG 1982

The first traces of divergences in thinking on the question of the content of sexuality within the women's movement became apparent during the 1982 Melkweg Women's Festival. From the very beginnings of this festival, the Melkweg had assumed a provocative and controversial stance. During the first Festival in 1977, porno movies were shown, provoking an angry response from the *Vrouwenkrant* (Women's Paper). In 1979, the organizers chose an advertising poster which didn't go down well: a close-up of female genitalia, known as the 'cunt poster'. But all the controversy did not prevent the Melkweg from continuing its daring approach. After a comparatively quiet three-year period, belly dancing, go-go girls and an exhibition of erotic photographs appeared on the programme. The intention behind these aspects of the programme was to break through taboos around the body. There was also a 'decadent night'- now a regular feature – during which eroticism played an important role. Alice Schwarzer talked about new femininity and sexuality, there was a lecture on prostitution, and women from the Study Group Sado-Masochism Association (VSSM) were also invited.

The organizers had decided they would fulfil a trendsetting role in the women's movement. They went in search – not only in the Netherlands – of things that concern and are relevant to women, and they then offered them to their audiences: a combination of 'politics, play, pleasure and work'.[2] The Melkweg presented play and pleasure as its specific innovative contribution, because 'there are numerous women who are occupied exclusively with the struggle'.[3] Moreover, to the Melkweg 'play and pleasure' also equals politics, especially for women. In addition, the organizers aimed to break through 'lack of understanding and taboos', the main target being the feminist taboo on (sexual) pleasure. The 1982 Festival was to be an event where everything was open to discussion, 'a festival without borders'.[4] As it turned out, these choices did not appeal to all those attending: during one of the performances beer glasses flew through the auditorium.

We will now try to unravel the conflict. A number of negative responses will be discussed with reference to articles in the

THE BODY

Vrouwenkrant, the *Vrouwenweekblad* (Women's Weekly) and *Vrouwentongen* (Women's Tongues). Subsequently, we will examine positive reactions to the Melkweg Festival.

Negative reactions

Apparently, the poster is supposed to appeal to women's emotional experience. Two beautiful, thin, shapely and wholesome women – one face cannot be seen at all, the other is expressionless. It is not their personalities (e.g. that they were good at something) that is important, but their bodies . . . . The two women in the poster didn't look much like women involved in some political action.[5]

Sex is not a feminist issue

The *Vrouwenkrant* criticized the fact that there was suddenly so much interest in sexuality within the women's movement.[6] Feminism is, after all, a struggle against the 'oppressive circumstances of women', and that is a political and economic issue. While it is certainly true that women are always defined as sex objects and that definition is also oppressive, feminists should avoid this aspect for that very reason. Too much attention to sexuality distracts attention from the real problems. And who says economics is boring and sexuality exciting?

Similar reactions were carried in the *Vrouwenweekblad*: 'Why were there no workshops on women's work/unemployment, single women (with children) who cannot survive on social security, housing shortages and the countless forms of male aggression (from sexual violence to murder)?'[7]

This view sees the primary task of the women's movement as struggling against the oppressive circumstances of women. Others see this main task as a reason to divide sexuality into two aspects. Feminism should not be concerned with the how, why and wherefore of sex. But, in contrast, the struggle against sexual violence is a feminist issue *par excellence*.

In *Vrouwentongen*, Tilly Janssen was also reluctant to dismiss sexuality as a relevant feminist area. After all, sexuality is 'the representation of male dominance, of male violence'. Feminism should be concerned with sexuality in as far as it has an oppressive function.[8]

166

Oppression of women through sexuality

The fundamental power inequality seems to have been traded in for the liberal principle: to each her own. Sexuality is no longer an area of struggle in which the women's movement has to fight against male dominance, but a place where lust, desire and affection have their fling.[9]

What the Melkweg saw as 'political' was seen as apolitical by its opponents. At the Festival, sex 'was taken out of its context and isolated',[10] the context being a feminist theory in which oppression is the central concept. Tilly Janssen believed the Melkweg denied the power relations between the sexes and, according to her, exhibited ignorance and *naïveté*. She pointed out that this liberal attitude ignores 'the threat of male violence on the streets, in families, in work situations, etc.'. The *Vrouwenweekblad* emphasized continually that the sexual feelings and fantasies of women are themselves suspect. They are seen here as products of oppression. This model can also explain the fact that at the women's festival 'a large number of women were getting the hots from a porno show, which . . . was supposed to show how disgusting porno is'.[11]

The social determination of feelings should be examined continually from a feminist point of view. Why feminist mistrust is more valid than unfeminist feelings does not become clear.

Feminine sexuality

Does all of this mean that women, particularly feminists, cannot or are not supposed to have any pleasure in sex? By searching for a specifically feminine sexuality, the writers in *Vrouwentongen* and the *Vrouwenweekblad* think they can sidestep a number of problems. Some see sexuality as something that is present, but has been oppressed for centuries; others take the view that a feminine sexuality is something that has never come to development as a result of all that oppression.

Here, too, the analysis of sexuality as a patriarchal product occupies a remarkable place. On the one hand, the feelings of women are shaped by patriarchal society, but, on the other, there is still something existing outside that patriarchal bastion on which women can base their search for, or the development of, a feminine sexuality. The impossibility of change implicit in the feminist analysis is passed over in various ways. Some argue the existence of an autonomous 'self' alongside the socially determined: 'Sexuality is formed by society, by environment and by ourselves. We can, therefore, develop something new ourselves.'[12]

Another writer introduces 'rationality' and 'feminist theory' as a solution to this problem. To prevent a lapse into the old male forms, feelings and new erotic forms are tested using feminist theory, which limits the options considerably. Feelings of lust evoked by a striptease or low-cut dress are not valid: 'I would be disgusted by my feelings, because they do not match my feminist ideas.'[13] According to this concept, a feminist has a rational part and an emotional part. The former can evaluate the latter, but how the two relate to each other remains an unanswered and even unasked question.

Often the question of the development of a new feminine sexuality is avoided by formulating it in a negative way. Feminist analysis provides definitions of male sexuality: 'lusting after an object without content'; 'objectivizing the female body', 'seeing sex as divorced from other activities'. Women's sexuality is then defined as the opposite.

Women's sexuality may be more than the traditional feminine tenderness, but feminism imposes conditions. Sexuality as it exists in a patriarchal society remains defined by the concept of oppression. But a dividing line is drawn between male and female sexuality. Some terms belong in the male sector: oppression, violence, inequality, objectivization, lust and power. All the rest lies on the other side of the border, and still has to be explored. In this view, feminine sexuality is only conceivable as tender, non-objectivizing sex with women in equal relationships: 'vanilla sex'. Power, a characteristic of male sexuality, cannot have a role in such relationships, and that is what makes sado-masochism, for example, so problematic for many feminists.

Sado-masochism

Sado-masochistic women demand precisely what we have just defined as male and oppressive, and then present themselves as feminists. This was the very reason why the programming of a sado-masochistic item in the women's festival fitted so neatly into the aims of the Melkweg. It offered the opportunity to claim pleasure that was taboo, to turn 'politics' into play, and designate the unacceptable as 'new politics'.

However, the extent to which 'old politics' still dominated the discussion was evident in the way the VSSM sold its product: 'SM is diametrically opposed to sexual violence and has as few points of contact with porno as other forms of making love . . . an SM game is only possible between partners who strive after equality in their relationship.'[14]

Apparently, even to the VSSM, the status of SM as a sexual practice depends not on, say, how pleasurable it is, but on the extent to which it meets the criterion 'non-oppressive'. And the verdict 'oppressive' is quickly reached by its opponents; in principle, all situations where there is any question of power or inequality can fall under this umbrella. Using the same theory which unmasks feelings as unreliable, the voluntary aspect can be questioned: 'through the women's movement we have realized that what can appear voluntary can also be called rape'.[15]

A kind of 'profession of faith' was now demanded from SM women who wanted involvement in the women's movement: 'In my opinion, if there are aspects of SM other than those designed to keep women in their place, the confirmation of role divisions, SM women should clearly and openly distance themselves from violence against and oppression of women.'[16]

That 'oppression' was of primary importance to the discussion in 1982 is also apparent from the fact that those who believe SM and feminism can go hand in hand used the concept in their arguments. For example, Dubbeldam emphasized the similarities of both by stating: 'We are fighting for the same ideals, the liberation of women from their oppression, the rediscovery of our own sexual experience.'[17] Thus, just like their opponents, SM women appear to base their views on a specific 'feminine sexuality', but to them this has a different content.

Positive reactions

There were also positive reactions to the 1982 Melkweg Women's Festival in feminist circles. Some certainly saw the Melkweg's approach as breaking through taboos. The 'feminist norms' which emerge from the negative reactions are seen as at least as limiting as traditional social norms.

Following the festival, *Katijf* ran an article which questioned the link of sexuality with sexual violence.[18] Feminism has limited women's sexual options to 'cuddling sex', and in doing so has confirmed traditional social norms: women are also conditioned by the women's movement to see sex only in the context of love, as expression of intimacy.

Under the title 'Bad girls & sad girls', *Diva* published a relatively enthusiastic report of the festival. It was the only feminist journal to do so. The tenor of its criticism, in as far as it criticized, was that the Melkweg hadn't gone far enough. All the organizers had done was pick up on a trend and for real 'bad girls' like the writers, the action was pretty tame.

With some relish, however, de Wit and Koelemij established the effect of many of the performances on the 'sad girls' – a 'hefty collision between fantasy, physical reactions and feminist norms of body and lust'.[19] In their article they introduce a positive use of the term 'lust' and advocate an open debate on lust and its feminist criteria.

The impulse provided by the festival report was followed up in an article by de Wit on the three go-go dancers who performed at the Melkweg.[20] She accuses the women's movement of moralism and locates its cause in the differentiation between lust and eroticism made by feminists. These are the self-same terms that are used by others to distinguish male and female sexuality. According to de Wit, the exploitation of, rather than the fight against, feelings of lust can be an important tool for women in developing individual autonomy.

Moralists versus liberals

In the foregoing we have seen how, in discussions generated by the 1982 Melkweg Women's Festival, a contrast emerged between two 'parties' with differing attitudes to sexuality as a feminist issue. These parties were quickly labelled moralists and liberals. Moralists are so called by their opponents because they see sexuality as a source of women's oppression and derive from their stance limiting norms for new forms of eroticism for women. Feminine sexuality is defined by them as the reverse of oppressive male sexuality.

In contrast, the opposing view is that this norm limits feminine sexuality too much. The taboo on feminine sexuality which exists within the women's movement has to be broken down. Women should demand pleasure, and their choice should be broadened to include more than the flavour of vanilla. Moralists, however, see this kind of attitude as trivializing the struggle against women's oppression in general, and against sexual violence and pornography in particular.

MELKWEG 1985

The undiminished interest in the question of sexuality at the women's festival took on rather different forms in 1985. The basis had changed: 'Everything that occupies or concerns women should have a place at this festival and we'd prefer to anticipate trends.'[21] This would, of course, require a different programme from the one presented in 1982: striptease alone could no longer generate uproar. Now a few porno films were on the agenda, a world champion body builder ran through her poses, there was a porno reading, a woman on a bed of nails, a workshop for erotic writing, and the, by this time, traditional 'decadent night' included a panel discussion on sex.

The number of reactions to the festival in the feminist press was considerably lower than in 1982, and the reactions were less negative. The *Vrouwenweekblad* was the only publication to criticize the festival fiercely, focusing on the panel discussion on sex in particular. *Diva* also offered criticism, but in the reverse sense: the Melkweg didn't go far enough. All in all, the 1985 festival appeared to be a less controversial event than that of 1982.

Sex panel

Characteristic of the atmosphere in 1985 was the panel discussion held during the festival. This launched a number of subjects that were new to the debate on feminism and sexuality. One of the most prominent new items in 1985 was the 'sex industry': whores and porno stars are allocated a pioneering role in the liberation of feminine sexuality. Their experiences with sex can serve as an example for other women.

Only foreign women with experience in the sex industry were invited to form the panel. Pat Califia is an active SMer and writes SM stories. Kathy Acker has worked in the sex industry and writes porno stories. Candida Royalle is a former porno star and now makes porno movies for women, and Xaviera Hollander, better known as the 'Happy Hooker', wrote a bestseller on her (pleasant) experiences as a prostitute. The final panellist, Gayle

Pheterson, a socio-psychologist who fights for the rights of pros-
titutes, seemed a little out of place. Moreover, she was an exception
in a different sense – her participation recalls the feminist struggle
against oppression.

Marjan Sax, in the chair, asked panel members such questions as:
'why are you so interested in sex?' 'Do women want porno?' 'Do
we as consumers want to make use of existing facilities, or do we
want our own brothels?' and so on.

About-face

In view of the subjects discussed by the panel, the speakers, and the
terminology used, we can conclude that between 1982 and 1985 an
obvious turnaround took place in the discussion of feminine sexuality. Old taboos seemed to have been swept away. If oppression was
the key word in 1982, it had been replaced by lust and pleasure in
1985. There was little difference of opinion among panel members on
the idea that no limitations should be placed on feminine sexuality.
Differences of opinion in this tolerant atmosphere remained latent;
there was more talk than discussion.

However, it struck us that in this liberal discussion there were
still rules and taboos with regard to the way one could talk, and
what could be said. We saw quite a few forms of moralism in this
apparently liberal discussion. This indicated that the discussion
wasn't quite as 'over' as it seemed . . .

Oppression as taboo

Finding 'moralist' aspects in the liberalism that appears to have
achieved consensus in 1985 is not difficult. References to oppression
as a criterion for testing feminine sexuality, frequent in 1982, was
now taboo. Anyone who wanted to go into the relationship between
feminine sexuality and oppression might have found herself in the
following situation:

Gayle Pheterson: Just one more remark on the sexual violence
issue. As we all know, the blame for the
abuse we suffer always ends up on our own
shoulders. At the end of the day, the woman
in the porno movie gets the blame for the
rape of a 'good woman'.

Marjan Sax: Yes, yes, good.

      . . . and she moved on to a totally different subject.

Yet it cannot be said that the whole idea of oppression of women through sex has become obsolete. The issues of feminine sexuality and sexual violence have simply been disconnected – but the problem remains.

Like equals?

Another form of moralism can be discerned in the way discussions on feminine sexuality are carried on, or rather not carried on.

> In this women's festival we want to explore the fears and fantasies of women with regard to 'public sex' and pornography, the various experiences of pro-sex feminists, and the options for developing an 'autonomous feminine lust experience'. For this reason, we have included a number of items on the programme which have to do with sex, either directly or indirectly. For example, we want to experience with you an erotic performance 'in the flesh' . . . . We would also like to watch certain movies with you (yes, so-called sex films).[22]

Although, on the one hand, there is a suggestion here that women can now sit down as equals around a table to discover what their sexuality is, on the other, the Melkweg appeared to see its relationship with the public as educational.

> Do you remember the last women's festival in 1982, when the beer glasses sailed through the auditorium as we staged a striptease just for women? Well, hopefully we're all a little wiser. A number of things have also become clearer.

And anyone who hadn't reached that superior level would be better to stay at home:

> All items are intended for women with a positive attitude to sex and eroticism (and not only in theory, but especially in practice) and who won't immediately start looking for limitations.

Moreover, they were wheeling in 'experts' who knew better than any other women what feminine sexuality was and could be. As we have seen, women with 'practical' experience have more right to a hearing than those with 'theoretic experience'.

Xaviera is perhaps the world's only professor of sex whose qualifications were gained purely and solely from practical experience. She knows what she's talking about!

The extent to which someone does not meet traditional expectations with regard to feminine sexuality was also an issue. The criteria which had been considered valuable in 1982 were abandoned. Thus, the Melkweg was certainly moralistic when it suggested that the question of what feminine sexuality is can best be answered by a lesbian, polygamous SMer who has been employed in the sex industry for years. The voice of a monogamous, heterosexual scholar serves primarily to demonstrate what feminine sexuality is not.

Femininity and femininities

The argument in 1985 against the moralism of 1982 was that the criteria which result from the analysis of women's oppression through sexuality limit feminine sexuality. Moralists make a strict distinction between what is masculine and therefore to be rejected, and what is feminine. However, the definition of feminine sexuality thus remains traditional and, as we have seen, begins to function as the norm. In 1985, many people wanted to get away from these norms and the analysis that produced them. But this aim placed participants in the discussion in the following dilemma: on the one hand, liberalism does not allow any fixed definition of femininity – the thinking that (almost) anything goes is based on the idea that feminine sex is (almost) unlimited. Assuming that feminine sex is one thing and therefore not something else, establishing norms then means limiting what is allowed. On the other hand, feminine sex is precisely what has to be found – only by discovering feminine sexuality can you become sexually liberated. In the discussion this is often solved by alternately arguing in favour of both positions – suggestions with regard to what femininity could be are offered, but these are immediately followed by reasons why we cannot yet know these things.

In this way, feminine sexuality has been elevated to a great mystery: even the experts, who by reason of their position should be able to dictate what feminine sexuality is, keep the question open by beginning, ending or otherwise larding their truths with pronouncements on the oh, so unknown or mysterious nature of feminine sexuality.

> We still have very little idea of what is meant by women's sex. Really, we know so little about our own sex.
>
> (Candida Royalle)

> I've really been talking about sex since I was eleven. And yet, every answer I've tried seems incomplete, maybe not true at all, or maybe true, but perhaps everything else is true.
>
> (Gayle Pheterson)

> Well, now that we know that sex is such an unspeakable, unclear, wide-ranging thing . . .
>
> (Pat Califia)

The idea of feminine sexuality as some kind of buried treasure is the most important delay mechanism in the discussion. But how do they know that the sex to be discovered is a valuable treasure, and not just an old cheese roll?

> So, sexuality is a very complicated subject. It's not just about what we want, but, to me, I often have this hatred of my own sexuality, because it's a hatred of all manipulation, of all the ways in which I have been imprisoned. I'm in a double bind which is, I think, very close to my identity.
>
> (Kathy Acker)

They know this because they have all caught a glimpse and that glimpse turned out to be a combination of lust and oppression. Oppression functions here as something that makes sex an even bigger mystery, as something 'deep in yourself', and thus plays a central role in the jumping back and forth between the two sides of the dilemma sketched above.

The dilemma of the necessity and the impossibility of defining femininity also emerges as a result of the question on why it is a good thing to set up a sex industry for women. According to Candida Royalle, that could create preconditions in which feminine sexuality could be discovered by women.

> Statistics show, at least for America, that around 50 per cent and sometimes more of the people who rent and buy porno are now women. So, of course my theory is that if they're looking at the male stuff, let's try and give them something

to look at that is more to their own liking. Now, of course, we don't really know. It's all experimental.

If women are buying as much porno as men, it seems remarkable to conclude that they want something different. But there is apparently an assumption here that feminine sexuality is different from male.

> The problem is that the production of sex films has been male dominated. And men's sexuality seems to have been based on power, on games of power . . . . The only way to change that is to get women to do it themselves . . . . I am not going to do scenes with women until I can get actresses who really like each other. And I think that's what women want to see. They want to see genuine instead of artificial or make-believe sex . . . . If we have women's porno, then maybe we'll get to see more than just a series of close-ups of genitalia and 'cunt shots'. Maybe we'll get something more interesting and artistic, hopefully.

Thus, feminine sex is: not based on power; more 'real' (not artificial); not only genital. The panel discussion also indicates that the feminine sex industry will be free from coercion, hierarchy and humiliation.

This construction of femininity is reminiscent of nothing other than the great opponents of unlimited exploration of 'the autonomous feminine lust experience' who still ruled in 1982. What is masculine and what is feminine appears to have been maintained. Only one thing has changed: lust, which was once a characteristic of masculinity, has now been annexed by femininity.

The Melkweg organizers and the panel members emphasized the fact that no single feminine sexuality exists. As if to allay the fear of coming across as moralistic, the endless possibilities of feminine sexuality are trotted out. All women are different and feminine sexuality is different for every individual woman.

This is another point of argument used to support a women's sex industry. The sex industry offers an option not for the discovery of uniformity in feminine sexuality, but for the discovery of its diversity.

> The specific nature of a woman's desire is important, as is the fact that preconditions don't allow us to find out what those desires might be. We don't have enough resources to really have the kind of freedom that would allow us to be as diverse as I think we would like to be. So, what I'd like to see for

women, is more in the direction of material conditions that
would make it possible for us to start exploring our fantasies.

(Pat Califia)

... the truth in women's land. And how confused and shocked
we were ... when we found not one but many truths. And
the more we learned to accept and value the many faces of
the truth, the more fascinated we became by the diversity in
characters.

(Melkweg announcement, 1985)

Is the assumed multiformity of feminine sexuality perhaps the
explanation for the lack of discussion? But if no limitations are
placed on the construction of what the feminine is, what then can
'feminine' refer to?

I don't think there's that much difference. We're all women,
all people.

(Pat Califia)

I think generally everyone does have the same desire. It's like
what Pat said, I think that it'll become more specific. For
instance, just personally, my main scenario – I think of it in
terms of scenarios – I really get off on being rejected.

(Kathy Acker)

Thus, in the plea for endless diversity in women and their lust
experiences, the concept 'feminine' disappears now and then as
easily as it emerges.

In the liberalism of 1985 we find on the one hand a point of view
which in fact makes a discussion on the distinctiveness of feminine
sexuality superfluous; if all people, including women, had the chance
to discover or develop their own individual 'scenario', then it comes
down to no more than women catching up on this point. On the
other hand, to accommodate the discussion on 'what women want',
the liberals continue to talk about a known or still to be discovered
(truth about) femininity. In doing so, of course, emphasis is placed
on the point that this does not mean that norms are now being
imposed on feminine sexuality.

In our view, both this dilemma itself and the fact that it cannot
be discussed, can be explained by the way in which the moralism
problem is defined by liberalists: that feminine sexuality is limited

as soon as norms appear on the horizon. But does the application of norms in itself have to be limiting for feminine sexuality? If we look at the discussion in 1982, those limitations appear to result more from the fact that the masculine and the feminine are segregated in opposites, and what is feminine is then determined and fixed by that segregation. The rejection of all norms implies the rejection of a strict division between masculine and feminine sexuality, but also produces a new problem: discussions on norms are taboo; no one wants to appear moralistic. In the meanwhile, norms definitely exist regarding what 'feminine' is. That is even a precondition for the discussion on the possibilities of feminine sexuality.

Diva – non-moralistic?

The only participant in the discussion not struggling with this dilemma was *Diva*. This journal neither appeals to a feminine sexuality nor to a sexuality that needs digging up, nor to a backlog women have to make up. At first sight, *Diva*, the Melkweg and the panel members appear to deal with their (common) opponents' moralism in the same way: they drop all norms. However, in *Diva*'s case a different evaluation of the problem lies at the root. On closer examination, *Diva*'s 'solution' is also different. It does not advocate mining for feminine sexuality, but undermining it, and argues against every definition of it.

This explains *Diva*'s changed attitude to the Melkweg festival. If *Diva* was the only positive voice in 1982, in 1985 it published one of the few negative reactions to the festival: 'Candida Royalle . . . didn't dance or sing badly, but we're still waiting for a really hard porno show, a lesbian live show, or in any case something new compared to 1982.'[23]

Just as in 1982, it can't go far enough for *Diva*. However, like the Melkweg, *Diva* does not only advocate more (kinds of) sex for women, it is also looking for continual innovation. Every fixation on women's sexuality has to be broken down: a sexual experiment should not lead to pronouncements on feminine sexuality, it should only generate a subsequent new experiment. Whereas in 1982 *Diva* was still calling for clear pronouncements on lust and its feminist criteria, by 1985 discussions appeared to have been relegated to the 'outdated' category.

But *Diva* does support the project for the development of a sex industry for women. This should be aimed at developing stylish ways of sexual enjoyment. And not because men have them, nor because women would want something different or do it differently, but because innovation is an aim in itself.

In fact, *Diva* has drawn the most extreme conclusions from the point of view that the panel members represent, but cannot maintain for the sake of the discussion: if you drop all norms for feminine sexuality, you have to relinquish all references to women and femininity.

> [We] propose . . . the following approach. Drop the formula 'all women'. What we're concerned with here is spiritual affinity, ideas and style. . . . Germans in overalls with no money, the consumer types who are too stupid to realize how special the Melkweg festival is, should park themselves in front of their TVs and follow it all from a distance.

Diva is explicitly proposing the exclusion of the category 'sex': 'In contrast, we see many an interested, elegant man or transvestite fitting better into the ambience.'

Conclusion

Between 1982 and 1985, a shift took place from 'oppression of women through sexuality' to 'liberation of women through sexuality'. This change can also be seen as an expansion of the answer to the question of what women may do and should do with regard to sexuality. In this sense, there is a shift in the answer, but also an observable continuity in the proposition itself. This explains in part the current silence around this subject: more and more was allowed, and ultimately (almost) everything was allowed, so there remained (almost) nothing to say about the subject.

However, although we showed that in 1985 'anything goes', we also saw that there are still all kinds of moralism hidden behind this liberalism. It is not the case that what is claimed about feminine sexuality has become totally arbitrary. The taboo on the establishment of norms ultimately means a taboo on the discussion itself.

In the first place, there is a taboo on the sexual violence problem. The analysis which once indicated the way in which feminine sexuality should develop is now working in the opposite direction. Secondly, in 1985 there turned out to be 'experts' who knew 'the bottom line' on feminine sexuality better than other women. A third kind of moralism is most problematic for the liberalists: the limitation of feminine sexuality by prescribing what it is and (still) may be. That is also the moralism of conservatives, of 'traditional' 'anti-sex' feminists – the same people on whom they have just declared war. Apparently, the liberalists are equally prone to pronouncements on what feminine sexuality is. However, factual pronouncements in this discussion have always formed the basis for norms and this link remains unbroken by the liberalists. It appears impossible to discover more forms of feminine sexuality without appealing to femininity, and that in its turn implies that some matters are more feminine, and therefore better, than others. But there is now no way to discuss these things.

Diva is the only exception here – there is neither a sexuality nor something feminine to be discovered. The journal rejects explicitly any attempt to search for a feminine sexuality, and also dismisses discussions in terms of what is allowed and what is not. But the problem is that Diva goes no further than that. Not talking about femininity, about what is allowed and what sexuality is, means not talking at all, only changing. To *Diva*, feminism is no more than continual experiments and trying out new things, and certainly not hanging around too long on specifics. *Diva* also has nothing to say about the direction of change, limiting itself to choices dictated by 'style' and 'taste'. However, these remain empty criteria; they are not defined in any way. Yet, they work for the 'real' feminist: only those with taste – and that can include men – are allowed to participate. It will be clear that *Diva* contributes to the fizzling out of the discussion.

Thus, there is a taboo on saying 'something is not allowed' and why that something isn't allowed. In the meanwhile, the norms which definitely exist have gone underground. In short: the discussion is not so much over, but has become stranded on its own preconditions.

NOTES

This chapter was originally published as an article, '. . . En lust voor ons allen. Het einde van de seksualiteitsdiscussie in de Vrouwenbeweging?' in *Tijdschrift voor Vrouwenstudies*, 33, 1988, vol. 9, no. 1, pp. 58–74.

1 Our thanks to Tjitske Akkerman, Irene Meijer, Agnes Sommer and Tsjalling Swierstra.
2 M. Strooband and W. Dorsman, 'Combinatie van spel, plezier en

werk' ('Combination of play, pleasure and work'), in *Diva*, no. 4, 1984, pp. 4–5.

3 Melkweg Report, 1982.
4 Festival flyer, 1982.
5 Roswitha and Jeanette, 'Rookgordijn om festival' ('Smoke screen round the festival'), in *Vrouwenweekblad*, 2 October 1982.
6 'Honderd jaar sexualiteit' ('A century of sexuality'), in *Vrouwenkrant*, no. 87, 1982, pp. 14–15.
7 Roswitha and Jeanette, op. cit.
8 T. Janssen, in *Vrouwentongen*, nr. 2, 1982, pp. 16–18.
9 Ibid.
10 Marjet, 'Ja, en dan die sexualiteit' ('Yes, and then there's sexuality'), in *Vrouwenweekblad*, 2 October 1982.
11 Tilt, 'Decadent night', in *Vrouwenweekblad*, 9 October 1982.
12 Jet, 'Sadomasochisme', in *Vrouwenweekblad*, 9 October 1982, p. 10.
13 A. Bontje, 'Sexualiteit en onze normen, uit het patroon gerold' ('Sexuality and our norms – rolling out of pattern'), in *Vrouwentongen*, 1983, no. 3, pp. 8–9.
14 VSSM announcement, 1982.
15 Jet, 'Sadomasochisme'.
16 Irene, 'SM vult lacune op in seksualiteitsdiskussie' ('SM fills hiatus in sexuality discussion'), in *Vrouwenweekblad*, 9 October 1982, p. 8.
17 J. Dubbeldam, 'Verslag van diskussie op vrouwenfestival' ('Report of discussion at women's festival'), in *Kerfstok*, October 1982, pp. 5–7.
18 M. Bots and M. Prinssen, 'Als het alleen maar zacht is... wordt ik heel ongeduldig' ('If it's only soft . . . I get very impatient'), in *Katijf*, no. 12, 1982, pp. 8–13.
19 P. Koelemij and B. de Wit, 'Bad girls & sad girls, vrouwenfestival op het scherp van de snede' ('women's festival on a knife edge'), in *Diva*, no. 5, 1982, pp. 3–4.
20 B. de Wit, 'De politiek van de heupbeweging' ('The politics of the hip movement'), in *Diva*, no. 1, 1983.
21 Melkweg announcement, 1985.
22 Melkweg announcement, 1985 (the following quotes come from the same source).
23 B. de Wit, 'Unknown gender of wij vrouwen' ('Unknown gender, or we women'), in *Diva*, no. 5, 1985, pp. 18–22.

Part IV

FRENCH THOUGHT
AND
PSYCHOANALYSIS

INTRODUCTION

Although French thinking has sent 'a fresh southern wind'[1] through the ranks of Dutch women's studies scholars, its primary effect has been to force the issue of whether an ontological difference exists between men and women (Irigaray). Following in the wake of interest in Foucault's questioning of the Western subject, interest in the psychoanalytical theory of Lacan, which examines the basic form of the subject and designates it as masculine, also flourished in the Netherlands. However, the phallogocentric principles of this thinking were soon criticized with the help of Derrida and Irigaray's work. Rina van der Haegen, who introduced Irigaray's writings in the Netherlands, attempted in her 1989 Ph.D. thesis (University of Nijmegen), *In het Spoor van Seksuele Differentie* (On the track of sexual difference), to articulate 'the feminine' beyond the dominant, masculine order by applying this French thinker's mimesis strategy. According to Irigaray, mimicry of the masculine norm offers an opportunity to break open the patriarchal discourse, so that space is created for a 'double syntax' in which the 'invisible feminine' can also be expressed.

By elaborating on Lacan, but also as a criticism of his theory, Irigaray distinguished both a masculine and feminine subjectivity. This met with resistance from many a researcher, and as a result psychoanalysis, including Irigaray's variant, was again criticized, this time from the deconstructivist approach of thinkers such as Derrida and Kofman. This in its turn led to a confrontation, with a choice between adhering to identities, as expounded in the notions of Lacan and Irigaray, or rejecting and suspending every identity. Thus, the title of a recent article by Veronika Vasterling reads; 'Lacan or Derrida, psychoanalysis or philosophy?'[2] In the end she chooses the 'absolute identities' of psychoanalysis rather than Derrida's 'absolute difference philosophy'. According to her, the complete de-bordering and blurring of meanings of signs in Derrida precludes the criticism of discriminating demarcations of a temporary identification of sign and meaning. For this reason, she accepts the psychoanalytical model in which the phallus applies as transcendental signifier and through which every meaning process can be put on hold, even though only temporarily, and its empiric conventions analysed. Other researchers, however, have never accepted the phallic premises of psychoanalytic theory and continue to draw inspiration from Foucault and later Derrida.

The way psychoanalysis is applied in Dutch women's studies research is too diverse to constitute a national trend similar to those advanced by Teresa Brennan as French, American and English in her *Between Psychoanalysis and Feminism*. While Brennan places, 'very roughly' as she herself says, the defence of Freud and Lacan under the British flag (Juliet Mitchell and Jacqueline Rose), she allots criticism of psychoanalysis to French theorists such as Irigaray and Cixous, and, following them, to American feminists.[3] The articles in this section represent a number of positions assumed in this debate by Dutch researchers. In this sense, the Netherlands is unique in that all the major influences – British, continental and American – are all represented and are often brought together in thematic discussions. Both Karen Vintges' and Angela Grooten's contributions focus on the theme of 'scopophilia', although each has a specific approach. Joke J. Hermsen's article can be seen as representative of Dutch interest in French philosophy in which thematic propositions are of first importance.

In Chapter 11, 'Coming to your senses . . .', Angela Grooten elaborates on the feminist conflict around the symbolic order of language, in which only the Law of the Father is said to apply, using the theme of 'scopophilia' in relation to feminine subjectivity. According to Freud, the privilege of seeing, of the scopic, forms the transition from the pre-Oedipal to the symbolic order and through its link to the visible, male sex, the basis of our phallically delineated culture. The answer to whether there can be any question of an own, intrinsic feminine visual pleasure and style within the phallic order of the symbolic, as argued by Irigaray and Cixous, has to be negative, according to Grooten: 'the symbolic order is scopophilic, post-Oedipal and defined by the father'; 'she' cannot encompass the 'all' of the pre-Oedipal, motherly. But fortunately, there is still a lot going on beyond the phallus.

Like Kristeva, Grooten argues that the pre-Oedipal, 'earlier' senses do not disappear from the symbolic order of language. Semiotic elements of language, such as sound and rhythm, which through their reference to the pre-Oedipal identification with the mother are termed 'feminine' by Kristeva, find their resonance in the symbolic order of language. According to Kristeva, a poetic and artistic use of language goes beyond and undermines its symbolic laws so that a stronger *'disposition sémiotique'* comes into being. In her *Révolution du langage poétique*, she points out the importance of these violations which can have a 'revolutionizing' effect.[4] Following Kristeva, Grooten proposes a similar aestheticization of language by emphasizing a 'rhythmic style of music, poetry, literature' in the otherwise 'inevitable logocentric approach to reality' – a 'creative and pleasurable style' which is not the sole preserve of woman, but which probably belongs more to the 'order of the daughter' than to that of the son.

In Chapter 12, 'The vanished woman and styles of feminine subjectivity', Karen Vintges departs from psychoanalytical theory and uses Foucault's later work[5] to develop a feminist subjectivity which is not based on an essential feminine subject or identity. Foucault's work has been influential in women's studies research in the Netherlands since the early 1980s. In contrast to feminist research in the US – books such as *Feminism and Foucault: Reflections on Resistance*,[6] where the work of Foucault is subject to more pragmatic questions on the possibilities of 'feminine resistance' to the patriarchal order – in the Netherlands his historical and especially his discourse analyses are of importance. Foucaultian discourse analysis offers feminist researchers the opportunity to analyse not only theoretic practice but also concepts such as 'woman' or 'femininity' as cultural constructions. While most Dutch women's studies research has concentrated on Foucault's earlier works, Vintges' contribution discusses how, in his later texts, Foucault reacts against the modern subject as true identity, thus offering space for constructions of subjectivity which are no longer the product of a 'True Discourse on Man', or in Vintges' case, on Woman. According to Vintges, by 'exposing the space of ethics as independent discourse resort', in principle Foucault has provided an opportunity for the development of a feminist subjectivity which presents itself as an ethic around being-a-woman without having to be based on a specific feminine identity. In more recent research, Karen Vintges articulates the life and work of Simone de Beauvoir as an example *par excellence* of such a feminist aesthetic existence.

The work of the French philosopher Sarah Kofman also demonstrates a resistance to every accretion to a feminine or masculine identity. Joke J. Hermsen's contribution, in chapter 10, 'Baubo or Bacchante? Sarah Kofman and Nietzsche's "affirmative" woman', shows how this French thinker uses Nietzschean and Derridean interpretations to try and transcend the binary man–woman opposition. Kofman is concerned with tracing those places in texts where the authors have lost 'the power' over their thinking and can only express what to them is 'firm and settled' (Nietzsche). It often proves that in these cases their attitude to women is at issue. However, Kofman is not satisfied with merely locating these places. She delves relentlessly into the 'firm and settled' nature of these thoughts and undermines them, especially where they concern sexual difference. Precisely because in these areas nothing can be firm and settled, and sexual difference exists by the grace of the indecisiveness and elusiveness of the difference, Kofman has indicated, following Derrida, the impossibility of abolishing sexual difference in masculine and feminine identities. In her chapter, Hermsen goes in search of the method Kofman applies in order to disseminate the man–woman dichotomy to such an extent that a polymorphous scale of sexualized positions emerges which, in a Nietzschean sense, asks for affirmation. She shows that Kofman has left behind the problem of identity, encapsulated in the question: 'Who/what am I?', in favour of a polyphonous, affirmative subject who no longer says I–woman or I–man, but 'we–woman, man, lesbian, homosexual, heterosexual, etc.'

NOTES

1 R. van der Haegen, in *In het spoor van seksuele differentie* (On the track of sexual difference), SUN, Nijmegen, 1989.
2 See *Krisis, Tijdschrift voor Filosofie*, no. 34, March 1989.
3 T. Brennan (ed.), *Between Psychoanalysis and Feminism*, Routledge, London, 1989, p. 2. According to Brennan, this division of minds and continents primarily comes down to two positions which can be taken with regard to the symbolic order and the position of the phallus as transcendental signifier within that order. Whereas French and American feminists 'try to find ways around the male dominance implied by Lacan's symbolic law', it constitutes a problem for Mitchell because the desire to undermine the symbolic, phallic order is, in fact, impossible as 'without a symbolic law human beings cannot function'.

4 J. Kristeva, *Révolution du langage poétique*, Editions du Seuil, Paris, 1974.
5 *L'Usage des plaisirs* and *Le Souci de soi*, Gallimard, Paris, 1984; [English translations by Robert Hurley,] *The History of Sexuality*, vols II and III: *The Use of Pleasure* and *The Care of the Self*, Random House, New York, 1985.
6 Irene Diamond and Lee Quinby (eds), Northeastern University Press, Boston, 1988.

10

BAUBO OR BACCHANTE?

Sarah Kofman and Nietzsche's 'affirmative' woman

Joke J. Hermsen

'We no longer believe that truth remains truth when we remove its veils; we have lived long enough to still believe that. Nowadays, it is an accepted matter not to want to see everything naked, not to want to get into everything, and not to want to understand and 'to know' everything. 'Is it true that the Lord God is everywhere?' the girl asks her mother, 'but I think that is very wrong.' A tip for philosophers. We should honour shame (chastity) much more behind which nature keeps hidden her mysteries and myriad uncertainties. Perhaps truth is a woman, who has reasons for keeping her reasons to herself. Perhaps her name is, to use Greek once more, *Baubo* . . . ?'[1]

What is the relationship between Nietzsche's thinking and the image of woman which it expresses? Although at first sight this relationship appears rather problematic and ambivalent, Sarah Kofman, long before the *Spurs* of Derrida, has shown the 'anti-metaphysical' nature of Nietzsche's thinking on woman. In her deconstructive readings of Nietzsche, Freud and Plato we sample the omnipresence of Nietzsche which she sometimes plays off against the old metaphysical concepts, and sometimes against the so-called objective truths of Freud. Although she uses Nietzsche to criticize Freud's psychoanalysis, as is apparent in *L'Enigme de la femme*,[2] she is not afraid of applying this psychoanalytical instrument to Nietzsche and others. She thus attempts to trace the area (in a philosopher's thinking) where he/she loses control over thinking and can only discern what is to them 'indisputable'. Often, it appears that the philosopher's attitude to women is at issue, or as Nietzsche put it:

190

'In the case of every cardinal problem there speaks an unchangeable "that is I"; about man and woman, for example, a thinker cannot relearn but only learn fully – only discover all that is "firm and settled"' (*Beyond Good and Evil*, 231).

From Nietzsche's numerous, heterogeneous texts, but also from the work of Freud and Derrida, Kofman distils what we could call the 'Nietzschean' woman. This woman is affirmative, narcissistic and knows that because of her veiled self-satisfaction she can be mysterious and therefore seductive. These characteristics are personified by Baubo, who in Greek mythology is the life-affirming woman *par excellence* and as a result symbolizes life itself. In this chapter I will discuss primarily those texts in which Kofman explores and discusses the image of this affirmative woman – 'La femme narcissique' in *L'Enigme de la femme*, 'Baubo' in *Nietzsche et la scène philosophique*[3] and 'Ça cloche' in *Lectures de Derrida*.[4] Whenever we are in danger of losing the thread of this newly woven image, we will fall back on a number of conversations with Sarah Kofman that took place in Paris and Amsterdam.

FREUD AND THE NARCISSISTIC WOMAN OF LOU ANDREAS-SALOMÉ

In *L'Enigme de la femme*, Sarah Kofman provides a new reading of and commentary on Freud's texts on woman and emphasizes especially the complexity of these writings. Her reading of Freud can be called 'deconstructive' in the sense that she opens up Freud's text so that she can get at the fundamentals of his discourse. She fills the open places with her own interpretations and carries through certain of Freud's reasonings until they disintegrate. As she often borrows Freud's own words, it is sometimes difficult to know who is actually speaking – Freud or Kofman. As a result, it would appear as though the numerous ambivalences and contradictions which Kofman wants to demonstrate in his work, are exposed by Freud himself, and this method is advantageous to her own interpretation.

Kofman sees one of these ambivalences in Freud's text *Zur Einfuhrung des Narzissmus*.[5] Freud delineates an image of woman here which is in contradiction to the image we generally find in his texts, namely the image of the castrated woman, who is seen as lacking or deficient, who suffers from penis envy and is only a lesser version of man. The narcissistic woman described here, however, bears no resemblance to this stock image and for this reason Kofman sees a glimmer of light in Freud's otherwise rather 'phallocratic' discourse on sexual difference.

In *Zur Einfuhrung des Narzissmus*, Freud demonstrates important differences between woman and man in their development of an original narcissism. From adolescence, man transfers his narcissism to an external object which he subsequently overvalues, thus impoverishing his Ego and libido in favour of this object. In contrast, during post-pubertal development the narcissistic woman will witness an expansion of this original narcissism because she does not transfer love of herself to an external object, but is sufficient to herself (*Selbstgenugsamkeit*). She knows no need of loving, but wants solely to be loved by others; the man who can satisfy this demand will please her. Freud describes the great attraction (*Reiz*) these women have for men. The man, who has lost his own narcissism and is searching for an external love object, will be jealous of the narcissistic woman's self-love, and will envy her self-satisfaction. He is jealous of her independence and to him she is an enigmatic and mysterious creature because he does not understand how she has retained her self-love. He desires her because of this narcissism.

According to Kofman, this is a great reversal in Freud's discourse. In his other texts, woman always envies the man his penis, and here we see a reversed state of affairs: it is man who envies woman her narcissism. Freud compares the narcissistic woman to a child who can be self-absorbed for hours, and with the predatory animal, the cat and the criminal, who all have in common a measure of self-satisfaction, or independence and inaccessibility. It is these comparisons which, according to Kofman, give Freud's text a Nietzschean character. She even asks herself whether Freud was inspired by the Nietzschean model of the narcissistic, affirmative woman. He wrote this text in 1913, when he was closely involved in a dialogue about the subject of narcissism with Lou Andreas-Salomé, and she is believed to have talked to him about Nietzsche's affirmative woman. Kofman points out that thanks to Lou Salomé, Freud, who always claimed he had hardly read any of Nietzsche's work, was able to arrive at a different image of woman through Nietzsche. Kofman points to various examples which she believes demonstrate similarities between Freud and Nietzsche. The latter also compared woman to a child, a predator and a cat: 'She has the same sharp eye as an eagle, is as brave as a lion and still she remains an innocent child.'[6] The remarkable thing about this quote

Figure 10.1   Lou Andreas-Salomé (1906); the narcissistic woman *par excellence*?

is that it is how Nietzsche described Lou Salomé to his friend Peter Gast. Thus, she could indeed have played a double role: telling Freud about Nietzsche's affirmative and narcissistic woman and functioning herself as a prototype for this kind of woman.

In her essay 'Der mensch als Weib'[7] ('The human being as woman') published in 1899, Lou Salomé sketches this image of the feminine ideal. The ideas behind this text were developed many years earlier during her stay with Nietzsche in Tautenburg. As a result, they exhibit a number of similarities with Nietzsche's ideas on the *Ewig-Weibliche*. In 'The human being as woman', Lou portrays the woman as a creature who rests-in-herself and continually repeats and affirms herself, who is sufficient to herself and appears a true incarnation of Narcissus. In contrast, the man is a dissatisfied creature who continually strives after new, external goals in order to rid himself of the feeling of being incomplete. The man is a restless careerist who tries to rediscover his Ego, which has been expelled from oneness with the mother, in all kinds of professional specializations, whereas the woman is the *geniessende Mensch* (the human who enjoys), who is *heimisch* (at home/comfortable) in herself, and approaches the original state of the *Ganz im All* (all in all). It should be noted here that the differentiation made by Lou in *Weib-Mann* does not refer to differences in the social realities of men and women (*Mann-Frau*), but that *Weib* is a symbol for the ideal state of human beings to which both men and women aspire.

In the text, the *weibliche* ideal is linked exclusively to the term narcissism. According to Lou Salomé, the background to every narcissism is *die imaginierte infantile Einheit mit der Mutter* (the imaginary infantile unity with the mother), which is experienced as a *ruhen im Mutterschoss* (resting in mother's lap). The breach with this 'mother's lap' is more violent for men because they must turn away radically from the female sex in order to acquire an own identity. The man compensates the loss of unity with the mother through his urge to achieve which leads to power over things, so that he once again has the feeling of being 'everything'. The woman does not have to relinquish the mother in such a radical manner, and is therefore closer to the original unity.[8] Only in cases of negative mother relationships, Lou Salomé believed, will women also force the breach with the mother and subsequently attempt to reattain the original 'everything state' by means of the same urge to achieve that is characteristic of the man. Lou Salomé raised these same ideas in her conversations with Freud.

However, according to Kofman, the similarities between the images of the narcissistic woman described by both Freud and Nietzsche, and the influence of Lou Salomé on Freud ended quite quickly, because Freud then fled from the positive image of woman which he created in the narcissistic woman. He apologized for 'attempting to drag the woman down', and she suddenly appears as immoral and reprehensible. It seems as though he is gripped by a certain fear of the *'unheimliche'* and elusive narcissistic woman, and goes on to condemn narcissism on moral grounds. He subsequently indicates how she can transform her immoral self-love into a love of an external object. And what could be a more suitable state than pregnancy? Thanks to her child, the narcissistic woman is able to love an external object because she can always consider her child as part of herself. Pregnancy is seen as a saving path, which can turn her reprehensible narcissism into a respectable love for others. According to Kofman, this means in effect that the woman should love in the same way as the man so that she can comply with our ethic. This is where all comparison between Freud and Nietzsche ends for Kofman, because didn't Nietzsche challenge all our moral and ethical beliefs?

Little remains of the narcissistic woman in Freud's work. The mysterious woman who wants to keep her secret to herself, and in this sense is like the criminal who does not want to reveal a secret, is transformed by Freud into an hysteric. An hysteric who is ill because she remains silent. Freud, who cannot bear the inaccessibility and self-satisfaction of the narcissistic woman, will make her 'better'. He will attempt to break her silence, so that she will become accessible to him and will then reveal her secret. He will give her back the word, but, according to Kofman, this word is 'poisoned'. It is poisoned by the so-called truths of Freudian psychoanalysis, that is penis envy and the castration complex. If psychoanalysis wants to give back the word, then it does so 'in order to steal it more easily, to make her word subservient to that of the master'.

Psychoanalysis will not cure woman, it will poison her with a discourse in which she is 'cadaverized' as an incomplete man. Obsessed by his *idée fixe*, Freud tries to tether the enigmatic character of woman so that he can get a better grip on it. According to Kofman, this is why he departs from the image of the narcissistic woman and replaces it with that of the hysteric, who is dependent on psychoanalysis for her 'cure'. That is why Freud first indicates a lack, declares her 'sick', so that he can then 'cure' her.

195

Sarah Kofman's criticism of psychoanalysis ties in with the critical texts of the *écriture féminine* writers. In their writings, both Hélène Cixous and Luce Irigaray have made similar attacks on the phallocentric thinking in psychoanalysis.[9] They also demonstrate that in psychoanalytical theory woman symbolizes what is *not*, what is lacking. In Freudian thinking, the phallus is the primary sex and woman will always be relegated to an emptiness, to a lack, which makes her subordinate the superior male sex.

In spite of similarities in their criticism of psychoanalysis, Sarah Kofman wants no part of the *écriture féminine*. She accuses these writers of trying to reverse the masculine–feminine pair in favour of the feminine only, which will only lead them to the same metaphysical pitfalls as the logocentric thinking of psychoanalysis which also sets one of the oppositions above the other. In contrast to Irigaray, who continues to adhere to a fundamental distinction between the sexes, Kofman attempts to find a method which transcends this opposition and which will carry a double confirmation of both sexes. She believes Nietzsche's philosophy offers at least a starting point for the development of the method she seeks.

NIETZSCHE AND THE AFFIRMATIVE WOMAN

In *Eperons. Les styles de Nietzsche* (*Spurs*), Derrida has shown that Nietzsche gave a typology of various women. According to Derrida, there is in Nietzsche's work 'no essence of woman, because woman disperses and disperses herself, automatically. She devours . . . every essence, every characteristic'.[10] In his work, woman is 'a name for the untruth of the truth'. There is 'no woman, no one truth of the one woman', but in Nietzsche's texts various kinds of women are observable.

Derrida has classified these various types of women in three groups: (1) woman as lie; (2) woman as truth; and (3) woman as affirmative force. For a better understanding of this last category, we should relate it to the other two. Woman as lie is the castrated woman, who does not have the truth and who is despised and condemned by man who sees the phallus and the truth as his attributes. Woman as truth is the castrating woman, because she threatens the man whom she has deprived of the truth. In this case, as in the first category, the man still believes in the truth and woman is identified with this truth. In Derrida's view, both woman as lie and woman as truth are still imprisoned in the 'phallocentristic' space because there is still belief in only one truth. Both are also linked to castration. In the first case, because she is the non-truth and is therefore castrated herself. In the second case because she is seen as the truth, and therefore threatens and castrates the man who does not possess the truth, because truth is seen as the phallus.

The third type, however, and this is the type Sarah Kofman advocates, the affirmative woman, is no longer seen as the truth or the non-truth, but as life and affirmative force in life itself. She 'affirms herself in herself and in man', and is no longer affirmed by man. The affirmative woman appears to be the enigma, the mystery of life itself.

Nietzsche's affirmative woman is a chaste woman because she has no intention of raising the numerous veils that encircle her, thereby exposing herself. She maintains this chastity because by doing so she increases her mystery, and thus her power of attraction. She wants her veils because she knows there is no truth behind them, only more veils. As Nietzsche put it: 'We no longer believe that truth remains truth if her veil is ripped away.' Nietzsche wants to retain the veil, as does the chaste woman. 'Is truth perhaps a woman who has reason to keep her reasons hidden?'[11] The affirmative woman does not want the truth, because nothing 'has been more alien, repugnant, inimical' to her than the truth.[12] What she does want is illusion, the lie and the beauty, and in that sense, according to Kofman,[13] she is like the artist who loves illusion and prefers pretence above truth.

Nietzsche's artist is the person who repeats reality by selecting it, doubling it, accentuating and veiling it. There is no real reality. And everyone has their own reality. But the metaphysician refuses to recognize this and will always go in search of that one reality, that one truth, and will attempt to lift the numerous veils that shroud it. The artist refrains from this course because, like the affirmative woman, he knows there is no single truth and therefore prefers the illusion. However, those who want to find the truth deny that truth is an absence of truth and that life is illusion and a lie. Thus, to Nietzsche, life is synonymous with woman: 'life is a woman', and 'her great art is the lie, her supreme concern is appearance and beauty'. Sarah Kofman thus evokes a different image of Nietzschean woman than the misogynist vision so often cited by feminists.

Nietzsche in his turn has little good to say about feminist women: 'Woman wants to be independent: and to that end she is beginning to enlighten men about "woman as such" – *this* is one of the worst developments in the general *uglification* of Europe.' Those women who, like men, go in search of the truth, go in search of their own essence and want to lift their veils, will stumble into the same pitfalls as their male counterparts who have been looking for the phallus behind the veil for centuries. If these women also go in search of the same thing, they will be acknowledging their castration and thus denying their affirmative power which transcends this search for truth and is able to affirm life itself. If they want to lose their chastity, if they want to remove their veils, they will transform themselves into degenerate women who, instead of affirming themselves, go in search of the phallus they do not possess.

'*Mulier taceat de muliere*', exclaims Nietzsche; woman should remain silent on the subject of woman if she wants to retain her power and her mystery. But what does that power consist of? If she may not emancipate herself, what can the affirmative woman do? We can guess the answer, of course, and it is confirmed by Nietzsche: 'her first and last profession: which is to bear strong children'.[14] Is this no more than sending woman back to the sink, as we saw in Freud? An introductory question to Sarah Kofman: Is the affirmative woman no more than a housewife and mother?

> If Nietzsche polemizes against feminists, then he does this to demonstrate that they see themselves as castrated men and thus lose all their feminine power. The feminine, creative and affirmative power is indeed primarily the power to bear children. The first affirmative woman is the mother. But there is more. Nietzsche also compares the woman to life and the artist. She is the creative force who can affirm herself and life in all its forms.[15]

The image gradually becomes clearer. We now see an affirmative woman who affirms herself and life and who sits playing with her chaste veils, enjoying life. But how much enjoyment can she get out of those veils? Wasn't it Freud who saw this chastity as one of the main causes of the backward intellectual development of women? And in his famous text 'On female chastity', didn't Nietzsche himself show concern for the lot of women relegated to chastity: 'The education of prominent women has something inconceivable, something astounding .... Everyone agrees they should be brought up as ignorant as possible *in eroticis* ....'[16] It is chastity which made them willing victims of men. How do we reconcile this condemned chastity with that other, celebrated chastity of the affirmative woman? Sarah Kofman:

There are two types of chastity in Nietzsche's texts, just as there are also two kinds of veils, of masks; that of the weak and that of the strong. The chastity of the weak is not self-chosen, self-desired chastity. The affirmative woman chooses her chastity, her veil or mask, because with it she has the power of seduction. Just like the artist, who also veils reality so that it can be made more attractive, the affirmative woman wants her veils.

If you want to respect feminine chastity, then you have to keep a distance, you have to make sure you remain with the illusion, with the superficial, with the mask. According to Nietzsche, the true philosopher is not the metaphysician who wants to find the truth behind the veil or mask, but the philosopher who wants the illusion and dares look at the abyss of life. To Nietzsche, the Greeks were the true philosophers: 'Oh, those Greeks! They knew how to *live*: that is why it's essential to remain virtuously on the surface, the fold, the skin, and to adore appearance . . . .'[17] Nietzsche called himself a disciple of the Greek god Dionysus. He admired his cult because Dionysus was the god of masks, of wine and of fertility as creative force. Following Nietzsche, Sarah Kofman calls the affirmative woman Dionysian.

BAUBO OR BACCHANTE?

Sarah Kofman ends her article on Nietzsche's image of woman with an excursion into Greek mythology to discover a woman who could act as model for the affirmative woman. Nietzsche himself gives rise to this when, in the same introduction, he writes that life is called 'Baubo'. Baubo is able to make Demeter, goddess of fertility, laugh again when she is mourning for her daughter Persephone. Demeter has not eaten or drunk anything for nine days and as a result the fertility of the earth is endangered. Baubo lifts her skirts and shows her belly and sex on which a likeness of Iacchos, another of Demeter's children, sometimes identified with Dionysus, has been painted. Through her laughter, Demeter remembers her own sex and her own fertility. Baubo manages to break through Demeter's mourning so that the earth's fertility is no longer threatened. She is also showing the goddess the power of her sex which can scare off Hades, the god of the underworld who has stolen her daughter.

According to Kofman and others, Baubo is one of the Greek words for the female sex organ. Nietzsche is said to have seen life itself as the female sex organ, or in any case as female fertility.

However, the word Baubo comprises more, and here we approach the relationship with the god Dionysus. When Dionysus' lover, Proshumnos, died, he replaced her with a wooden phallus which was meant to comfort him. This wooden phallus, which Dionysus subsequently carried with him, is called Baubon. Thus, Baubo(n) can be seen as a symbolization of both sexes, and Kofman points

Figure 10.2 Head of Dionysus (Museum of Corinth, Greece)

out that we can see Baubo as 'the female *doppelgänger* of Dionysus', who, thanks to her intervention in the feminine and the masculine, and thanks to the confusion she causes in the masculine–feminine opposition, because she is both the one and the other, transcends the metaphysical opposition.

The affirmative woman is like Baubo: she is the symbol of fertility and of the eternal return. She is no longer imprisoned in the masculine–feminine opposition, but has transcended it. She is affirmative in the sense that she says 'Yes!' to life and to herself, and, in addition, she is Dionysian. But what does that mean, what is the 'Dionysian' character of the affirmative woman? Kofman:

> The Dionysian character of the affirmative woman means the total confusion of the metaphysical masculine–feminine opposition. Dionysus can no longer be termed immortal or mortal, masculine or feminine. That does not mean he is a synthesis of the two, but that he is both to an equal extent at various moments. The affirmative woman is dionysian because she carries in her the contradictory presence of the opposite, not in a synthesis of that contrast, but in a movement which transcends that contrast. In our terminology, we can no longer label that movement masculine or feminine, nor can we indicate it with terms like these, because then we will always lapse into metaphysical oppositions and hierarchization. Like Dionysus, it is total confusion.

Kofman believes the affirmative women is also a bacchante in a sense. She is like the Thracian women who trekked into the mountains to celebrate wild feasts in honour of Dionysus. The Bacchantes were 'ordinary' housewives and mothers, who gave themselves up to ecstatic expressions during these feasts, and in their extreme exaltation even killed animals and their own children. By killing an animal and then clothing themselves in its hide, they were able to merge with their god Dionysus. By throwing off the yoke of daily care and grind, in their frenzy they could transcend life and death, reaching the divine. During these feasts, the loving mothers were transformed into frenzied women who thus represented the contradictions of life – a life that consists of both pleasure and suffering, of happiness and sadness, and that needs affirming in all its forms. The affirmation of both happiness and sadness is, according to Kofman, the Nietzschean way of life, and it is in this sense that Nietzsche's affirmative woman resembles a bacchante. Without

201

doubt, Nietzsche's projection of his *amor fati* in the image of the affirmative woman was again inspired by Lou Andreas-Salomé. She once sent him a poem in which she expresses this double affirmation of joy and pain. Nietzsche admired it so much that he even set it to music and gave it the title 'Hymn to Life': 'To live, to think for a thousand years / Oh, enclose me in both arms: / If you have no more happiness to give me / Then you always have your pain.'

The affirmative woman is both Baubo and bacchante. She sows confusion within the masculine and the feminine oppositions and she affirms 'life in her savagery and cruelty, but also in her fertility and eternal cycle'. She breaks out of the rut of daily life. Through ecstatic exaltation she is able to break through the morality and restrictions laid down by society, so that she can become godlike or Dionysian. She exhibits narcissistic traits, as we have already seen in Freud, because thanks to her veil she is mysterious and self-sufficient and uses this to seduce the other. In a sense, she is also criminal, because she wants to keep her mystery to herself, and is unencumbered by morality.

By interpreting the Nietzschean, affirmative women in this way, Sarah Kofman's main priority appears to be to cast doubt on Nietzsche's misogynist reputation and, following his philosophy, to question metaphysical oppositions. She attempts to provide an impulse towards thinking in terms of sexual difference outside the metaphysical dichotomies. But the affirmative woman can no longer be denoted in our terminology and this raises the question of whether we can actually speak or think about her, or merely dream about her. In order to find an answer to this question, we should examine more closely a stage (called fetishistic) which precedes affirmation and which Kofman has found mainly in the work of Jacques Derrida.

THE TINKLING OF METAPHYSICAL SHARDS

In 'Ça Cloche',[18] Sarah Kofman gives a lecture on *Glas*, in which she sees a figurative representation of the Derridean ideal, namely a generally accepted form of fetishism. It is primarily the fetishist's indecisive behaviour and eternal oscillation between the true object and its replacement which appeals to Derrida. The fetishist sexualizes a specific object that has no sexuality of its own, and allocates to this object the same sexual characteristics as those of the desired person. In this way, he replaces the desired person with a sexualized object, knowing that this object is not the person. Thus, the fetishist oscillates continually between the true object and its replacement, and is indecisive in his choice between the two.

In *Glas*, Derrida sets out two parallel columns of text and is, according to Kofman, like the fetishist who cannot choose one of the two, but wants both. For this reason, the whole of the *Glas* text is no longer open to one unequivocal interpretation, because the reader is obliged to move between the two columns and cannot decide to settle on one. This *mise-en-scène* characterizes the eternal oscillation in Derrida's texts. 'Oscillation is my emotion', writes Derrida, but what does one gain from this oscillating game, Kofman asks, and what is Derrida's aim here?

Firstly, there is never a single goal, but always at least two. Like the fetishist, Derrida always plays on 'two tableaux or between two tableaux' simultaneously. His *Glas* text depicts these two tableaux: there are two texts which together provide a double writing practice (*écriture*) and a double view (*regard*), which makes the text impregnable. But as the text cannot be grasped by anyone, will it be remembered by anyone? Who is the actual loser in this double game? According to Kofman, it is the fetishist, Derrida, who loses as he will never be able to truly enjoy because, just as in the text, he has split his desires. If you split your desires into a duplication, you will always oscillate between two poles and will never be able to enjoy but only 'play as if you were enjoying'. And Derrida admits that: 'I divide my actions and my desires . . . I will always elude you, I simulate continually and never enjoy . . . I pretend that I enjoy. . . .'[19] The text and the writer are indecisive, oscillate between two texts, but they are also double because they are not one column but two at the same time. Kofman maintains that what is applied to a text here, can also be applied to sex. Derrida's two columns are not opposed to each other, they are next to each other and they are both heterogeneous. The one column does not speak the same language as the other, does not have the same rhythm, but they still communicate with each other and refer continually to each other. Each column, which at first sight appears unconnected to the other, is always linked to it, 'flows over into the body of the other'. According to Kofman, Derrida has broken with 'phallogocentrism' because he has put an end to the radical man–woman opposition in which both have a specific essence. One sex cannot be seen as separate from the other, does not have a strictly defined framework, but oscillates between both sexes.

Does this fetishistic oscillation also determine the character of the affirmative woman? Kofman:

> No, because the fetishist is still caught up in the opposition, even though he may not necessarily be in a fixated position. The affirmative woman has transcended this opposition because it no longer exists. But she can transcend it due to the oscillation introduced within the opposition. Derrida's generalization of fetishism topples a hierarchy in favour of the least esteemed term, the feminine, and thus allows an equality of terms.

I need to point out here that the interviews with Sarah Kofman as well as her book on Derrida date from the period *before* Derrida changed his 'oscillating-between-two-sexual-poles' position into a more qualified one, as he argued in his text on Heidegger: 'Geschlecht: sexual difference, ontological difference' from 1987.[20] In this text Derrida stresses the positivity of the *neutral* aspect of Heidegger's notion of *Dasein*, in order to be able to transcend the binary opposition Sarah Kofman accused him of, and to 'open up thinking to a sexual difference that would not yet be sexual duality, difference as dual'. This neutrality, however, does not amount to desexualization; it is rather according to Derrida 'not unfolded with respect to *sexuality itself*, but strictly on *sexual duality*'. The neutrality of Heidegger's *Dasein* presupposes a pre-dual sexuality, that has not yet been 'taken in', i.e. has not yet been determined in an oppositional duality: woman or man. And Derrida states: 'If *Dasein* as such belongs to neither of the two sexes, that doesn't mean that its being is deprived of sex. On the contrary, here one must think of a pre-differential, rather a pre-dual sexuality'. Derrida points out that Heidegger by emphasizing the neutral aspect of *Dasein* does not want to deny that everyone's own body is sexed or that there can be *Dasein* without a body. On the contrary, 'it is its own body itself, that draws *Dasein* originally into dispersion and *damit* into sexual difference.' Given that the body occupies an a priori fixed position within the dualistic scheme, dispersion and therefore difference is in fact not possible. Derrida needs to posit this pre-dual neutral sexuality to be able to think sexual difference at all. A neutrality which according to Derrida 'leads back to the "power of origin" which bears within itself the internal possibility of humanity in its concrete factuality'.

I could illustrate this in saying that although my sex is the sign that

204

signifies me, 'I' does not a priori coincide completely with the sign of my sex. My sex is indeed a *spur*, a trace left on me, an important one, but which the 'symbolic order' tends to fixate into an identity or into an 'essence' of my being. However, as Kristeva puts it, the subject is 'a subject in process', because 'the unconscious and semiotic processes constantly undermine this fixation',[21] so that 'I' constantly has to relate myself in new ways to the sign of my sex. If the subject does not coincide completely with her/his sex, if he/she carries always a differentiating force, this means that the subject is never a closed sexual identity, but constantly creating the conditions for her or his own being-woman or -man. Sexual difference in this way is not thought as the difference(s) between man and woman, but as the distance(s) between the subject and the sign of her/his sex. A distance that makes differences possible at all, a 'spacing'[22] that can be created if one starts thinking from a pre-dual and *only* in that sense 'neutral' sexuality.

Before Derrida, Sarah Kofman had already pointed out this notion of neutrality, this *Neutre*, and thus departed from the problem of identity which results in the question 'Who/what am I?' in favour of the multi-voiced, affirmative subject who no longer says I–man or I–woman, but 'we–woman, man, lesbian, homosexual, heterosexual, etc.'. The opposition man–woman is comprised in the 'we' without them becoming one, but they belong to each other through the differences which separate them. They are different in their belonging to each other, and therefore they must continually affirm themselves and their differences. Kofman sees the first impulse towards this affirmative stage in the work of Maurice Blanchot, who writes about the *'immense parole'* that always says 'we': 'What she is to me: the "we" that holds us together and where we are neither one nor the other. . . .'[23]

Through the image of the affirmative woman, Sarah Kofman has attempted to 'disseminate' the man–woman dichotomy so that a polymorphous scale of sexualized positions emerges which all ask to be affirmed in the Nietzschean sense. The affirmative woman says 'Yes' to herself, and 'Come' to the other. She knows that the other in the 'we' is radically different, but she also knows she is irrevocably linked to the other. Sarah Kofman's affirmative 'we–woman, man, lesbian, homosexual, heterosexual, etc.' has restructured Derrida's indecisive oscillation between two poles in favour of a kaleidoscopic affirmation of countless differences. What 'we' can do with this seductive image is a question which now opens up discussion.

'We' will finish with a poem Rainer Maria Rilke wrote a century ago for Lou Andreas-Salomé in which he, like Sarah Kofman, is astonished by 'we'.

Ich habe das 'Ich' verlernt und weis nur: wir.
Mit der Geliebten wurde ich zu zwein;
und aus uns beiden in die Welt hinein
und uber alles Wesens wuchs das Wir.

Und weil wir Alles sind, sind wir allein.[24]

NOTES

This chapter was originally published as an article, 'Baubo of Bacchante? Sarah Kofman en de affirmatieue vrouw', in *Tijdschrift voor Vrouwenstudies*, 31, vol. 8, no. 3 (Sept. 1987), pp. 318–33.

1 Author's translation from the foreword of F. Nietzsche, *Die Frohliche Wissenschaft*, Kroener Verlag, Stuttgart, 1976.
2 *L'Enigme de la femme*, Galilée, Paris, pp. 60–77; English translation, *The Enigma of Woman*, Cornell University Press, Ithaca, NY, 1985.
3 *Nietzsche et la scène philosophique*, UGE, Paris, pp. 263–304; English translation, *Nietzsche's New Ideas*, Chicago University Press, Chicago, 1989.
4 *Lectures de Derrida*, Galilée, Paris, 1984, pp. 115–45; English translation, 'Ça cloche', in *Continental Philosophy II – Derrida and Deconstruction*, Routledge, London, 1989.
5 *Gesammelte Werke*, Part 10, Imago, London, 1942; Frankfurt am Main, 1978.
6 Letter to Peter Gast, 1881, in F. Nietzsche, *Sämmtliche Briefe*, Walter de Gruyter, Berlin and New York, 1986, part 6.
7 Included in Lou Andreas-Salomé, *Die Erotik*, Ullstein Materalien, Frankfurt, 1985, pp. 7–45.
8 According to Lou Salomé, the artist is also in search of this original unity and in his work tries to cancel out the dichotomy between life and death. He is close to the narcissistic, *weibliche* ideal precisely because of his 'feminine' aspects, but he will have to go in search of it: he must create in order to *'wider zu leisten'* (regain) the original state of childhood
9 H. Cixous, *La Jeune Née*, 10/18, Paris, 1975, and *Portrait de Dora*, Editions des Femmes, Paris, 1976; L. Irigaray, *Speculum de l'autre femme*, Minuit, Paris, 1975.
10 *Spurs*, trans. Barbara Harlow, University of Chicago Press, Chicago, 1970. See, for an interesting communication on this text, Gayatri Chakravorky Spivak, 'Feminism and deconstruction, again', in Teresa Brennan (ed.), *Between Feminism and Psychoanalysis*, Routledge, London.
11 F. Nietzsche, *Frohliche Wissenschaft*; English translation, *The Gay*

Science trans. W. Kaufman, Vintage Books, New York, 1974, fragment 339.

12 This and the following three Nietzsche quotations are from Nietzsche, *Beyond Good and Evil*, Penguin, Harmondsworth, 1973, fragment 232.

13 'Baubo', in *Nietzsche's New Ideas*.

14 Nietzsche, *Beyond Good and Evil*, fragment 239.

15 This and subsequent passages are from an interview with Sarah Kofman in Amsterdam and Paris, 1987.

16 Nietzsche, *The Gay Science*, fragment 71.

17 Ibid., Introduction.

18 In *Lectures de Derrida*. This paper concerns Derrida's *Glas*, published by Galilée, Paris, 1974.

19 Quoted in *Lectures de Derrida*, p. 141.

20 Published in *Psyche: Inventions de l'autre*, Paris, Galilée, 1988. English translation in *Research in Phenomenology*, vol. XIII, pp. 65–83. All references come from the English version. See also G. Spivak's comments in 'Feminism and deconstruction, again', Teresa Brennan (ed.), *Between Feminism and Psychoanalysis*, Routledge, London, 1989.

21 Julia Kristeva, *La Révolution du langage poétique*, chapter A.1, 'Sémiotique et symbolique', Editions du Seuil, Paris, 1974.

22 Derrida speaks of the *Erstreckung of Dasein*, 'a spacing which comes to extend the *There* of Being, between birth and death'. In 'Geslecht . . .', p. 77.

23 M. Blanchot, *Le Dernier Homme*, Gallimard, Paris, 1957.

24 See, for an English introduction to the works of Lou Salomé and English summaries of most of her written texts, Angela Livingstone, *Salomé: Her Life and Work*, Moyer Bell Ltd, New York, 1989.

11

COMING TO YOUR SENSES . . .

On the scopic order and woman's disorder

Angela Grooten

Anyone who speaks in public will frequently glance round the hall at the audience. Seeing the listeners from a distance helps presentation. However, if the speaker could smell, feel or hear the audience, this would be very distracting. People cannot close off their senses to sound and smell – they are exposed to the penetration of sensations through nose and ear, and they cannot prevent feeling things touching their skin. In contrast, the gaze can be averted, and the eye can be closed. The mouth can be opened for tasting, or closed to refuse food; be opened to speak and closed to be silent. There are differences in sensory sensations and they have consequences.

In our culture the visual sense enjoys the highest regard. This has far-reaching effects. Even so, it seems to me difficult to consider the order of the scopic without remaining aware of feeling (the aesthetic) and touch (the kinetic), smelling and sniffing (the olfactoric), hearing and listening (the acoustic), savouring and tasting, or the speaking, chatting and singing of the mouth. You will have realized that I distinguish between active and passive sensory observations. This distinction is also applicable to the visual sense: there is the passive, uncontrolled seeing of something, and the active, scrutinizing way of looking at something. This latter way of looking, the examining eye, which is conscious and concentrated, and especially the exceptional lust which arises during active looking as well as the infatuated repetition of the gazing which brings with it this extra pleasure, is termed 'scopophilia'.

'Scopophilia' has the connotation of being rather a 'dirty' word. It indicates a perversion of looking, an excess of lust, a surplus, a fetishization of the image. For this reason, in the following pages I

208

will indicate the order of neutral seeing as 'the scopic' and the order of the over-valued looking as 'the scopophilic'.

Over the last few years, the concept 'scopophilia' has popped up in texts by women culture theorists and academics such as Luce Irigaray (France) and Evelyn Fox Keller (United States) who are trying to develop a feminist philosophical critique of our modern western culture, albeit from very diverse points of departure.

Luce Irigaray attempts, particularly in *Speculum de l'autre femme* and in *Ce sexe qui n'en est pas un*, to demonstrate that Freudian thinking on female sexuality is dominated by the lust economy of the penetrating look. She protests against the fact that the woman thus appears as a 'hole', and she tries to undermine the scopic dominance of the One, visible, phallic sex by setting it against an autonomous economy of flowing, streaming. When women are denied their own pleasure within the male order, this is because Freudian theory reduces the meaning of the woman's body to that which cannot be seen. Irigaray wants to distort the importance of the mirror image for the constitution of the male sexualized subject into a parody effect.[1]

In 'Gender and science', Evelyn Fox Keller is irritated by her observation that natural science activities have become linked to masculine characteristics. She attempts to subject this phenomenon to analysis by considering the objectivization and detachment from things, the distinction between mind and nature (matter) and the way researchers in modern technological sciences stay out of involvement. Using Chodorow's cognitive-psychological theories on the ego-borders of mothers and sons, she tries to explain that detachment and objectivization of things are inculcated in boys in particular. In 'The mind's eye', Fox Keller and Christine Grontowski examine how since Plato an over-valuation of the eye has been developed and sight has became elevated as noble sense above the lower, non-reflective senses. They consider too how the contemplative focus of the mind on ideas and knowledge became the most elevated which had to be striven after by the subject, and that the visual metaphor for knowledge and insight in things has dominated the modern period since Descartes.[2]

That our modern western culture is dominated by male signs, values, standards, and masculine views, options, perspectives and analyses is for these and other critics both evidence and grievance at the same time. To them it is also clear that this attitude to nature and the world has resulted in a sadistic manipulation of it, a subjection, domination and exploitation. Links are made between patriarchal supremacy and the eye's dominance over other senses, with the over-evaluation of the scopic dimension in our culture. The image rules, the representation, the visible sign, the symbol, mediation, abstraction.[3]

THE LOFTY EYE AND BASE LUST: SUBJECT–OBJECT

The work of Plato and Aristotle marked the transition in Greek philosophy to an esteem for the contemplative use of the mind in search of abstract knowledge. Since that time, and especially after its festive revival during the Enlightenment, and in nineteenth-century Idealism, which was concomitant with the celebration of the subject's power and rationality, seeing has been linked with the most elevated activities of the human mind. Light is linked to truth, contemplation to insight and understanding. Ideas and analytical logic celebrate their power over things. Abstraction, distance and sublimation of material and physical matters adorn spiritual man. In science and technology man trusts to progress through his ability to penetrate the laws of nature. This occurs through inspecting nature via instruments such as micro and macroscopes, lenses, glasses, electronic and other optical devices. The visual metaphor still governs advanced western science. For example, in particle and astro-physics one speaks of 'windows' on the heavens through infra-red, radio and X-ray beams besides optic monitoring. Insight into objects in nature offers man the possibility of understanding, control, manipulation and subjection of these for his own benefit. The observer's ability to perceive and his own consciousness do not much form part of the discussion yet. There is distance between subject and object.

Sigmund Freud had a great reverence for the attainments of human culture, the abilities of the reasoning mind and empirical science. On the other hand, he had a sharp ear for the complaints, the suffering and the imperfection of people's existence in modern culture because his mind was open to the vicissitudes the body had to endure before a human subject is inserted into culture and all the primal is subjected and sublimated. According to him, the insertion of a child into culture is a liberation from direct and total fear and physical dependency. This is rewarded with the admittance to the realm of the mind, consciousness, identity, language and communication, domination, control and detachment with regard to subjection to direct physical pulses. Nevertheless, Freud always stressed the price that had to be paid. The 'discontent' remains within the subject as a scar marking the relinquished realm of unmediation, omnipotence, aggression and death wish, and of totalizing sensual satisfaction.

In spite of his 'modernism', to Freud the becoming of a reasoning subject is always besmirched. In his theoretic model, the realm of sublimation, the laws and the ideal, in short the realm of mature, 'elevated' cultural man, is analogous to the realm of the Father, the authoritarian Patriarch who lays down the law in society. In the course of becoming adult, the human subject must, in one way or another, assume a position with regard to the authoritative structure of reality. An order governs here thanks to specific differences, possibilities and impossibilities. The sex difference (the fact that human beings have to assume a sexuated subject position), the generation difference (the fact that humans cannot retain a total unity with the mother), and mortality are the greatest shortcomings of being, linked to the physical existence of man (the 'Real' in Lacan). These are articulated in one or other symbolic way in the rules and taboos of every culture. Every human subject has to determine his position with regard to these articulations or 'laws'. This position with regard to the symbol of power, the father, or the Phallus, and with regard to the relative powerlessness of the Ego, is castration and it is reflected in the composition of the subject's structure.

The form of recognition-under-protest of the law of the father, which results in an acceptance of and participation in the social game, is called the neurotic position by Freud. So this is the most common and normal and desirable position for the subject: culture cannot demand more than a recognition and acceptance of the laws by the subject, and the subject had better do so for his own sake. This position of recognition-under-protest of the order is post-Oedipal, which means the child has arrived in a stage of its development in which it has left the private domain of the mother in order to enter the order of the paternal laws of language and social ideals.

The young child's pre-Oedipal attachment to the mother can be sketched, but only in *retrospect from* the position in the communicative order, as a situation of a duality between mother and child in which both are complete for the other, and both perceive each other in imagination as interchangeable. There is no detachment in such a relationship, no mediation, abstraction or symbolism, no temporal or spatial function. It is a totalizing, bodily-sensual subjection with an all-or-nothing character in lust or suffering.

The half-recognition (denial or rejection of the prohibition of the father and his symbolic order) can result in a respectively 'perverse' or 'psychotic' structure in the subject. The positions 'neurotic', 'perverse' and 'psychotic' are defined in psychoanalysis precisely that way – as acceptance, denial or rejection of the paternal law and the own lack, the 'castration'. In this case, when these terms are used in relation to the human subject they do not apply in the moral sense of 'sick' or 'inferior', but are no more than definitions within a theoretic model.

The female theoreticians who used the concept 'scopophilia' as handle for their critique of this patriarchal culture were inspired by Freud. And indeed, to Freud the *Schautrieb* (the urge to watch) is one of the most important urges.[4] There are more, but this *Schautrieb* is linked directly by him to the motor functions for manipulation of objects. He discusses the typical instinctive polarities of sadism/masochism alongside voyeurism and exhibitionism. An important similarity between both instincts is distance dividing the eye and the object. This distance means the object can be perceived and makes its manipulation possible.

Most characteristic of a drive is its *compulsion*, the motor momentum or the sum of the force or active energy. A drive, and libido in general, is in origin a piece of activity; passive instincts are only drives towards a passive goal. Thus, Freud's pleasure economy is defined as masculine (also in the woman), because borrowing from biology he links activity to masculinity and passivity to femininity. But he also points out that both polarities occur in the subject and initially have no psychologically sexuated meaning.[5] Freud sees the urge to rule, the need for control, for (motor) domination and manipulation as belonging to the culture-creating attitude of the active person (= masculine). The link with the modern western attitude of the mind towards nature (= passive object, feminine) will be clear: looking to grasp, and that in order to subject and to control.

According to Freud, different stages can be distinguished in drives. The first is an active one, located on one's own body: the auto-erotic or primary narcissistic stage. When the child has grown there follows a focus on an object outside itself whereby the child has become the subject. This is an active form of sensory urge. After this, the child can abstract from itself and from the agency outside itself (mother) and it can imagine these as being subjects or objects of the drive; as a result it can conceive of itself as an object for an external subject. This stage is again passive, but now secondary. According to Freud, this last active and passive form of the urge always coincide. The primary narcissism is covered over and 'forgotten' by these later positions of active subject and passive object.[6]

In Freud's earlier work, *Drei Abhandlungen zur Sexualtheorie*, he designates seeing as derived from touching.[7] Voyeurism in children is specially aimed at seeing and touching genitals and excretory organs, and a curiosity remains linked to this which can change into inquisitiveness, and even into intellectual acuteness and theoretic creativity. Particularly in the male child, an active involvement in the mystery of where babies come from, and later the mystery of the sex difference (castration), can lead to development of the intellect.[8]

PERVERSE PERSUASION

When a development gets stuck somewhere before reaching the ultimate adult sexual goal, in other words in an earlier partial drive somewhere on the body (oral, anal, olfactory or on a certain part of the body other than the genitals, or on other organs or senses), and when there is a libidinal over-valuation of such an object or stimulation, which was in fact intended for hetero-genital satisfaction, then Freud talks of Perversion.[9] Perversion, according to Janine Chasseguet-Smirgel, is by definition anally coloured,[10] but also has aspects of the preceding sensory phases. When feeling, or smelling or hearing the object remains more important than the achievement of the genital-sexual goal, then there is a question of perversion or a kind of fetishism. This 'wrong' object (= from the Latin 'pervertere') is then charged with all the drive energy: the fetish, which can be oral or anal, acoustic or olfactory or tactile or scopic or all at the same time.

According to Freud, the choice of a sexual object similar to one's own image, homosexuality, is in this sense also a perverse position. Initially, he called it 'inversion'.[11] The difference between the sexes, *hetero*-geneity, is denied and replaced by a *homo*-geneity, a likeness. The loved object has to be overcharged with libidinal energy, like a kind of fetish, in order to sustain the denial of the heterogeneous goal (which from the point of view of the accepted sex difference is actually 'superior'); this attitude comprises simultaneously both an acceptance and an excessively vehement denial of this 'superiority of the goal'.[12] The perverse position is a natural stage in the development to adult subject, and something remains of it in every person. Thus, it is the rule rather than the exception, and it is usually combined with the most 'normal': neurosis. Perversion and neurosis are each other's negatives, they always coincide in one or other combination, as recto/verso, in every person. If we now look at the *Schautrieb*, then the sadistic form of it is the *Schaulust*, voyeurism, and the masochistic form is exhibitionism. Now, our scopophilia is this voyeuristic pleasure, this peeping activity charged with excessive lust. A good translation alongside voyeurism could then be 'leer lust'.[13]

HOT AIR

For further considerations on the scopic order and on cultural problems for the woman, we have to examine something else more closely. That is the relationship between the scopic and the phallocratic character of the cultural order: that of patriarchal authority. This is connected to the description of the rules, laws and norms of society as a language, a structure of symbols and signs and abstractions. Through cultural agreement, meaning is assigned to the order of signs and symbols. This is no more than an unspoken gentleman's agreement which is to every subject's advantage, but which has to be paid for. And through the common acceptance of that meaning, these signs acquire real exercised power in socio-historical reality. This agreement, this game, this cultural sublimation thus consists of abstraction of the unmediated being by means of symbols, signs, language. This order forms a third dimension alongside the physical two-dimensional mother–child unit, a symbolic space with an order of laws and norms which creates distance and which is authoritarian; reality which exercises power to which each child has to subject itself and into which it must insert itself. It has to play the game of communication and action because it is the only possible game. The phallic third point of the Oedipal triangle or the third dimension provides the subject with space to liberate itself from the polymorphous, unarticulated dual symbiosis with the mother and to distance itself from this deadly embrace. This whole system of signs and language agreements has to be guaranteed by a basic value, a primordial sign, and an ultimate warrant which secures the meanings in the game at the beginning of the chain structure. This basic value can perhaps be compared to the bars of gold in the vault at the Netherlands Bank on Amsterdam's Frederiksplein, or those in Fort Knox in the US, which guarantee the total paper money trade throughout the world by means of an agreement on their 'real' value. This trade also consists of no more than a belief in these agreements, and thus causes their actual fulfilment. So it is speculation in fact, a trade in hot air, but it has real power and real economic, political and social consequences. Now according to the psychoanalytical theory of Jacques Lacan, the Sign of Signs (the $ – which can also be read as the 'split Subject' – or the f – also to be read as the crossed out phallus) is the Phallus, the patriarchal power sign *par excellence* and by agreement.

No one, however, possesses the Phallus, neither father nor mother, neither man nor woman, boy nor girl, young nor old, dead nor alive. The existential lack, the real, takes care of that. But everyone covets it, it is promised to some, and some fantasize that they have it, others that they are it. Some signs represent a social agreement with a promise of the power of the Phallus: the visible label on the body of men: the penis, that carnal organ which can be seen. Through this social agreement it seems that the man is on the side of power; many believe this categorically, especially men. And feminists.

The game played by the subjects of phallic power is, according to Lévi-Strauss, guaranteed by the objects of value they exchange among each other – the women. Why is the female body value object in this game? Because there is 'nothing' to *see* on their body. But there is therefore more to fear! Within the scopic, at least, the female body is a direct reminder of the sign that can be lost. When this threatening body can be dominated, possessed and traded, then at a symbolic level the fear can be allayed, and the illusion of superiority, of 'whole-ness' can still be fostered. That's where the sometimes fetishistic, false veneration of the female body by men comes from. But both sexes know unconsciously that this game is based on speculation, hot air, and know the vulnerability of the artificially sustained illusion. The market can collapse. The first Sign, the Phallus, that figures as anchor, as fixed beacon lighting up all other meaning relationships, has no meaning in itself. It is empty. It is a hollow sign, an empty set, according to Lacan. The Phallus is a fraud, the symbolic meanings in culture are based on nothing. This undermines the power which is grounded in meaning. Culture is phallic, but fraudulent. The Phallus is a 'fallusy'.

Cultural law, the symbolic order of language, the logical rules and principles of reality are described in psychoanalysis as phallocratic, the reasoning subject as masculine and the passive object as feminine. Psychoanalysis is the myth of this power structure: in the crucial metaphor of castration upon which everything turns. Under threat from this or under pressure from fear of it, people rally to the Law of the Phallus, that patriarchal sign. The primacy of the scopic in Freud's model becomes clear in his much disputed assumption that seeing the absence of a penis in a girl causes horror and shock in both sexes, followed by fear or jealousy with all the later consequences for the position in culture.

To Freud, the desirability and superiority of the visible sex is beyond dispute. At the same time, in his theory he lends a willing ear to the symptomatic complaint of the sensory. But only within scopic primacy can the authority of the Father threaten effectively (thanks to the existence of the female body), through the creation of a real power difference allied to a corporeal difference ('lack'): castration = the making invisible of the sign that contains the promise of social power. The Phallus is no more than a signifier and it can only play its hollow role within the symbolic order of which it is the ultimate guarantee. Outside of this order it is pointless. The often heard question 'Why the Phallus as Sign of signs, why sexual difference?' now shifts to: 'Why the scopic above the direct senses, the *intelligibile* above the *sensibile*?' and is thus as unanswerable and indisputable as sexual difference itself.

The inserted subject, which is culturally (that is linguistically) active, perceives 'reality' (as produced), acts therein (as desired) and strives after its social ideals, is by definition masculine by structure. That means that every person who uses language, has a cognitive consciousness and an ('neurotic') unconscious in which the fortunes of their repressed drives are represented, is 'masculine' in structure. He/she always has a simultaneous subject and object position (the bisexuality of Freud); an active attitude in culture, and a passive one in which he/she sees him/herself as the object of the Other's desire.

Seen this way, masculine/feminine, subject/object, active/passive are a question of terminology for positions within the individual. Once inside the psychoanalytical model, this nevertheless often leads to confusion and reasonings based on pure metaphors and tautologies, which in their turn generate more.

In the unconscious, all kinds of positions can be assumed with regard to constitutive castration. This trial of the existential deficit applies to every person to an equal extent, to men and women, to rich and poor. It has nothing to do with biological sex. And the freedom of choice for the subject in her/his unconscious position to withdraw from castration, and to deny or to refuse it, is equally great for all individuals.[14]

A VISIBLE AND A TANGIBLE DIFFERENCE

The castration problem breaks down into two fundamental elements: the difference between the sexes and the generation difference. These differences produce social problems for those with a 'wrong' (per-verted) body in this scopic and masculine culture: those who are invisible, on whom there is nothing to see, who are 'without', 'her without . . .': women.

And the subjects just go on looking at the objects! Through frequent and fascinated looking, watching, scrutinizing, leering, thinking, mustn't the enigma reveal itself, the secret become open to analysis, the fear averted?

What is a woman? *Was will das Weib*? In this respect modern science looks in a way like a Don Juan. This attitude *compels* him to look under every woman's skirt to see if 'it' is really true (that Nothing). The compulsion to ascertain, to convince himself time and again that he is 'whole', to shudder in fascination for 'it', to test his fundamental refusal to believe over and over. It's a perverse addiction, resulting in a programme of repetition that causes a waste of energy.

FEMALE NEUROSIS

Within the paternal order of the scopic she, 'the one without . . .', has difficulty with the invisible body. What should she do in order to appear, to become visible? According to Freud, there are only two ways within the neurosis: either identification with the ideal image of the other's object of desire: passive narcissism, frigidity or 'normal' motherhood, or, the second way, provocation of the other's (sadistic) activity, through which one becomes – as object and symptom of the man – visible: masochism or hysteria.[15] Little remains for woman within the paternal order, which is post-Oedipal (post-dating the castration complex), than to become visible, that is to figure within the scopic, the phallic. That can only be achieved as derived function of the male subject's desire, thus indirectly still via the visible symbol. Post-Oedipal problems are of symbolic, communicative nature, and of the patriarchal order (neurosis = protest against the law, but acceptance of it). The conflict with the scopic dimension of the patriarchal order also manifests itself in the neuroses of women: she figures as lack in the formation of her symptom. Hysteria, the female neurosis *par excellence*, is characterized by a symbolic representation of the question: 'What is a woman?' No one knows the answer, no man, no woman. A solution could be: put on the theatrical play of the ideal image of woman: the way the man fantasizes his fetish. The 'actress', acting and dolled up in an excessively feminine manner, is a masquerade of phallically determined sexuality (Lacan). She is staging a 'performance', an act which attracts the attention of men and seduces their desires (assumed by her and him). Within the scopic, her body is 'wrong', faulty and lacking. This is why the symptom often manifests itself on the scopic plane: hysteric blindness, or paralysis, or fainting, or a dramatic outward expression of suffering.

The hysteric does not know what a woman is, nor what she desires. She has no image of her own. She does not know which mask to wear, in what she must shroud herself, in order to exist 'truly' for the other (and thus for herself). In masculine culture she is like the mirror image of a vampire: invisible (except for its mask and clothes), masked to suggest something of an own face. But which mask? Which role, which face? Poor vampire. Woman does not appear within the scopic, but within the scopophilic: as fetishized image of the other's, and thus of her own, desire.

FEMININE PERVERSION

Within the perverse structure, there is a possible way out for woman via the denial of the scopic lack: the masculinity complex or even female homosexuality. In culture, not only is every woman by definition of the wrong 'persuasion', she is always partly so because the turning away from the mother (in order to make the transition to paternal sexuality) required by Freud never takes place completely. Even mirroring, the girl is after all similar to her mother's image. That is why she knows as no other that there is more than phallic lust. And that is why, unlike the boy, she does not have to surrender body and soul to the game of the scopic symbol: society. For her, yet another dimension of sensual pleasure is open, that is the advantage of the perverse position. The disadvantage lies in the price which has to be paid according to the rules of the game. For woman, the chosen symptom within the perversion is, although often of a scopic nature, also carried directly on her body.

The effects of, for example, enslavement (which is also a form of fetishism) are visible in thinness or fatness or paleness. In addition, absorption in an overwhelming compulsive–obsessive action programme which defies communication can often make its telling mark on outward appearance: for example, the disappearance of the subject in the caricature house-slave-with-a-cleaning-obsession. These effects form mute traces, a silent exclamation mark as action programme which manifests itself directly in reality in a struggle with aggression, destruction and death. At this level there is no longer any question of a mediated game still requiring any symbolic communication with the other, as in hysteria; it is beyond discussion, the unmediated act in the real is a deadly serious matter on and against the own body.

The non-visual, unmediated senses are prominent in the perverse universe. This is well illustrated by the example of Anorexia Nervosa and its fetishistic aspects: addiction, orality, anality, scopophilia with regard to outward appearance, expulsion, compulsion, repetition, totemism, silence, disavowal, superiority, amorality, stubbornness and so on. The playing field here is a bisexual position in between the maternal (via the prescopic tie of refusing food and keeping silent, among others) and the paternal (via the seduction of his commanding authority and glance!).[16]

Thus, suffering is woman's only option for appearing in culture, a passion, passivity, in the order of the scopic, for which she has the wrong, 'cock-eyed' body. In the order which is not hers, there is no opportunity for authentic pleasure or a desire of her own. The only possible pleasure is masculine, voyeuristic, sadistic. According to Lacan, she will therefore be obliged to go and stand on the side of the man, and as a speaking subject she does just that.[17]

A FEMINIST LUST?

However, this is not a hopeless story on the damnation of real women in this culture. After all, everything is possible in the subject's psychological structure, all positions, from the psychotic to the neurotic, can be assumed in the unconscious; the actual fact of biological sex difference can be disavowed and even rejected psychologically. The masculine position as subject in culture can be assumed by anyone who makes that choice, begins to speak the language, plays the game, goes out in public, and lashes out according to the rules. Woman can thus go and stand on the man's side, and vice versa. Because of the ability of the unconscious to make choices, corporeal woman does not have to be reduced to a passive object in culture. Identification of women with that passive position, and subsequent indignant feminist protest against it, would unintentionally come down to biologism à la 'anatomy is destiny', and furthermore to a reduction of the extra-symbolic to the phallic, in other words to a confirmation that there is actually only one sex, the male, which would mean sexual indifference.

On the one hand, biological women have to do more social penance for their taking up of a subject position with a masculine desire, because of the extra handicap of the visibly wrong body in such an undertaking. Woman adds her psychological suffering to the 'real misery' in order to bear it.[18] Lacan explicitly sets against this the existence of an extra pleasure dimension for the subject-on-the-side-of-the-woman: beyond the Phallus.[19]

Whether an own, intrinsic feminine style of conduct is possible after all within the patriarchal order of the symbolic, the scopic – whether the status of either scopophilic masculine subject or masochistic suffering object can be avoided – seems a contradiction in terms of the accepted definitions and the descriptions used. Every human being – biologically female or male – is an active subject within the symbolic order, as regards unconscious structure and active desire for the cultural ideal. If that order is defined as scopophilic, then communication within it will have to be effected in the form of images and representation of images by all subjects, including corporeal women. As this order is patriarchal and post-Oedipal, it cannot describe 'all' of the pre-Oedipal maternal stage. That is why 'The Woman' does not exist (within this order which is the only communicative one), according to Lacan.[20] Culture will always be limited to providing only partial meanings for concrete appearances in reality, and Lacan believes this has nothing to do with a body's anatomical equipment. So there is no own feminine pleasure under the scopophilic, the phallic, yoke.

FATHER IS ONLY A SYMBOLIC FUNCTION

But there is more than the paternal. There is more than the scopic domain. There is more than neurotic suffering. There is more than the sexual difference at symbolic level. There is also the tangible generation difference at the level of the Real: that between mother and child. There is also a *maternal dimension*. A pre-Oedipal stage in which the 'earlier' senses than the visual played their role, a perverse universe without scopic differences, without heterogeneity and sexuatedness, but with homogeneity and polymorphousness. There is also an audible domain and a domain of scents. A realm of rhythm and sensitivity, immediate feeling and perception. A domain of tasting, touching, smelling, hearing, of direct, overwhelming sensations. Realms not abstracted via a symbol or sign, not provided with a social meaning authorized by third parties, outsiders. A realm of physical pulsation, rhythmicity, repetition, directness, totality, without distance in place or time, without control and without any chance of returning to it through an image.

The activity and passivity of these earlier senses have very different characteristics indeed from those of the visual sense: the latter can be closed off, controlled, averted. Distance is required in order to look at the object. That distance makes possible abstraction and manipulation. The ear and the nose and the skin know no control option, no distance from the object; their experience is immediate, direct, here and now. It even goes round corners. Feeling and hearing is direct contact. Closing off and keeping distance, and thus manipulation and control, are not possible.

The direct, unmediated sensory bond with the mother – which can only be presumed in retrospect – took place in rhythmic presence and absence, satisfaction and depletion, separation and reunification, sound and silence. That all took place before the Grand Entrance of control through distance by means of the intervention of the father, the third term. Not all can be said about that symbolic situation either. The senses' sensations preceding the eye's domination cannot be described adequately in language. Oneness with the mother can no longer be remembered because its sensory nature cannot be coded in abstract language. The pleasure of the musical rhythm of sounds, of caresses and scents, takes place beyond language, that abstract communication in signs, that repeatability and remembrance in visual representations. Sensory pleasure lies beyond the realm of the Phallus, of the scopic. It cannot be discussed other than in deficient adjectives, subjective metaphors, suggestive comparisons. Feelings of nostalgia and utopia can only be indicated vaguely, and the same applies to bereavement, melancholy, depression or overwhelming emotion.

   In their desire for insight, understanding and control, the therapist and the scientist ask: 'What does woman want?', 'What is woman's discontent?', and they bid her: 'Well then, describe to us your pleasure beyond.' It is impossible to express it in the language of the Father. Yet that does not mean it does not exist.

TALKING ABOUT MUSIC? A LOT OF OLD COCK

How can one adequately express the taste of wine? By describing its colour? How does one describe a colour exactly? A scent? Everyone knows the hilarious adjectives and metaphors that are uncorked in attempts at communication during wine-tasting sessions. But that's debatable. How do we communicate adequately on the poignancy experienced while listening to a piece of music? There too we find a similar impotence in the totally clumsy and deficient adjectives and imagery – often ridiculous, and subjective, and totally unscientific, unrepeatable and untestable, but sometimes aesthetic and poetic. Moreover, such experiences of a direct, sensory nature do not lend themselves well to remembering, unless they are told to a third person, in a secondary processing in language, and have therefore been encoded in linguistic representations. Just compare what happens with dreams when they are recounted or remembered upon waking. Who can still remember the taste of that sumptuous dinner long ago? But you can remember how the table was decorated. Who can call to mind that specific timbre that made a musical performance so memorable? But you can remember how the light fell on the musicians. Who can still feel after a while that certain caress, or re-experience from beginning to end the time the 'earth moved'? But you can remember the clothes the lover (no longer) wore. Who can remember how it felt to be high? But you can recall what you talked about? Who can explain exactly in a conversation, with words, the precise sequence of a motor skill such as skating, skiing, playing the piano? You usually have to get up and demonstrate the movement. That is where the remembrance is, in the senso-motoric memory which never fades. (The same applies to the olfactory memory, which is also buried deep but never dims.) Sensations in both these categories can awaken very deep, 'forgotten' associations and experiences from the distant past. They can evoke an indescribable, overwhelming feeling, a nostalgic undirected desire. Usually, these experiences are overgrown by retroactive meanings and designations, by symbolic reductions and fixations. The symbolic overwrites the category of the unmediated Real. It becomes invisible, and it cannot be talked about or explained. But that does not prevent it from existing, as Freud's teacher Charcot said.

Who can consciously call to mind the total pre-Oedipal bond with the Mother? But its loss is felt afterwards in depression, in melancholia, in nostalgia. According to Freud, woman especially dwells under the sign of mourning. The pleasure of the physical bodily experience, in the union and reunion, is also felt, but defies description; a pleasure beyond the phallus, beyond language. Who does not know the joy of sporting exertion, of being absorbed in the harmony and rhythm of the body-in-surroundings? (The current addiction to sport experiences such as running could be seen as an example of a pleasure programme acting directly on the body itself.) Who doesn't recognize the unthinking joy of playing a musical instrument, say a piano, or singing? During activities of this kind there is no symbolic reflection, and yet they are immeasurably complex. They are a rhythmic process of unmediated interaction between senses, instrument and perceived product. The intervention of any cognitive reflection would be too slow, banal and distracting. Music is an automatic reflex. That pleasure is sensory, but not scopophilic.

In this kind of process of a surrounded body-in-action, we can no longer talk of a subject/object division in the modern sense. In such a process of technical skills acquired through protracted sensory practice there is no question of abstract control, secondary symbolic representation, communication or reflection, nor of a hierarchical dichotomy of differences between One and Other, a cognitive logic of *a* and *not-a*; let alone of only one significance of sexual difference. Modern western discourse knows no representation, no visual meaning for an important register of life.

PRACTICE MAKES PERFECT

If we want a useful metaphor, perhaps we have to go back to the image of pre-Socratic Greek philosophy which predates the subject/object division. This contained an ideal of 'Quality'[21] and 'Virtue' in the sense of 'skill', in a model of wisdom consisting of practised pleasure in aesthetic, musical, physical, social, rhetorical, literary, gymnastic, culinary, scientific, erotic experiences, etc. That could (but didn't have to!) lead to a stylish way of life in which no one-sided interest was attached to logical reasoned knowledge and public objectivity, nor to official prestige or status in culture. In this sense, wisdom is something other than knowledge. Wisdom and motor skill are only acquired through prolonged sensory practice; time cannot be hurried. Factual knowledge and insight can be acquired instantly through logical reasoning, analysis and cognitive control. But even though you may understand, while sitting in an armchair, the mechanical principles of skiing, sailing or horse-riding, you still can't do them when you actually try for the first time – even the know-it-alls will spend a lot of time automatically leaning to the wrong side! Knowledge and understanding are not all there is. There's the body as well. Socrates led the way in a respect for the primary register and in a scepticism for the symbolic game. He also wanted to enjoy himself in all ways and refused to lay down his ideas in written form. He undermined power, obviousness, identity and certainty and, in the first place, himself. No one thanked him for it.[22] Such a Socratic model of lustful style does not place the exclusive focal point on strict logical-analytical reflection of subject to object, but also values a bodily wisdom acquired through time, experience of life, and practice. And there is no question of a subject action or an object passion.

The style of a primary pleasure can be sought, heard or felt perhaps, but it cannot be described objectively or (psycho)analytically.

This other lust – linked by Lacan to the mystical experience – is thus not reserved exclusively for people with a woman's body; doesn't everybody have other senses and a feeling body in addition to eyes and brains? Didn't men also have and lose a mother? Aren't all fathers sons? Don't sons also know the pleasure of singing, sports, making music, dancing, doing carpentry or knitting?

Perverts, artists, aesthetes, culinary fetishists, specialists in the *ars amatoria* – all celebrate in refined stylish and 'elevated' pleasure the nostalgia for the indescribable, unforgettable but not-rememberable, invisible mother. Along with the melancholics, they too make an incomplete transition to the phallic register, and remain sceptical, perverse and creative in making aesthetic marginal notes on it. The established order is thus 'improved' according to their own insight (superiority!).[23] Seen in this light, a creative and pleasurable style belongs not so much to the (father's) 'son', but to the order of the (mother's) 'daughter'; as a beauty of rhythm and pulsation which still resounds and is remembered in the body when the subject has already made the transition to the paternal dimension; an embellishing perversion of the ordinary neurotic position.

The inevitable logical, theoretic approach to reality should be adorned with beauty. Not for the aesthetics in itself, but because it is really more adequate: a lusty decoration of rationalist metaphysics – by introducing a rhythmic style of music, poetry, literature – is needed to teach us more about reality. In the Socratic sense, of course.

Is it not peculiar that at the end of his life, Freud, that sexist patriarch, was confronted with the paradox that his theory on woman's lack was itself lacking, and in respect to this greater truth took a step back? He rightly abstained from theoretic comment with the words:

> However, you should not forget that we have only described woman in so far as her essence is determined by her sexual functions. Although it is true this influence is very great, we should not lose sight of the fact that the individual woman can otherwise be a human creature. If you want to know more about femininity, then consult your own experience of life and turn to the poets, or wait until science can provide you with more profound and better connected insights.[24]

NOTES

This chapter was originally published as an article, 'Horen en zien Vergaan', in *Tijdschrift voor Vrouwenstudies*, vol. 27, 1986, pp. 271–90.

1 L. Irigaray, *Ce sexe qui n'en est pas un* (This sex which is not one), Minuit, Paris, 1977, pp. 25–6, 29, Dutch translation 1981; and *Speculum de l'autre femme* (Speculum of the other woman), Minuit, Paris, 1974; on similarity as structuring principle and the specular metaphor in western thought, see also R. van der Haegen, *In het spoor van seksuele differentie* (On the track of sexual difference), SUN, Nijmegen, 1989, pp. 48–55.

2 E. Fox Keller, 'Gender and science', and E. Fox Keller and C. Grontowski, 'The mind's eye', in S. Harding and M. Hintikka (eds), *Discovering Reality*, Reidel, Dordrecht, 1983.

3 Light metaphysics is acknowledged as fundamental to western thought. The light image is the absolute metaphor for expressing man's insight into the essence of being of all existing things. In this terminology, the basis and origin of all beings is true and essential light, and its 'image' is perceivable light. For the reasoning mind, this primordial light makes possible clear insight into existing things; seen ontologically, the a priori illuminating and radiating structure of intelligence is its counterpart. Thus, light, being and intelligibility are connected metaphysically from the early pre-Socratic Greeks such as Parmenides, via Plato, for whom the highest aim was to contemplate the essence of being as pure truth and goodness: as known/seen inner radiance to be perceived by the soul's eye: reason. This *intelligibile* is set against the less elevated activity of the non-visual, direct and tangible senses: the *sensibile*, what can be felt, what can be perceived sensorially. Aristotle builds on this Platonic division and it is continued in history through the thinking of the Christian Fathers, such as Augustine, the medieval schools of thought, Descartes up to the Enlightenment, and Kant's *Critique of Pure Reason* with its metaphors for insight, clarity and true, rational knowledge. See J. Ritter (ed.), *Historisches Wörterbuch der Philosophie*, Wissenschaftliche Buchgesellschaft, Darmstadt, vol. 5, 1980.

4 S. Freud, *Triebe und Triebschicksale* (1915), in *Studienausgabe*, vol. III, Fischer, Frankfurt, 1975, p. 92; see, for the English translation, *The Standard Edition of the Complete Psychological Works of Sigmund Freud* (abbreviated *SE*), J. Strachey, A. Richards *et al.* (eds), Hogarth Press, London; vols I–XXIV, 1953–1974; vol. XIV, *Instincts and their Vicissitudes*, pp. 109–41. See also J. Lacan, *The Four Fundamental Concepts of Psychoanalysis* (trans. A. Sheridan), Penguin/Peregrine, Harmondsworth, 1986, pp. 67–78.

5 Ibid., p. 97; see also S. Freud, *Drei Abhandlungen zur Sexualtheorie* (1905), in *Studienausgabe*, vol. V, p. 123; see *SE*, vol. VII, *Three Essays on the Theory of Sexuality*, pp. 123–244.

6 S. Freud, *Triebe und Triebschicksale*, pp. 92–5.

7 S. Freud, *Drei Abhandlungen*, p. 66.

8 Ibid., pp. 98, 100, 109.

9 Ibid., pp. 60ff.

10 J. Chasseguet-Smirgel, *Creativity and Perversion*, Free Association Books, London, 1984, *passim*.
11 S. Freud, *Drei Abhandlungen*, p. 48, notes pp. 56–8.
12 A. Grooten, 'Aberraties en kreaties' (aberrations and creations) (review of J. Chasseguet-Smirgel, *Creativity and Perversion*), in *Psychologie & Maatschappij* (Psychology and society), 34, 1986, p. 115.
13 Since this article was written in 1986, several publications on film theory, women and the psychoanalysis of vision have appeared. See J. Rose and J. Mitchell, *Feminine Sexuality. Jacques Lacan and the Ecole Freudienne*, Macmillan, London, 1982, p. 168; J. Rose, *Sexuality in the Field of Vision*, Part II, Verso, London, 1986; M.A. Doane, 'Veiling over desire: close-ups of the woman', in R. Feldstein and J. Roof (eds), *Feminism and Psychoanalysis*, Cornell University Press, Ithaca/London, 1989; K. Silverman, *The Acoustic Mirror*, Indiana University Press, Bloomington/Indianapolis, 1988.
14 J. Lacan, in J. Rose and J. Mitchell, *Feminine Sexuality*, p. 168.
15 S. Freud, *Ueber die weibliche Sexualität* (1931), in *Studienausgabe*, Bd. V, pp. 279 and 281; see *SE*, vol. XXI, *Female Sexuality*, pp. 221–47.
16 On anorexia as the feminine symptom of pure will, see P.L. Assoun, *Freud et la femme*, Calmann-Levy, Paris, 1983, pp. 134–9.
17 J. Lacan, in Rose and Mitchell, op. cit., p. 150.
18 P.L. Assoun, *Freud et la femme*, p. 178.
19 J. Lacan, in Rose and Mitchell, op. cit., p. 144.
20 Ibid., pp. 149–52.
21 'Quality' is R. Pirsig's reading of the sophists' and Socrates' *arete*, the classical concept of 'virtue', meaning 'being good' at something. A good English translation is skill, but it also refers to mental exercises, in R. Pirsig, *Zen and the Art of Motorcycle Maintenance*, Corgi, London, 1978.
22 For Foucault's respect for the Greek style of a 'beautiful life', see Karen Vintges' contribution to this book, pp. 228–40.
23 For the link between creativity, aestheticism and perversion, see J. Chasseguet-Smirgel, op. cit.; and A. Grooten, op. cit.
24 S. Freud, 'Die Weiblichkeit', in *Neue Folge der Vorlesungen zur Einführung in die Psychoanalyse* (1932), Fischer, Frankfurt, 1981, p. 110; See *SE*, vol. XXII, *New Introductory Lectures on Psychoanalysis*, lecture 33, 'Femininity'.

12

THE VANISHED WOMAN AND STYLES OF FEMININE SUBJECTIVITY

Feminism – deconstruction and construction

Karen Vintges

How does the development of a feminine culture relate to the deconstruction of femininity? Does deconstructive thinking mean that we can do no more than deconstruct the meaning of femininity, and that we cannot work on feminist style development? I began to ask myself these questions because of a number of experiences I had recently which were linked to the deconstructivism of French philosophy. However, the primary reason was the attempts of women to develop a pornography of their own, and the criticism, based on deconstructivist thinking, these attempts evoked. In the framework of this theme, the development of feminine visual pleasure, I want to try and answer these questions. My main concern here is the theoretical legitimacy of the construction of a feminine style. Psychoanalytical theory is often advanced as a foundation for the so-called 'feminine', and thus for a specifically feminine way of looking, which can give rise to 'new forms of visual pleasure'. The premiss here is that there is a male way of looking, which is characterized by an active, voyeuristic position, and a feminine way which is described as a passive, narcissistic position, and that these continue to exist alongside the sexual division in our society. This premiss presupposes an *essential* difference between real, living men and women. But I have my doubts about this approach. In her chapter, Angela Grooten demonstrates that Freudian psychoanalysis cannot underpin such a difference between men and women as two different essences, because the masculine and the feminine, and in this connection the masculine way of looking and its so-called feminine counterpart, are not unequivocally divided between the sexes. Masculine and feminine are used, in fact, as terms which signify different positions in relation to culture, and personally I believe it would be much better if this was expressed in other terms; it would perhaps be better to stick to the terms 'symbolic' and 'imaginary'. But would this get us anywhere in our examination of the question of ways of looking and visual pleasure of real women? No. And in this connection it would seem to me more sensible to drop the whole psychoanalytical project altogether.

For an analysis of the difference between men's and women's ways of looking and visual pleasure, an historical (rather than a general) approach seems to me the most preferable: we would then try to trace (instead of presupposing) and indicate differences in the level of visual practices through concrete research. We would be concerned with different (sub-)cultures among men and women, with traditions and conventions which determine what and how people look, and *which* subjects and images evoke visual pleasure. You can, for example, perceive pornography as such a male visual culture, although women are fast making up lost ground in this area. Women often have a much better developed visual sense of fashion or interiors – at least that is my experience.

But what about the further development of a feminine visual pleasure? If you don't want to fall in with the psychoanalytical discourse as foundation for a feminine visual pleasure, and even reject this theory in so far as it postulates an essential difference between men and women, and if all that remains to you are then historical and social differences between men and women, how can you validate the *development* project, the *conception* and *discovery* of new forms of feminine 'imagery'? After all, the historical and social differences could boil down to no more than 'reproductions' of that which already exists, and thus cannot form a validation for such a cultural-feminist project. Wouldn't this approach imply dumping an important cornerstone of feminism, namely the development of a feminine culture and a language (in this case a language of images)?

Modern feminism wants to be more than an emancipation movement. It is not simply striving after social equality between men and women, and the abolition of women's oppression. Feminism also seeks to be an instrument of cultural criticism and to offer alternatives to the dominant culture. And it is this cornerstone of feminism that concerns me here. My question is: how can we validate theoretically the development of feminism as culture, or rather sub-culture, if we do not want to use as point of departure an *essential* feminine position in or outside culture, in other words a feminine subject? I will use 'French thinking' as the basis for the examination and application of this question, and the most recent work of Michel Foucault for the answer.

FEMINISM AS DECONSTRUCTION OF THE SUBJECT WOMAN

One of the most important, and perhaps even the most important, themes in contemporary French thinking is the attack on the central notion of Man in our culture: a creature who is gifted with a will of his own, his own desires, his own consciousness – the so-called subject. We see two ways of attacking this subject.

Firstly, there is the strategy designed to *decentre* the subject. For Althusserians, the primary factor here is that the subject is not the controlling principle in society and in social development, but is itself only one part and effect of it. Lacanians remove the subject from its central position in the psychological structure. The unconscious shouldn't be forgotten, and the subject is only one – imaginary – aspect of the psychological structure. Luce Irigaray, and Julia Kristeva and Hélène Cixous in their early works, take this psychoanalytical decentring of the subject as point of departure. They argue that what lies outside the subject form is feminine. Because it has been excluded from culture, the feminine is culture-critical above all.

A second strategy for assailing the subject which can qualify as *deconstruction* of the subject comes down to the assertion that the subject does not exist. There are positions or roles in social practices and discourses which have a subject form. But there is no subject-being which precedes or is a mean of all those different positions, no agency which (subsequently) goes through life as subject. Nor is the body such an agency. It consists of a multitude of intentions, energy streams, sensations and actions, and these are addressed and articulated differently in different discourses. All that remains are different subject positions: the subject itself is fragmented. The principal proponents of this deconstructive view are the authors Michel Foucault, Gilles Deleuze and Felix Guattari.

In feminist journals such as the British *m/f* and the Dutch *Tijdschrift voor Vrouwenstudies* this latter view has been elaborated into the question of the feminine subject. If we assume that a unified subject does not exist, then we can no longer speak in terms of a feminine subject. There are only feminine positions, roles and places in practices and discourses, which offer and structure being a woman: as a consequence research is advocated on the way in which these various woman-positions are structured, or how they look in our society. Instead of assuming that there are women who are subsequently confronted by all manner of practices and approaches, the relationship is reversed: which woman-positions do we find in our culture?

It is from this notion that I advocated above an historical approach to differences in masculine and feminine viewing positions, instead of presupposing them as givens. But from the starting point of this view – from a denial of the existence of women as unified subjects, with an essentially identical subjectivity – how can you find room for a construction of a feminine (visual) culture? In Foucault's most recent line of reasoning there is such space, as I will try to demonstrate here. But first I want to discuss more specifically his early study *La Volonte de savoir*,[1] and the Nietzschean view of the subject and subjectivity which it contains, and which, in my view, has been adopted by the feminist journals mentioned above.

SUBJECTIVITY AS EFFECT OF NORMALIZATION AND DISCIPLINE

In his first book on sexuality, Foucault examines the way in which sexuality in our culture has been talked about since the nineteenth century. His reversal of the repression hypothesis is probably well known by now: sexuality is not repressed but produced! There is an incredible increase in talk and knowledge about sexuality in the form of the so-called *scientia sexualis*: discourses such as psychology, psychiatry, pedagogy, medicine, and all the practices and technologies surrounding them, force us to talk about sex: what do you like best? how often? with whom or what? And so-called truths are elicited from us on 'our sexuality'. But what is actually happening is that they are produced through confessional techniques, and thus we are allocated a sexual identity (homosexual, heterosexual, paedophile, sadist, masochist, etc.). Allocated, because sex does not actually exist. Foucault states:

> All along the great lines which the development of the deployment of sexuality has followed since the nineteenth century,

one sees the elaboration of this idea that there exists something other than bodies, organs, somatic localizations, functions, anatomo-physiological systems, sensations, and pleasures.[2]

What has been lumped together as 'sex' is in fact a multitude of factors. Sex has thus been created as a unit, and sexual identity has been made into the most important subject form in our society. Everyone is required to speak out about his or her sexual nature, sexual preference and desires. Foucault sees this as normalization and discipline: we are subjected to and judged by the power of the Norm (which determines what is normal, what is deviant), and held in check through the determination of our identity.

In other studies, on punishment, medical science, psychiatry among them, Foucault has also attempted to demonstrate that standardized subject forms are imposed on us in all kinds of ways, and that herein lies the greatest power effect in our culture: countless technologies, techniques and practices – interwoven with the humanities – produce subject positions which we have to assume on pain of exclusion and/or other sanctions. The fact that we live in these subject positions and experience ourselves as subjects, forms the mechanism of *the* dominant power type in our society, characterized by Foucault as normalization and disciplinary power. This view of being a subject as effect of disciplinary power is also the central theme in Foucault's *The History of Sexuality. An Introduction.* Foucault himself said this work was intended primarily to reveal the interior subject positioning, which he believes takes place in our culture primarily via the deployment of sexuality. In this study, he comes very close to the image of man developed by the authors Gilles Deleuze and Felix Guattari in *Anti-Oedipus.*[3] They also argue that what are in fact multiplicities become caught in subject forms, and thus subjected to the existing order. In this respect, they see the psy-complex (all psychological technologies, practices and techniques) as the main culprit. This imposes the subject form, in the form of the psyche, and thus constitutes subjectivity.

In a recent article, Peter Dews has emphasized the Nietzschean background of Deleuze's and Guattari's thinking, and that of Foucault in *The History of Sexuality. An Introduction.* 'Nietzsche's central argument,' writes Dews – and he refers to the second essay in *Zur Genealogie der Moral* –

is that a reflexive relation to the self and in particular an internalized moral control of behaviour, can be inculcated through threats and violence . . . . This task is accomplished by enforcing a block on the spontaneous expression of instincts, since 'all instincts that do not discharge themselves outwardly turn inward – that is what I call the internalization of man: thus it was that man developed what was later called his "soul".'[4]

By paraphrasing the above, we can argue that to Deleuze and Guattari what is now called the psyche came into being through the blockage of spontaneous expression of desires. The psy-complex, and in particular psychoanalysis with its oedipalization of desire, plays the leading role here.

Foucault sees internalization – the constitution of an inner space, of a subjectivity – as having taken place via the effect of the deployment of sexuality. We can now ascertain that every normativity (the construction and application of norms and values, and of giving meaning in general) in this thinking emerges as a subjection to the existing order: after all, normativity falls back on things like a consciousness, or a subjectivity, which in Nietzschean terms stands for the internalization of spontaneous life forces (a slave morality), and thus only reinforces what has to be broken down. Direct, uncoded life should be put in the place of man and morals, which in Foucaultian terms stands for discipline and normalization. It is this equating of normativity with normalization which is adopted in articles in *m/f*. For example, Parveen Adams and Jeff Minson write: 'The implication of Foucault's position is that the domain of morality, the realm of values, is dissolved.'[5] In this framework they problematize a feminist politics which is based on a struggle for rights of women, and thus is founded on general ethical principles, and on the notion of the woman as subject. 'There is a price to pay for returning to such traditional and conventional ground . . .' they warn us.

Further discussions in *m/f* frequently refer to the difference between theory and politics: at a theoretic level, the subject woman has to be deconstructed; at a political level, a feminist movement has to start from and appeal to the subject woman, otherwise you would shatter feminism.[6] In her introduction of *m/f*'s deconstructionist view in the Dutch *Journal of Women's Studies*, Mieke Aerts also brings up the difference between theory and politics, but at the same time puts forward the fact that a deconstructionist view can also have consequences for a view of the women's movement.[7]

The philosopher Anjes Manschot-Vincenot attempts to draw consequences for the sexuality discourse in the women's movement from Foucault's text. She writes: 'Now, we could ask ourselves whether, in the line-up of father confessors, medical men, psycho-analysts, and sexologists, the scientia sexualis has been destroyed by feminists, or has only been complemented and perpetuated . . . . In that case, it would be no more than a palace revolution . . . . A new creed replaces the old, norms are modernized, new exclusions emerge.' But she goes on to postulate that Foucault cannot have intended this because the people who are now getting a hearing were formerly excluded: 'In my view, it cannot have been his intention to lump together the interests of those who used to have the stage with those who have now taken the microphone.'[8]

In fact, Manschot-Vincenot has formulated a critique of Foucault because *The History of Sexuality. An Introduction* leaves no room for any other conclusion: feminists speaking about sexuality is in itself a form of normalization. This conclusion derives from the equating of normativity and normalization in Foucault's book. But does deconstructive thinking imply that *every* new production of meaning concerning women and femininity – in other words fem-inism as sub-culture – has to be rejected as a new normalization and discipline? To my mind, in his most recent work Michel Foucault has broken with the Nietzschean equalization of normativity and nor-malization and has handed us the instruments for a solution to our femininity dilemma. It is a solution which builds on deconstructive thinking and does not fall back on old theoretic solutions.

SUBJECTIVITY AS EFFECT OF AESTHETICS OF EXISTENCE

Foucault's recent studies of sexuality, *L'Usage des plaisirs* (*The Use of Pleasure*) and *Le Souci de soi* (*The Care of the Self*),[9] comprise a revision of his earlier hypothesis that talking about sexuality dates from the sixteenth century only, and became intensified from the nineteenth century onwards through the humanities. We find discourses which problematize sexual behaviour in Greek and Roman writings, and these form the topic of the two books mentioned above. This 'discovery' of Foucault's means, in fact, that he departs from an important hypothesis in *The History of Sexuality. An Introduction* – that the discourse on sexuality coincides with the constitution of the modern subject and that *every* discourse on sexuality has a normalizing and disciplinary effect.

In the books mentioned, he brings to our attention the so-called prescriptive discourses on sexuality in Greek and Roman culture: 'that is, texts whose main object, whatever their form (speech, dialogue, treatise, collection of precepts, etc.) is to suggest rules of conduct . . . . These texts thus served as functional devices that would enable individuals to question their own conduct, to watch over and give shape to it, and to shape themselves as ethical subject.'[10] Foucault calls these ethical discourses: he reserves the concept ethical – as distinct from moral – for those discourses which construct a relationship of the self to the self, and are therefore aimed at the concrete shaping of an own existence. Foucault also calls these arts-of-existence discourses, aesthetics of existence, or self-practices. He describes them as follows:

> What I mean by the phrase are those intentional and voluntary actions by which men not only set themselves rules of conduct, but also seek to transform themselves, to change themselves in their singular being, and to make their life into an oeuvre that carries certain aesthetic values and meets certain stylistic criteria.[11]

So we are concerned here with a type of discourse, or 'discursive practice', which comprises an ethic which has an *aesthetic* thrust, thus producing the term 'aesthetics of existence'. In history we find many examples of this type of discourse and on numerous themes. Foucault wanted to describe only those related to sexuality. His books demonstrate how extensive these prescriptive discourses were in antiquity and the extent to which sexual behavioural rules had been worked out in detail. But we should note that this concerns discourses which are aimed solely at Greek – free – *men*. At the same time, we should take into account the locality aspect: these were arts-of-existence discourses which were designed by and for a specific group and were not aimed at people in general.

But even for the target group itself, there is no question of a general normative claim. Those among the male population who did not keep to the prescriptions of the arts-of-existence discourses were not seen as people who deviated from the norm and who had to be readjusted through re-education or other 'social work' measures, but as 'over-confident': 'It was a personal choice for a small elite. The reason for making this choice was the will to lead a beautiful life, and to leave to others memories of a beautiful existence,' according to Foucault in an interview in 1983.[12]

The most important characteristic of these arts-of-existence was that they functioned independently, separate from religion or the juridical-political system. In the interview cited here, Foucault argues that it is precisely the independent status of Greek aesthetics of existence which should inspire us. He is not looking for a revival of these Greek ethical discourses – they were too focused on master/slave thinking for that – but we could apply the *type* of ethic we find there:

> My idea is that it's not at all necessary to relate ethical problems to scientific knowledge . . . . For centuries we have been convinced that between our ethics, our personal ethics, our everyday life and the great political and social and economic structures there were analytical relations . . . . I think we have to get rid of this idea of an analytical or necessary link between ethics and other social or economic or political structures.[13]

So far my remarks have focused on Foucault's recent work. Unfortunately, the framework of this article does not allow me to go into the refinements he introduced in the form of a concept apparatus to analyse and distinguish this kind of arts-of-existence discourse, which in my view can be of great use. I will now try to extrapolate this thinking of Foucault to the question which is central to this article – the question of theoretic justification of the development of a feminist sub-culture.

In my view, Foucault's recent work offers clues to an answer to this question because it breaks the link between normativity and normalization. It advances the possibility of constructions of self-identity which escape subject-being as a result of normalization. He does this by indicating the possibility of *independent* ethical discourses which are detached from truth and science. After all, it was the humanities which created the modern subject through their production of truth about man (his desire, his 'self', his unconscious, his conscious, his identity, etc.). Rejecting this subject-being as self-reflective consciousness and true identity, Foucault sees space for and even advocates constructions of new subjectivity, applying Greek traditions of arts-of-existence and ethics.

In this way, Foucault makes possible a useful approach to our problem, an approach which can be described in brief as: the subject woman does not exist, long live feminine subjectivity! This approach contains a resistance to all discourses which attempt to postulate the truth about woman, and against all ethics and normativity with regard to women and femininity which are based on 'scientific knowledge' of what woman is, or what her characteristics are (her desires, her identity, her consciousness, her unconsciousness).

But feminine subjectivity has not been swept off the table by this. It is perceived as something which is perpetually construed and constructable. Foucault's latest work also provides us with a solution to the specific problem he saddled us with in *The History of Sexuality. An Introduction*, namely whether feminists' speaking about sexuality does not in itself link up smoothly with *scientia sexualis*.

This problem also shifts in a different direction now Foucault has amended his most important hypothesis – that speaking about sexuality coincides with the normalizing constitution of the modern subject. The Greeks already had discourses on sexual behaviour which were oriented towards a self-identity in this area; however, this was not based on the *truth* about the body and its desires. These discourses were aimed at constructing an *ethical* relation to the body. Thus, speaking about sexuality can also have this status and, from this perspective, the feminist debate on sexuality can be given a varied status. If we take this approach as point of departure, in other words if we assume that we want to develop cultural practices around woman and femininity which escape subject essentialism and the truth goal of *scientia sexualis*, but which link up with the Greek type of aesthetics of existence, what consequences will this have for a feminist development of style?

FEMINISM AS CONSTRUCTION

The first obvious consequence would be that feminist discourses comprise no claims to truth with regard to being a woman and femininity. Feminists should not have pretensions to truth discourses, but should give an ethical form to their discourse. They should present themselves as a discourse which comprises an ethic around being a woman; only in the name of an ethic around woman can they present their cultural constructions.

A second important point concerns the locality of a feminist aesthetic of existence. Firstly, as we have seen, the Greek aesthetics of existence only comprise an *ethic*: the relationships of the self to the self, and not an objective morality which extends to all aspects of the social sphere. Feminist constructions which articulate femininity should aim to be no more than the construction of styles of living, and not a morality with regard to all aspects of human life. In addition, they should present themselves as discourses which have something to offer *to those who feel attracted by them*, and certainly not as a compulsory morality for all women. This too, as we have seen, was inherent to the Greek model of aesthetics of existence. And finally, this approach implies there can be no question of *the* feminist ethic or way of living. Ethical discourses around being a woman can, of course, have very different contents. In this respect, feminism is more an umbrella name for all the different styles which want to offer an alternative to the dominant culture of femininity.

To summarize, I come to the question which was my original concern: how can we justify theoretically the cultural cornerstone of feminism, namely the development of alternative cultures and life-styles if we do not want to base this on theories which postulate an essential femininity, or solely on the *existing* social differences between men and women? In my view, Foucault has handed us the instruments to achieve this in his latest work. He has revealed space for ethics as an independent kind of discourse. Analysing the Greek traditions of arts-of-existence, he shows us space for constructions of self-identity which escape the modern form of subjectivity (that is, the self-examining subject striving after authenticity). I am of the opinion that in this way Foucault has opened up the possibility of a reconciliation between ethics and deconstructive thinking and that he makes possible a useful approach to our problem – how to develop a feminist subjectivity without the basis of an essential feminine subject. When we transform what has been made the truth of our identity into an ethical relation and also present and structure this as such, then speaking about being a woman can certainly be a pretext for a culture-renewal programme; in this way 'being a woman' can give rise to the design of new styles of life, forms of living and cultural 'images' and 'translations'.

Following this road means rejecting all discourses which attempt to postulate or discover the truth about woman, and all ethics and normativity with regard to women and femininity which are based on 'scientific knowledge' about what the woman is or what her characteristics are (her desires, her unconscious, her lusts). And this road also means: presenting oneself as a specific ethic on being a woman, as a feminist aesthetic of existence. How feminist aesthetics of existence are fleshed out, what they look like and will look like, remains a question of 'taste'. A 'taste' which can be acquired, argued and disputed in a permanent discussion – which is thus a political discussion!

EPILOGUE

To conclude I want to emphasize once again that I am concerned in this article with cultural feminism as distinct from emancipation feminism.

Feminism's striving after emancipation – as expressed, for example, by Simone de Beauvoir: women are also people and should not be stereotyped and discriminated against under the guise of a so-called femininity – certainly involves a far-reaching political programme. And this feminism is, and rightly, not averse to one general norm. But we are concerned here with a general morality which is posed in negative terms: women mustn't be discriminated against! Yes, indeed, it would be absurd to act the liberal here.

However, in this regard I am not concerned with emancipation feminism. When I talk about feminism as producer of alternatives to the dominant culture, I do not have in mind the far-reaching implications of emancipation feminism for our society. What I do mean is that feminism which will offer new cultural meanings in terms of femininity.

In this article I have only examined what I see as the desirable strategies and points of departure of such a culture feminism. It is not the case that I reduce all feminism to this. It is evident that consequences can also be drawn for emancipation feminism from an anti-subject, in this connection an anti-Woman, mode of thought. Such consequences – in practice often already implemented – are, for example, that general political slogans are abandoned, that political demands are formulated very pragmatically and concentrated on specific situations, that the aim is the removal of social obstacles which are especially impeding for specific groups of women. Is it necessary to add that the vanishing woman will still definitely be involved in emancipationary feminist politics?

However, the basis of my article is a plea to give culture feminism which speaks in terms of femininity the form of an ethic. When feminists (want to) invent new forms of imagination, of writing, of thinking, etc., then that would seem to me an enrichment of culture and as such more than worth working for. However, when they use this platform to speak as representative of the Truth about Woman, or of feminism, about how the world and mankind should look, as Marilyn French does, for example, in *Beyond Power*, then we are not dealing with an ethic but with a general, positive morality, not with normativity but with normalization. As the latter prospect makes me shudder, I advocate a limitation of pretensions of such culture-feminist projects: rather no morality, but an 'ethic', and rather an ethic moulded on aesthetic than on 'scientific' grounds.

NOTES

1 First published in French in 1976; Dutch translation by Peter Klinkenberg *et al.* – *De wil tot weten*, SUN, Nijmegen, 1984; English translation by Robert Hurley, *The History of Sexuality. An Introduction*, Pelican, Harmondsworth, 1981.
2 *The History of Sexuality. An Introduction*, pp. 152–3.
3 G. Deleuze and F. Guattari, *Anti-Oedipus*, Athlone Press, London, 1984.
4 P. Dews, 'Power and subjectivity in Foucault', in *New Left Review*, 144, March/April, 1984, pp. 82–3; published in Dutch translation in *Krisis*, vol. 17, 1984, p. 5.
5 P. Adams and J. Minson, 'The "subject" of feminism', in *m/f*, vol. 2, 1978, p. 53.
6 See, among others, 'Discussion', in *m/f*, vol. 7, 1982.
7 M. Aerts, 'Het raam van de studeerkamer' ('The study window'), in *Tijdschrift voor Vrouwenstudies*, vol. 2, no. 3, 1981.
8 Anjes Manschot-Vincenot, 'Dromen over een bloeiend sexueel leven. Kanttekeningen vanuit Foucault' ('Dreaming about a flourishing sex life. Notes on Foucault'), in *Wijsgerig perspektief op maatschappij en wetenschap* (Philosophical perspective on society and science), vol. 18, no. 2, 1977/78.
9 M. Foucault, *L'Usage des plaisirs*, and *Le souci de soi*, Gallimard, Paris, 1984; English translations by Robert Hurley, *The Use of Pleasure*, and *The Care of the Self*, Random House, New York, 1985; Dutch translation in resp. 1984 and 1985.
10 M. Foucault, *The Use of Pleasure*, p. 12–13.
11 Ibid., pp. 10–11.
12 'On the genealogy of ethics', in H.L. Dreyfus and P. Rabinow, *Michel Foucault. Beyond Structuralism and Hermeneutics*, University of Chicago Press, Chicago, 1983, p. 230; Dutch translation appeared in 1985.
13 Ibid., p. 236.

INDEX